EMOTIONS RE&SONS

EMOTIONS RE&SONS

An Inquiry into Emotional Justification

Patricia S. Greenspan

Routledge
New York, London

Published in 1988 by

Routledge
an imprint of Routledge, Chapman and Hall, Inc.
29 West 35 Street
New York, NY 10001

Published in Great Britain by

Routledge
11 New Fetter Lane
London EC4P 4EE

Copyright © 1988 by Routledge, Chapman and Hall

Printed in the United States of America

Library of Congress Cataloging in Publication Data

Greenspan, Patricia S., 1944–
    Emotions and reasons : an inquiry into emotional justification
    Patricia S. Greenspan.
        p.   cm.
    Bibliography: p.
    Includes index.
    ISBN 0-415-90049-2
    1. Emotions (Philosophy)   I. Title.
B815.G74 1988
128'.3–dc 19   88–12210

British Library Cataloguing in Publication Data

Greenspan, Patricia S., 1944–
    Emotions and reasons : an inquiry into emotional justification.
    1. Man. Emotions
    I. Title
    152.4

    ISBN 0-415-90049-2

For H & H

CONTENTS

ACKNOWLEDGMENTS

The first draft of this essay was written while I was on a twelve-month fellowship from the National Endowment for the Humanities in 1983–1984. During the academic portion of that year I was privileged to serve as Visiting Scholar at the University of Bristol, with the opportunity to escape distractions and seek out new sources of stimulation. A special research assignment from the University of Maryland Division of Arts and Humanities, during fall term, 1984, along with my spring term sabbatical in 1987, allowed some time for further drafts done in light of comments I received.

Although I have been working on it on my own time off and on since 1977, even this draft of my essay is not put forth as a finished product. I have not attempted to answer all questions but rather to pose some questions in a new way—and indeed to point up some new questions. Students often have remarked on the inexhaustible nature of the subject, in part a result of its multiple connections to more standard philosophic fields. Whether it seems frustrating or rewarding, this inexhaustibility also makes it impossible to acknowledge all debts to other authors. My notes below are therefore highly selective—if the term can be applied to something dependent on unreliable memory. In any case, I have not even attempted to cite overlapping works from other fields, including psychology, or works that reached me after 1984, except where they actually influenced my own thinking.

While my notes do cite some readers and others who provided me with specific points or objections, a number of people deserve mention here for general advice and criticism. Karen Hanson, who read the whole manuscript twice for Routledge & Kegan Paul, helped me both with astute objections and with the insistence that I not try to please everyone—or deal with all sources of displeasure within the scope of this essay. The essay begins *in medias res*, examining claims about the emotions that a linear approach might treat as "later" issues. To avoid treating them as afterthoughts, however—and in the belief that the more fundamental issues cannot really be settled in advance—I have resisted the temptation to shift the focus of my discussion onto its methodological and other presuppositions. Some of these are noted, as I proceed; but their justification is left to depend on their results. In immediate terms their upshot is an essay that many readers will find difficult; but my hope is that it yields enough of interest to be worth their labors.

It should be evident, too, that I did not think precision achievable at this stage of the subject, though I have tried to answer those objections I was made aware of. Substantial chunks of my first draft received comments from Daniel Farrell, William Lyons, and Adam Morton. Kathy Lossau, Linda Paul, and Sharen Taylor helped me make further corrections. Early versions of Chapters 2 and 4 were improved by the scrutiny of audiences at Bristol, Trinity College Dublin, Glasgow, Kings College London, Cornell, Cincinnati, and Memphis State. Chapter 3, Section (iv), was read in first draft form at the 1985 Greensboro Symposium in Philosophy, at the University of North Carolina at Greensboro, with Harvey Green as commentator. (Its penultimate draft was published, along with other contributions to the Symposium, in [Philosophical Studies], 50 (November 1986), 321–341. Copyright © 1986 by D. Reidel Publishing Company. Reprinted by permission.) I should add that earlier, unpublished papers, amounting to predecessors of Chapter 6, were tried out on groups at Pittsburgh, Oxford, California at San Diego, Johns Hopkins, Virginia, and Ohio State.

I owe further thanks, for practical assistance, to Maryland Philosophy Department Chairman Michael Slote, former Acting Chairman James Lesher, Routledge Philosophy Editors Maureen MacGrogan and Stratford Caldecott, and my grant referees Annette Baier, Alan Donagan, Daniel Farrell, Amelie Rorty, and Stephen Stich. Finally, let me thank Suellen Evans-Parzow for putting my first draft on diskettes, and Karolyn Marshall, Lorrie Lizak, and Lake Jagger for xeroxing my final draft, along with other special secretarial help as my deadline for submission approached. That deadline brought a number of points suddenly into focus, I should say. To some extent, I have tried to thread them back into my text; but rather than risking further complication of the argument, I have left some work to a later time—and, I hope, to other authors.

Washington, D.C.
January 25, 1988

I
EMOTIONS AS "EXTRAJUDGMENTAL" EVALUATIONS

1
Reasons to Feel:
Sketch of an Argument

In reaction to the Cartesian account of emotions as sensations, a number of contemporary philosophers have suggested that we explain them in terms of *evaluative judgments*.[1] Thus, fear is not to be construed just as a set of chills, shudders, and the like—introspectively identifiable events of feeling. Rather, it essentially involves a belief that danger looms—perhaps as a cause of sensation or its physiological underpinnings, but at any rate, as a necessary element of genuine cases of fear. This judgment is partly factual but also partly evaluative: It is about the likelihood of harm from some source, with "harm" understood as an evil. Its detailed factual content typically serves to exhibit an "object" of fear—something it is directed towards as a putative source of harm—and thus to distinguish the emotion from objectless sensations, of the sort that might be felt in reaction to the cold. But its negative evaluative content is needed to explain why it amounts to *fear* rather than some other reaction to an envisioned possibility, such as thrilled anticipation—and why fear amounts to a *reasonable* reaction in certain situations.

I grant these points to "judgmentalism," as I shall call this view; and I shall feel free to rely upon them without reviewing the arguments for them here. But I think they can be incorporated into a broader evaluative view, allowing for propositional attitudes that are weaker than strict belief: states of mind, like *imagining* that danger looms, that involve entertaining a predicative thought without assent. For judgmentalism, as I shall argue, does not do justice to the diversity of emotional phenomena. It also suggests an oversimple answer to justificatory questions, about the reasons for emotions and their role as reasons for action. With belief as the "intentional" component of emotion—the component that is *about* something, and hence is capable of misrepresenting its object— "emotional justification" would seem essentially to be justification for and by belief. I hope to lay the foundation for a subtler account, however, by bringing in a noncartesian element of object-directed *affect*, whose object is an evaluative proposition. Shudders and chills may be about some state of affairs, in short, and the same may be said of generalized comfort or discomfort. I shall use this fact, taken as a "brute" fact, to argue in Part II for a different approach to the justificatory questions on the basis of an alternative to judgmentalism as defended in Part I.

In this chapter I shall not attempt an argument, though, but just a sketch of one, presenting in compact form some points that will reemerge later in this essay with a more detailed treatment of cases.

Let me propose, then, that we look at emotions as compounds of two elements: affective states of comfort or discomfort and evaluative propositions spelling out their intentional content. Fear, for instance, may be viewed as involving discomfort at the fact—or the presumed or imagined fact (I shall say "the thought")—that danger looms. This gives only a general pattern of analysis and is meant to do no more; further specification must wait upon investigation of particular emotional states. But by breaking down emotions into layered affective and evaluative components, with the latter taken as objects of the former, the pattern should provide us with a way of approaching two main questions of emotional justification:

(1) How are emotions justified by the situations in which they arise?

(2) How does emotion function in the justification of action?

At the outset, bypassing issues of moral justification, I have two corresponding theses in mind, based on the interpretation of emotions as "propositional feelings":

(1) Although its appropriateness may be explained in terms of belief warrant, the evaluative component of emotions need not rest on reasons adequate for belief.

(2) The affective component of emotions gives them a special role to play in rational motivation, as "extrajudgmental" reasons for action.

But the two theses will turn out to exhibit some complex links. In particular, the full justification of emotions themselves will depend on (2), as well as on (1)—on the practical "adaptiveness" of appropriate emotions, or their instrumental value as spurs to action.

The implications of my argument will be seen more clearly as the two theses are defended in detail in light of my proposed analysis of emotions. Briefly, though, I hope to use the two theses, especially in my final chapter, to exhibit the special rational and moral significance of emotion as a supplement to judgment. The motivational influence of the full range of emotions will turn on (1), as we shall see, because of the importance of *imagination* to emotional evaluation—particularly evaluation from another person's standpoint, or "identification," which I take to be central to *moral* motivation. The greater part of this essay will focus on (1), since (2) presupposes the distinction it draws between emotion and belief. But my defense of (2) will eventually bring out my reason for stressing the distinction: It allows emotions a role in rational motivation that is not simply parasitic on that of judgment. For "judgmentalism" subsumes emotions under a conventional rational category at the cost of slighting their own role as reasons.

For the moment, an example should help to distinguish the two theses, as claims about *rational* justification, from the common view of emotions as features of fully human sensitivity or the like. Let us look at one of the less sentimentalized cases of emotion: wary suspicion, in regard for one's own self-interest. Suppose I am involved in a business transaction and seem to "pick up on" something about the salesman that puts me on guard about his trustworthiness. My suspicion, in this case, supposing that it does count as a state of feeling, amounts to one of the milder varieties of fear. It is important to my argument here that such states need not be extreme—need not involve "states" in the sense of "agitated states" but simply current *conditions* of feeling. I am not "in a state," in the popular sense of the expression; and the feeling I have is neither very intense nor an experience of some particular sensations, like chills and shudders, that are characteristic of full-blown fear. We may grant, however, that my feeling does go beyond assent to a proposition: that X, the salesman, is likely to mislead me in some way that I would find injurious (injurious to my interests, that is). I am *uncomfortable about* that presumed state of affairs and thus am undergoing an emotion even though my discomfort might resist explanation in terms of any very specific mental event. Rather, it amounts to a general state of negative feeling, perhaps a kind of mental tension, directed towards an evaluative proposition of the sort that is characteristic of fear.

In standard cases the evaluative proposition will be one I take to be true. But in order to allow for the possibility that my emotion parts from belief, I shall use "the thought that [the proposition holds]" as a non-committal expression introducing the object of my discomfort, or what I am uncomfortable about. The expression should not be taken as implying that I am uncomfortable about the fact that such a thought occurs to me; indeed, the thought need not occur to me explicitly. Rather, the object of my discomfort amounts to the *content* of the thought: that I face a threat of injury from X. Because the affective component of suspicion is intentionally directed towards this evaluative component on my view, the emotion may be said to have a propositional "internal" object, along with the object given *in* the proposition, as the source of harm. This means that my suspicion is not just like chills or shudders, or even general discomfort, *accompanying* an evaluative thought in the way that a headache might accompany the thought that I am losing out in a business transaction with X. Even if it were "objectless," in fact—if its evaluative component did not pick out a particular source of harm—the emotion would have intentional content; for its affective component must at least be directed towards an *indefinite* proposition on my analysis.

The propositional object of emotional discomfort need not be an object of *belief*, however. In the present case we might suppose that I reject the corresponding judgment, since I think I have reason to believe, and no good reason not to believe, that X is entirely trustworthy. He has been highly spoken of by others whom I trust, and I cannot say what it is about his manner on this occasion that stands behind my feeling to the contrary. Indeed, I cannot even say that the feeling is based on something about his manner: Perhaps I am simply uneasy in an unfamiliar situation. So I manage to dismiss the feeling—intellectually, at any rate—as a product of my own inexperience in business transactions. It does persist; but I "explain it away," resisting any tendency to take it as something that would survive the collection of further evidence. Although I keep thinking— entertaining the thought—that X is apt to mislead me, I do not *think that* he is, in the sense that involves assent to the content of my thought. Rather, the case supposes, I attribute it to my own imagination.

My "intuitive" suspicion may be *warranted*, however, even though I do not take it to be and even though the corresponding belief would *not* be, under the circumstances. There may be some features of X's way of presenting himself that do back up my reaction, that is, but are not perceived clearly enough to justify a belief that X is untrustworthy. All the evidence I have—including any memories of my similar reactions on past occasions—counts *against* that judgment. And yet my emotion may be appropriate, not just because in this case it happens to fit the facts, but rather because it is here "controlled by" some relevant features of my perceptual situation. I might have at least prima facie evidence for belief, if I were able to specify those features at least roughly; but as things stand now, I do not know enough about the "subliminal" sources of my emotion even to attribute them to its object. I am reacting to something about X's eye movements, say, something whose relevance to untrustworthiness could be explained by a developed science of "body language," if there were one. But from my current evidential standpoint the emotion would seem to be best explained by my own uneasiness. So it seems that the emotion may be appropriate in a case where its corresponding belief is neither warranted nor held.

Some would insist that "belief" be widened to make this out as a case where I do hold—unconsciously, perhaps—that X is untrustworthy. I shall attempt to answer them in Part I, as I exhibit the advantages of my broader view in application to other sorts of cases. For the moment let me just say that I am suspicious of this apparent appeal to simplicity. Its use in defense of a neatly reductionist theory runs the risk of slighting the special rational significance of emotion. If we are to address the question whether emotions add anything of value to beliefs in this and other cases, it would be well to avoid transferring their intentional content to some attenuated notion of belief. I shall eventually argue, in Part II, that what emotions add to beliefs depends on their partial justification in *extraevidential* terms—in terms of practical "adaptiveness," or a kind of instrumental value that is not properly brought to bear on assessments of belief warrant. This means that in at least some cases an appropriate emotion may be one that parts from warranted belief. But to make out this rational possibility as a real one, we need to put some limits on the attribution of beliefs. In general, it seems that belief is just one propositional attitude among others. In the present case we may speak of the subject as "feeling as though" X is untrustworthy—meaning "feeling" in the broad sense indicated earlier, not so easily picked apart from thought and *possibly* involving belief. Where it amounts to an emotion, though, it also involves an affective state directed towards the corresponding evaluative proposition, which may be held in mind without assent.

This compound feeling sometimes includes or yields an action requirement—a negative evaluation of alternatives to action—as an object of discomfort. In such cases, I want to argue, the emotion may also supplement belief in adding immediate "pressure" towards action. Thus, in the case of suspicion, as long as I am uncomfortable at the thought that X is likely to injure my interests, my discomfort puts me on guard against that possibility. It extends to a negative evaluation of failure to watch X carefully and thus adds a rational motive—the improvement of my present state of feeling—to any independently perceived (or imagined) need for watchfulness. If only to calm myself, in immediate terms, I ought to pay particular attention to what X says and does. This example should indicate how the special motivational force ascribed to emotions depends on my account of emotional discomfort as *object-directed* and hence as serving to hold an evaluation in mind more reliably than beliefs and objectless sensations. The content of even an acknowledged belief need not be an object of current attention; and unpleasant sensations that merely accompanied it might very well distract one from it or from a requirement to act in light of it. By itself, the evaluation of X as untrustworthy may be said to give rise to an action requirement, in the sense of a thought that I ought to keep an eye on X. But this is just what is sometimes called "a desire in the philosopher's sense," covering wants or preferences without any motivational force. Discomfort need not add pressure to this essentially affectless desire where it has no related intentional content but simply amounts to a further consequence of the same evaluation and hence a kind of affective *symptom* of emotion.

It would be no more than an incidental fact about my objectless discomfort, that is, that it would be relieved most naturally and effectively by *acting on* the accompanying desire, taking steps to falsify the evaluation that gave rise to it. Instead, consider how I might respond to a headache caused by the thought of myself as a hopeless failure in business. I might turn attention *away from* the evaluation. Perhaps I ought to work to get rid of the psychological causes of my reaction, calming myself independently of any attempt to lessen the likelihood of injury from X. The same might be said of object-directed discomfort, of course, in a case where my reaction is inappropriate—or where it would be practically maladaptive. I might be dependent on X for some benefit, say, in a case where he would notice and resent a guarded attitude. But let us restrict attention to a case like the present one, where my suspicion is assumed to be warranted and to have the usual sort of instrumental value, even if I have no good reason to think so. On the view proposed here, the emotion itself serves as a reason for action insofar as it yields discomfort *about* an action requirement. Discomfort at the thought that I ought to keep an eye on X—that there is a need to do so, which I have yet to satisfy fully—follows from my suspicion in its situational context and amounts to a *motivating* desire on this view. My discomfort apparently will continue unless and until I satisfy the requirement; so it adds a rational motive for action to that provided by affectless thought and desire, even in combination with affective emotion *symptoms*.

My detailed account of the special motivational force of the emotions will be postponed until I have considered some prior questions about the nature and justification of the emotions themselves. But it will often be anticipated in what follows, particularly in my treatment of the role of emotions in moral motivation; for on my account these issues turn out to be complexly intertwined. Indeed, even here, I really ought to qualify my reference to "the justification of the emotions themselves" as a prior question. This is meant as a reference to emotional appropriateness, taken as implying a kind of "backward-looking" justification— by the subject's "perceptual" situation, as I shall put it. The contrasting notion, of practical "adaptiveness," appeals to a kind of "forward-looking" justification, or justification by consequences—in particular, by the role of emotions as spurs to action. In fact, though, my account of the notion of appropriateness will turn out to rest on general adaptiveness; and a *full* justification of emotion will require adaptiveness in the particular case at hand. For the perceptual situation to which an emotion is appropriate justifies it only as an adequately grounded response. It is one that a subject *may* quite rationally forgo, if he can—in favor of belief, where belief is warranted, or some propositional attitude short of belief but not involving comfort or discomfort.

Consider the case of suspicion once again, and extract my evaluation of X as untrustworthy—a "feeling" of sorts, though not yet an emotion, on my view—from its overlay of discomfort, or feeling *tone*. Even on our assumption that I have adequate grounds for the emotion, the evaluation without the discomfort would do just as well for noninstrumental rational purposes—as a "representation," let us say, of my perceptual situation. I may have "every reason" for feeling tense about a threat of injury, but for representational purposes I have no *compelling* reason. The claim that I actually ought to *feel* suspicious in my business dealings with X must rest on some view about the practical insufficiency, without emotion, of my concern for my own interests. An evaluation, especially one from which I withhold belief, is unlikely to have the same grip on my behavior in the absence of negative feeling tone; and it is this fact that lets us complete our justification of the emotion. Appropriateness is not enough to mandate feeling, in short. Where there are no moral "reasons to feel," as in this case, we need to bring in practical adaptiveness.

"Adaptiveness" and Rational Self-Interest. It may already be evident that the term "adaptiveness" covers a range of possibilities, some of which turn out to qualify its initial contrast with "appropriateness." Distinctions will be introduced as needed via qualifications of the term: "General adaptiveness," for instance, will be used to refer to the instrumental value of an emotion *tendency*, as distinct from the value of an instance of emotion in the particular case at hand. But the term "adaptiveness" will itself remain broad; and as with some other terms to be introduced later— with scare quotes as occasional reminders—it is semi-technical in the sense of being derived from, but extended beyond, *fairly* ordinary language. In this case its basis is biological talk—also broad (meaning "functional" as opposed to "dysfunctional") but currently familiar on a more specific application (meaning something like "functional in promoting the survival of the gene pool"). In case the reader expects the term to be given a similarly narrow reading in what follows, I should stress here that I mean to retain even its extension to questions of *social* value. I do think that at least some emotion tendencies are of basic evolutionary importance, as I shall indicate briefly in my treatment of morally significant emotions. But of course I am in no position to substantiate a claim of this sort, except by providing an occasional speculation about how a given emotion might serve communal ends. In any case, the term "adaptiveness" also refers to other sorts of instrumental value, under-

stood as value as a means to some good—initially in application to a particular emotion instance, and indeed a particular self-interested agent, as exemplified by the case of intuitive suspicion.

A familiar philosophical term for what I have in mind here is "utility," of course, and readers are welcome to substitute this if they can cancel out misleading overtones. However, some who find the term acceptable in ethics seem to have more trouble reconciling the thought of "useful" emotions with the view of them as typically resistant to rational control. It does seem clear that emotional response can often be brought under *indirect* control—by controlling what one thinks about, say, or by rehearsing certain thoughts or activities to inculcate new habits of response. My eventual account of the practical adaptiveness of emotion will appeal to this possibility; but it will also assume resistance to *direct* control, of the sort that we have over action. In this respect and others emotion seems to stand *in between* action and belief, exhibiting some features of both categories; and partly to mark the contrast with action, I shall use a special term for emotional utility. As with "appropriateness" and belief, "adaptiveness" *can* be applied to action. But the fact that it is not the common term in philosophical discourse should actually be helpful in what follows, as long as the reader bears in mind the breadth of its intended meaning. In particular, though it does extend to the promotion of social ends, including group survival, I shall apply it in unqualified form to instrumental value for the agent.

My discussion of motivational force, in fact, will treat the self-interested standpoint as a rational basis for explaining some forms of altruistic motivation via the notion of identificatory emotion. I see no necessary conflict, however, between this approach and doubts one might have about the questionable status assigned to altruism by traditional views of rational motivation. No claim is made here that emotional concern for others would be *irrational if it were irreducible to self-interest. I do assume, though, that its explanation in terms of self-interest is needed to make it out as "rationally obligatory," or irrational for an agent to *forgo*—to provide a full justification for it, in short. My argument does not rest on a view of altruism as developmentally derivative or less certain in its origins than self-interest. But it does presuppose a view of self-interest as less easily shrugged off at later stages of development and hence as motivationally more reliable than altruism in standard cases.

At any rate, *emotional* concern for others, as I shall interpret it here, counts as a *subtype* of self-interest. It is important to my account of the special justificatory role of emotion as a supplement to belief that its "extrajudgmental" element amounts to an affective reward or punishment for the agent. One might indeed grant that the assignment of some weight to others' interests is rationally required on an intellectual level and still hold, as I do, that more is needed to give rise reliably to action on others' behalf. What overcomes moral *inertia*, on the view I shall propose here, is emotional identification. I shall therefore defend cases of identification as rationally appropriate, even though I take them to involve a conflict between emotion and belief. Since they also involve the reflection of others' interests in self-interest, my discussion of identification will serve to bring out the importance of emotions to moral motivation. I should stress, though, that the view proposed here is not intended as monolithic—on this question, any more than on the sense in which emotions are adaptive. Intellectual concern for others may be sufficient in many cases for action on their behalf; but I hope to make out emotional concern, and especially identificatory emotion, as socially adaptive partly because it reinforces moral reasons with self-interest. The latter will be said to provide a "rational" justification for emotion in the sense of "*purely* rational": independent of moral considerations, or appeal to others' interests as such.

This brief account of the role accorded to self-interest in my argument anticipates many later issues, to be brought together in my final chapter. For the purposes of this introductory chapter, let me end my discussion of "adaptiveness" by focusing on the self-interested interpretation of the term to illustrate its initial contrast with "appropriateness." An emotional or other reaction may be appropriate but not adaptive: It may be justified in "backward-looking" terms, by the situation in which it arises, without being justified in "forward-looking" terms, by its promotion of some end. Or vice versa: A reaction may be adaptive but not appropriate. Illustrations might be constructed from unusual variants of the suspicion case, such as one that surfaced above, where X would react badly to suspicion—and presumably would react well to a feeling of trust, even though only suspicion is appropriate. Similar examples will come up in Chapter 4, when I use the case to distinguish between *general* adaptiveness, as presupposed by appropriateness, and adaptiveness in the particular case at hand. But we can blur over the general/particular distinction for the moment if we choose an example where the conflict between appropriateness and adaptiveness is not based on unusual features of the situation. It should be helpful, too, if our example indicates that the conflict is not limited to strictly emotional reactions.

A familiar example is provided by the notion of *blame*, which may amount to a speech act, or an affectless attitude, as well as an emotion— a personal variant of anger, to be distinguished from impersonal frustration in Chapter 3. On any of these interpretations it might be argued that blame is *mal*adaptive in some cases where it is appropriate and that it is adaptive in some cases where it is *in*appropriate. The former claim seems clearly to apply to cases of extreme rage. While the evidential standards for this sort of anger might seem to be no less demanding than those for the corresponding belief, presumably they could still sometimes be met, for a case where rage, even if unhelpful, is fully warranted. At any rate, my own focus here is on less extreme states of anger. Supposing that the reaction is momentary and its manifestations controlled, "outwardly directed" blame might still be defended as a psychologically helpful reaction to a situation that *warrants* only a kind of impersonal frustration. Where something goes wrong, but through nobody's fault, blame may be useful to the agent in providing an external target for destructive energy. But even as judged by a less demanding standard of evidence than the corresponding belief, it may still be inappropriate—where its object, for instance, is inanimate and hence not a suitable target of revenge. I take it, then, that appropriateness and adaptiveness may be accepted as distinct notions, at this point, however they might later turn out to be connected in application to emotions.

So far, I have given a sketch of an argument, as promised in my chapter heading, along with an indication of some terminological and other basic assumptions underlying it, in the preceding subsection. I shall often use subsections, I should note, for a more sustained treatment of particular points or cases than would otherwise fit into the surrounding discussion. For more than most philosophical discussions, or those that are designed to present an argument, this essay often proceeds by a relatively open-ended sort of inquiry. Cases initially constructed to illustrate some point in my argument often turn out to be worth exploration in their own right and are mined for further points of interest, with a pause from the argument's main thrust. Many of these subsidiary points do play an important role in some later stage of the argument; but they emerge in the order of discovery—along with some points that do not advance the argument, except in very general terms by exhibiting the fruitfulness of its approach to the emotions. My subsections are meant to contain the splay somewhat; and I shall also provide occasional foreshadowing and summary to illuminate a general path through it. But my discussion will often diverge from this path to focus on fairly specific issues and emotions.

I have two main reasons for allowing, and indeed encouraging, this essentially nonlinear presentation of the argument just sketched. The first has to do with my skepticism—whose consequences will emerge in Chapter 3—about the standard logical ordering of the issues I shall address. But even apart from this, I take it that a central consideration in favor of any approach to the emotions should be its ability to "capture the phenomena." The latter include some not-so-ordinary, but not at all unheard of, experiential phenomena on which readers' intuitions may differ. I do count these appeals to intuition as arguments; and sometimes they amount to stages in my overall argument. But the lack of uniformity in experience, or in the ways we organize it, means that a kind of argumentative "overkill" is sometimes necessary in defense of a given point. On the question whether emotions must involve belief, most notably, I present a number of different sorts of cases in the expectation that some readers will reject some of them while others will be convinced at the outset. Secondly, then, my cases are meant to give rise to side-questions in the hopes of sustaining interest for those who need no further discussion of the general point at issue. My purpose in this is not merely entertainment: Genuinely philosophical interest can be found, as I think we shall see, in some rather particular questions on this topic. In any case, some of the answers to the more particular questions turn out to contribute to my main argument in ways I could not have plotted in advance or set into a neat ordering in retrospect.

What I have done instead on the level of chapter-by-chapter organization is complex. In my four internal chapters, I alternate between examining variants of fear, to develop my central views on the nature and backward-looking justification of the emotions, and applying my views to a wider range of cases, in search of both confirmation and the discovery of further issues. Thus, Chapters 2 and 4, though structured in the manner of an inquiry, with some tolerance for side-questions, should provide my discussion with a kind of thematic unity by focusing on a single class of emotions with the aim of refining and defending my central views. Chapters 3 and 5 begin by assuming the results of the immediately preceding chapters but then transfer attention to some diverse and problematic cases, teasing out further points from their detailed exploration. In Chapter 3 highlights of this broader discussion include: a distinction for anger and attachment-love between "full-fledged" and "deficient" cases of emotion; and a contrast between the more distant forms of pity and those that involve emotional identification. In Chapter 5: a defense of envy as sometimes appropriate, even on grounds of general social adaptiveness; and a defense of love and hatred as sometimes *both* appropriate, even where both appear to have the *same* grounds.

Chapters 2 through 5 will also contain some foreshadowing of my views on "forward-looking" emotional justification, since these turn out to be presupposed, in general terms, by the topics naturally treated earlier. In my discussion of anger, for instance, I shall suggest an account of how the emotion is socially "shaped" into its full-fledged form, which essentially involves a desire for revenge; and the account will imply a particularly close connection between the emotion and action. In my final chapter, when I turn to the issue of adaptiveness, this account of anger will provide me with an especially clear-cut example of a "pressuring" emotion made adaptive by behavioral control. But I shall also consider some contrasting cases—of other sorts of motivational force and of other sorts of reasons, besides practical adaptiveness, for requiring an emotion of an agent. Before approaching the topic, moreover, I shall bring together cases, and further variants of cases, from the wider range dealt with in my earlier chapters to confirm that an appropriate emotion, even if not rationally required, will come out as more than merely *understandable* on my view. Besides providing a bit of summary, this discussion will set the stage for the crucial argument of Chapter 6, which rests on the claim that something besides appropriateness is needed to complete the justification of emotions.

The upshot of my argument, stated briefly, will be this: emotions, conceived as comfort or discomfort directed towards evaluative propositions, *may* sometimes be rationally required, as *motivational* supplements to belief. But emotional justification in this sense can only be case-by-case, even as limited to appropriate emotions; for it demands more than the general sort of adaptiveness that stands behind my notion of appropriateness. Unless an emotion is practically adaptive in the particular case at hand, that is, there is no reason—apart from moral obligations, and the like—why one ought to feel it instead of simply holding in mind its propositional content without affect. But sometimes there *is* a "reason to feel"; and the core of my argument here will consist in an attempt to pin it down—to explain how emotions may be justified by their special role in rational motivation. The argument should serve to counter a long-standing philosophical tendency to dismiss the affective aspect of emotion—and with it, I would say, emotion—as at most a link in some causal chain that leads from belief to action. On the view I shall defend here, the intentional relation of affect and evaluation makes some emotions count as *motivating* reasons for action, whether or not they stand in the usual relation to belief.

2
Emotions Without Essences: Varieties of Fear

Before attempting to say more about justificatory issues, we would do well to enlarge our stock of cases in the hopes of settling on a workable analysis of emotion. In this chapter I shall focus on fear cases, illustrating their diversity in defense of a rather minimal analysis. The analysis is meant as a broad characterization of any given emotion, a "bare bones" breakdown into internally related affective and evaluative components, whose distinguishing features vary from case to case. For I hold that emotions, even those picked out by the same general term, may be manifested in different ways on different occasions—sometimes just in the effort it takes to *block* certain feelings, thoughts, and visceral or behavioral reactions. But without assigning them classificatory "essences," in the sense of necessary and sufficient conditions for the application of a given emotion term, we can use the pattern of analysis as a way of parsing ascriptions of emotion, exhibiting a common structure that allows for a limited analogy with belief.

Because the cases are so variable and what they have in common is rather abstract, their description in accordance with the pattern will often sound stilted or simply uninformative. I shall attempt to make up for this by alternating between the rather formal statement fitting the pattern and more common ways of speaking, bringing in distinguishing features of particular emotion instances. The varieties of fear seem to be relatively easily summed up in general, however, as involving discomfort at the thought that some form of injury is likely—if only injury to one's interests, as in the case of fearful suspicion. Since the content of the evaluative component of fear is taken as an object of its affective component, I shall also refer to it as an "internal" object "of" the emotion. But this is not to say, let us note, that the emotion is itself directed towards a proposition—that fear, on my view, is fear that injury is likely. Rather, what I shall call the emotion's "external" object—its object in the ordinary sense, or what it is *about*—will be given by some statement of its internal object as a putative *source* of injury. Thus, my earlier case picks out X as an external object of suspicion. This object may also be propositional— my suspicion also amounts, say, to fear that X will mislead me—but I make no claim that it must be. What I do claim is that fear may always be interpreted as involving *discomfort* about a certain proposition. Since it comes into the analysis of fear, this evaluative object of discomfort may be thought of as internal to the emotion. The emotion's external object, by contrast, is seen as standing outside it, as an object of its evaluative component: something the *proposition* is about.

The point of this terminology is to make it clear that the intentionality, or "aboutness," of emotions survives in cases commonly thought of as "objectless"—cases of anxiety, say, where there seems to be nothing specific that the subject is afraid *of*. Such feelings retain their difference from genuinely objectless *sensations*, as I shall go on to argue, even if we do not hold that they are caused by unconscious thoughts of specific dangers—though we might sometimes grant this, under conditions I shall also sketch. Put briefly, the distinction between "objectless" anxiety and the objectless sensations (a "pure" feeling of edginess, say) that are sometimes referred to as such is that the former, as an emotion, has an internal object. In standard cases of emotion, on my view, there are two layers of intentionality, with the second seen as adding something more specific to the first. First, the affective component, comfort or discomfort, has an evaluative proposition as its object. This is what is referred to as an internal object "of" the emotion, meaning an object of feeling internal *to* it. Secondly, the evaluative component of emotion, the proposition that *amounts to* its internal object, itself has an object, in the sense of something that it is about. This is taken as the external object of the emotion as a whole. Referring to both of these as objects of the emotion will at times be misleading; but here it serves to sum up briefly the layering of intentional states—unpleasant affect and negative evaluation—that together constitute fear, on my analysis. In "objectless" cases, I want to say, the evaluative layer adds nothing more specific to the affective, though it still provides an intentional link between feeling and the world— as my quotation marks around "objectless" here and elsewhere, are meant to indicate.

I now want to defend the complexity of my analysis, examining cases that indicate that simpler views would not apply to all varieties of fear. In particular, an insistence on belief, for the evaluative component, or characteristic sensation, for the affective component—or even a one-way causal connection between the two components—would rule out some nonstandard but imaginable cases of fear. These include cases that do not involve either conscious acts of evaluation or fullblown affective symptoms but still seem to count as "occurrent" emotional states despite their overlap with moods. My discussion here will be structured more around cases to be explored than points to be established; so its initial aim, in Section (i)—to undermine the view that emotions must involve evaluative *judgments*—will yield to some others and be followed up again later. For variants of my cases will also exhibit problems with the assumption that emotions must involve particular sensations, or even sensations with a certain causal history, as opposed to generalized comfort or discomfort with a certain evaluative object. The affective component of fear may be "tamped down" (ii) or directed towards an "invented" object (iii) so that its characteristic sensations of agitated discomfort are absent in some cases or are masked by another emotion in a way that also allows for *unconscious* fears. In some cases, for that matter, the emotion may be *pleasurable* on the whole; but it still involves discomfort at a negative evaluation, as I shall argue in Section (iv), while exhibiting the intended limitations of my analysis.

The cases I shall present here are meant to be realistically imaginable, for an agent who is basically rational, even if some of his emotional responses are *ir*rational. Because my eventual focus will be on action— and even at this stage I shall be bringing in some strategies for emotional control—I shall now speak of "the agent" rather than alternating between "agent" and "subject." On occasion, I should note, my "basically rational agent" will be myself: I shall include some first-person cases, since I think it important to provide confirmation from experience, at the risk of discomfiting a few readers. It *is* necessary, in discussing a subject of this sort, to go beyond the familiar summary of "our" intuitions about someone else's responses. Where irrational responses are in question, it is not always sufficient to imagine them "from the inside," relying on the reader to do the same. For the most part, however, psychological studies and clinical observations either fail to raise the questions I want to consider or are based on assumptions at variance with my answers. Cases from literature, where I can remember them, usually seem to be too dramatically complex to provide much evidence of the wide range of states that I want to count as emotions or much assurance of the agent's basic rationality. So I shall sometimes offer a bit of testimony; but to avoid misunderstanding, let me say at this point that the cases are meant to be rather *ordinary*.

(i) Evaluation Minus Judgment

Let me begin with a made-up case of phobic response that I introduced elsewhere in an argument against "judgmentalism," or the currently popular view that emotions always involve evaluative judgments.[1] It is a case that would apparently require *logically incoherent* judgments to explain the emotional and behavioral reactions of a basically rational agent. For the case assumes that the agent has no urge to warn others away from the object of his fear: Fido, a harmless old dog. Ever since an attack by a rabid dog, we suppose, the agent has felt fear in the presence of all dogs, including Fido, though Fido is well known to him. His fear, however, is centered entirely on himself, without any reasons, good or bad, for thinking that the dog threatens him any more than others. He does not just exhibit fear *symptoms* when Fido comes near— its characteristic sensations of agitated discomfort but without direction towards an evaluative object. On my view, where these amount to an emotion, they must be linked to a thought of danger from some source. The source may be something indefinite (where fear lacks an external object, as in "objectless" anxiety); or remembered (where fear awakened by Fido's presence is directed towards the dog that attacked); or, as in this case, perceived. Thus far, in requiring a danger-evaluation, I agree with the judgmentalists. But I question whether this persistent thought must amount to or rest on a belief.

The agent's fear of Fido, in this case, seems to be captured by a claim that he "feels as though" Fido is likely to injure him—as evidenced by his tendency, despite himself, to entertain that thought in Fido's presence. To insist that he must *believe* the thought, though, when he applies it only to himself, without appeal to features distinguishing his own case, seems to me to be a last resort from the standpoint of explanation. Logical incoherency is possible, of course; but I am assuming that the agent is functioning quite rationally in general, so that our ascription of beliefs to him ought to be governed by a principle of "logical charity." We need some special reason, that is—of a sort that I shall try to indicate later—for attributing to him an unacknowledged judgment in conflict with those he acknowledges. Instead of supposing that his beliefs come into momentary conflict whenever Fido comes near, it seems simpler, and preferable from the standpoint of rational explanation, to take this as a case where emotion parts from judgment. It exhibits the tendency of emotions, in contrast to a rational agent's beliefs, to spill over to and to fix on objects resembling their appropriate objects in incidental ways.

Some might object that a "basically" rational agent *would* feel an urge to alert others to an object of phobic fear; so let me now bring in a milder sort of case from my own experience: a somewhat phobic fear of skidding, ever since a car accident in a blizzard. This cannot be made as sharp as the Fido case, since "spillover" effects, assuming *some* degree of rational control, always involve at least a slight possibility of danger, just to the extent that they involve riding in a car. Perhaps the closest analogy to fear of Fido would be fear experienced while sitting in a motionless car in the snow. But though this did not result, the accident did give rise to a persistent fear of skidding and of the consequences of skidding in situations where it is clear that injury is extremely unlikely. On a later occasion, for instance, with someone else driving at a slow speed on an isolated road, a very slight skid and the momentary sensation of uncontrolled movement had me gasping audibly for a second out of fear. This was not a purely behavioral shock-response, like jumping in reaction to some sudden event, but without any thought of injury—even a thought that does not become explicit until later. It would be hard to make out as a conditioned behavioral response, moreover, since nothing like it occurred at the time of the accident. But as far as I can tell, it does not require explanation in terms of a current *judgment* that danger was imminent.

If anything was conditioned, it was the *thought* of danger or the tendency to call it to mind—something not quite explicit, but with clear-cut behavioral (and physiological) effects, in the later situation. This was based on a judgment made earlier, in the situation of my accident, presumably; but I would deny that I actually extended that judgment, *as a judgment*, to the later situation, even momentarily. Instead, I would say that the judgment gave rise to a sudden thought, logically unconnected to my current beliefs. I felt for a second as though danger were at hand—but *without* any urge to alert others in the car, as I would have been inclined to do in light of a universalizable belief that I was in danger. Given the rather trivial nature of this lapse from rationality and the fact that I would readily acknowledge it as such, it is unclear why I would conceal anything about it—from myself as well as from others. This includes even a suppressed urge that would let us back it up with an *unconscious* belief.

My danger-evaluation here may be thought of as "unconscious" in some sense since I did not become aware of it until immediately after the gasp-response—feeling somewhat sheepish about my excessive reaction but not particularly concerned to hide the thought that provoked it. To ascribe an unconscious *belief* to me, however, we would need some explanation of my failure to apply it to others, even at the time when I apparently applied it to myself. I take it that, for simplicity's sake, we ought to avoid exceeding the evidence in our appeal to irrational sources of motivation. So unless there is evidence of fairly deep cognitive disruption in the earlier situation—of a sort that might give rise to a *non*-universalizable belief—we ought to trust my denials in this case and in at least some imaginable versions of the Fido case as well. There is more to explanatory simplicity, in short, than theoretical neatness, or the sort of neatness that results from subsuming emotion under belief. Irrationality counts as a complicating factor from the standpoint of psychological explanation; so a simpler explanation will sometimes be one that multiplies mental subsystems—in this case, cutting off emotion from belief—rather than tolerating logical disorder within the system of belief.

I shall later cite some further cases, particularly of emotions based on fantasy, where judgmentalism seems to have counterintuitive consequences. But note that my treatment of these two cases, with its appeal to a principle of logical charity, does not commit us to accepting without question an agent's intuitions about what he believes. Nor does it depend on a view of belief as involving *certainty*. The belief corresponding to fear—the belief whose content is given by the evaluative component of fear—might sometimes be held tentatively, where the agent thinks he does not have adequate evidence for it. It amounts to a belief that injury is likely in the sense of "apt to occur"; and the agent might hold this in combination with a background belief that ascribes to him only slight evidence for it. But in these two cases, on our assumption, he thinks he already has adequate evidence for the *contrary* belief. He knows that Fido is *not* likely to bite him, for instance, though the thought still comes to mind and affects him emotionally. If we say that he also believes that Fido *is* a threat, then, we shall be ascribing to him a more extreme sort of irrationality than is necessary, lumping together all episodes of predication under the heading of "judgment" so that he comes out believing contrary judgments. We would do better, I think, to allow for some thoughts that are not logically connected to the agent's beliefs and hence do not count as beliefs themselves. This decision rests on logical charity, construed not merely as respect for the agent's system of beliefs—including any background beliefs *about* what he believes—but more fundamentally as a way of distinguishing that system from just any collection of predicative states.

(ii) Tamped-Down Affect

There is another version of the Fido case, designed to show that a case of occurrent fear need not exhibit the particular sensations characteristic of fear—or even, perhaps, any episode of sensation. I shall understand an "occurrent" emotion as a current condition of emotional experience, a "running" state—to appeal to the roots of both "current" and "occurrent"—if only in the sense that it runs through the present time. The contrast here is with merely "dispositional" fear, or the disposition *to* feel afraid—under certain conditions that may not be realized now or perhaps ever. For instance, even if the agent never has to deal with a dog again, he still "dispositionally" fears Fido and dogs generally. But though ordinary language makes no clear distinction and the occurrent/dispositional distinction may be interpreted differently, I want to make room for the case where the agent's fear of dogs is "activated," in present terms, while its manifestations are controlled. The point is to avoid limiting occurrent emotional states to states exhibiting full-blown emotion symptoms—states of extreme agitation, of a sort that are often maladaptive, in the case of fear.

An encounter with Fido is foreseen, let us suppose; so the agent has time for a rehearsal of alternatives for coping with the situation emotionally. He may manage to suppress the usual symptoms of fear by keeping himself, with a good deal of effort, from paying much explicit attention to Fido, though he knows that Fido is nearby. He does not feel *fear*, perhaps—a particular sensation, or collection of sensations, to which the noun would naturally apply—but I do want to say that he feels *afraid*, just insofar as he is edgily aware of the impression of nearby danger. He is uncomfortable "at the thought that" danger looms— the "thought" in my analysis pattern need not be explicitly entertained, remember— and this is enough for ascribing to him one of the varieties of occurrent fear. It is not as though he were emotionally unaffected by the situation— as he would be, say, if he had undergone successful treatment for his dog phobia, or if his short-term preparations for this situation had left him completely relaxed. Though a weaker fear term, such as "worry," might yield a more precise description of his present emotional state, it does seem to count as a state of "tamped-down" fear and not just a disposition to feel full-blown fear under certain unrealized conditions. He currently experiences discomfort at the evaluation characteristic of fear even if its characteristic affective symptoms are blocked. No doubt his fear would be more intense under other conditions—if he were not now working at controlling it by self-distraction. But the fact that he does have to work at this, at a cost in present discomfort, is sufficient for the ascription of occurrent fear, on my view, if his discomfort has the right sort of object.

Consider again my fear of skidding—a disposition, as ascribed to me now, to feel afraid when faced with the possibility of skidding. Since I occasionally have to commute some distance in an area where snow is handled poorly and since all-out fear symptoms are not a help while driving, my relevant experiences now fall into three categories: (1) *anticipatory fear*, the night before, as I watch the snow pile up and worry about the drive, imagining various possible accidents (with sped-up heartbeat and so forth); (2) *tamped-down fear*, during the drive, experienced as unpleasantly intense concentration on the task of avoiding skids (mentally sweating over it, let us say, with more than the ordinary degree of edginess); and (3) *full fear symptoms* (the gasp-response mentioned earlier, along with some physiological reactions), experienced when my tires fail to grip immediately. I would count all of these as occurrent fear states, with fear activated to some degree or other. They are certainly different from the purely dispositional fear of skidding that I have even as I write this, without any need to work at controlling fear symptoms and hence without discomfort of even a generalized sort. Although they differ importantly from each other, they can all be characterized in general terms as involving occurrent discomfort at a thought of danger.

In a way, the most clear-cut case is (1)—my long-term worry about the next day's drive—though it does not always involve the full set of fear symptoms and is directed in part towards imaginary objects. It amounts, at times, to a kind of fantasy-rehearsal of fear-while-driving, letting myself feel more than simple worry about the drive. The point, if I understand it, is to get the intrusive fear symptoms over with in advance, so that (2), my actual fear-while-driving, moves down in intensity to a state of productive worry. Unfortunately, this strategy does not help with (3), my reaction to a skid, though it makes (3) less likely to occur by preventing skids. But (3) is so brief and so much like a reflex that it is questionable whether it involves an *act* of evaluating the perceptual situation as dangerous. It is somewhat like jumping out of one's chair at some sudden event in a horror film—assuming also a jump in thought, since the "reflex" here is not just behavioral. Rather, it seems, a danger-evaluation has been framed earlier, in another situation, and is brought to bear on this one—though not as a current *belief*—by the perception of uncontrolled car movement.[2] In short, though none of these cases involves full-blown fear, of the sort that I might feel if the situation of my accident were repeated, my account of the emotion will include them all as occurrent fear states.

(iii) Invented Objects

To cover the varieties of fear, then, we must adopt an analysis that tells us very little, blurring together very different sorts of discomfort, different sorts of danger-evaluation—and sometimes, as I shall now argue briefly, different causal connections between the two. In standard cases the evaluative object of discomfort is also its cause. But discomfort can sometimes simply "take on" an object. Consider a case of initially objectless sensation—"pure" edginess, a result of drinking too much coffee—that *turns into* an emotional state by attaching to an available (external) object. The object need not be one that the agent would otherwise evaluate as threatening. Perhaps it is a task that he usually performs routinely—driving in good conditions, for instance—but in this case he comes to evaluate it in a way that would *explain* his feelings of agitation. We may think of the evaluation as an "invented" (internal) object of his anxiety, without which it would not amount to an emotion—even "objectless" anxiety, of the sort that one might feel if the evaluation were indefinite. In any case, if the evaluation lasts no longer than the coffee-caused affect that precedes it and if it does not seem to change the latter in quality, we would not have grounds even for a claim that the evaluation sustained or modified the affect. So here their usual causal relation would seem to be reversed.

Variants of the coffee-case may be used to illustrate and extend some of the main points made so far—eventually leading, via the notion of an invented object, to the acceptance of unconscious emotions in certain cases. In its present form, with *only* an invented object, it does not seem to require explanation in terms of unconscious anxiety or even the sort of unconscious *evaluation*—of failure as a threat, say—that may sometimes stand behind conscious anxiety. But it suggests that even conscious emotions may arise from some sort of unconscious need to connect up mental states intentionally. For what makes the agent's affective state come to be a state of occurrent *emotion* in this case is the fact that it comes to be object-directed. His initial, objectless edginess becomes anxiety by giving rise to a characteristic evaluation of some object of attention—or in cases of "objectless" anxiety just to an evaluation of something unspecified. The indefinite evaluation may be thought of as an intermediate stage in the search for something to explain the affect intentionally; and indeed the search may proceed even in cases where the agent is perfectly aware of the physiological causes of his feeling. For he may have other, more pressing objects of attention—or simply a tendency to look for something that his discomfort is about.

Thus, faced with the task of getting somewhere on time, an agent may know perfectly well that his sudden anxiety is the result of too much coffee without being able to banish the anxiety or to keep it from focusing on that object in particular. At times, he may "explain it away"; but he does not thereby turn it into something else—an objectless edginess that merely accompanies the thought of failure, say, in the way that a headache might accompany it. His state amounts to fear of failure, on the view defended here, as long as it involves discomfort at the thought that failure is a real threat—that it is likely to be realized and to prove injurious as things stand. We should note, in fact, that in this case he may withhold assent even from the specifically evaluative aspect of the proposition that constitutes the internal object of his fear. The physiological effects of drinking too much coffee may give rise to an exaggerated view of the *disvalue* of the envisioned threat—failure at a relatively minor task—as well as of its likelihood, the factual matter at issue in the previous cases. Where an agent is aware of this, we may have further reason for supposing that his danger-evaluation does not involve a belief.

Nor would the corresponding belief be *sufficient* for occurrent fear, let us also note—even if it did cause characteristic fear symptoms as well as generalized discomfort. We can imagine a case, that is, with all the elements of fear in place, exhibiting the usual causal connection but not the emotion since the requisite sort of *intentional* connection is missing.

We might suppose, for instance, that while I am driving in good conditions, a dispassionate judgment of slight danger reminds me so vividly of my accident in the snow that I briefly experience chills and shudders in reaction to my nonevaluative memories of being cold. Here a danger-evaluation causes my discomfort; but the result is not fear, since my discomfort is not *about* the evaluation—or, let us grant, about a fantasy-evaluation of the same general sort, based on imagining myself in the earlier situation. My discomfort is not directed towards any *evaluation*, that is, even a negative evaluation of being cold. But more to the point, it is not directed towards a danger-evaluation; so it does not yield fear, despite its causal connection to a danger-evaluation. To rule out such cases by insisting that the causal connection must be immediate, moreover—excluding any cases where the path from evaluation to affect is circuitous, as it is here—would seem to rule out some cases of genuine emotion. We might add a further stage to the present example, say, on the model of the coffee case, by supposing that I react to my discomfort by connecting it intentionally to the danger-evaluation that began my train of thought. Here my discomfort *takes on* an object and thereby does yield fear.

In the original coffee case, then, we should not be hasty about positing an unconscious evaluation just to save the standard causal account of emotional response. We need a special reason, I take it, for mistrusting the agent's denials that some prior danger-evaluation stood behind his reaction—for insisting that on some level inaccessible to reflection he already did see tasks like driving as threatening him with failure, say. My unconscious evaluation in the skidding case is not unconscious in this sense: After a skid, I can immediately identify what I have gasped *at* as a thought of danger, formed earlier and needed to explain my behavioral response. Since the coffee case allows for emotions with "invented" objects, it does provide the *basis*, as we shall see, for an argument that emotions sometimes involve unconscious evaluations in the deeper sense. But here, too, we need some reason beyond theoretical neatness for appealing beyond accessible consciousness. It would be a different story, for instance, if the agent's behavior exhibited a tendency to avoid tasks like driving or to look for possibilities of failure in general—and to withhold from himself such evidence of irrationality. We might then have grounds for positing an unconscious danger-evaluation that at least caused his coffee-induced edginess to focus on a particular (external) object. Without the behavioral evidence, though, appeal to an unconscious danger-evaluation would seem to be unnecessary to explain his sudden anxiety. Rather, we may grant that feeling sometimes just takes on an object, by prompting the agent to come up with thoughts that would link it to objects of attention. We might want to explain this "rationalizing" tendency by reference to some sort of unconscious evaluation—a negative evaluation, perhaps, of mental states that have not been connected up intentionally. But we need not posit an unconscious version of *the* evaluative *component* of the resultant emotion.

In cases where an unconscious danger-evaluation *is* operative, however, the same rationalizing tendency can result in *multiple* (internal) objects, with one invented to "mask" the other. I now want to show how my minimal account of emotions can use this fact to explain unconscious emotions—not as paradoxically "unfelt feelings," as Freud (on most accounts) thought they would have to be, but without emptying them of occurrent feeling either.[3] On my view, they involve feelings that are felt but misidentified, usually because of psychological barriers to acknowledging their objects. For there are some cases where the agent's conscious emotional reactions—their felt quality and evaluative content, as well as their behavioral consequences—are not adequately explained without reference to an unconscious emotion, in this sense. The agent may feel discomfort, for instance, but fail to recognize that it is directed towards a danger-evaluation and hence fail to see that it amounts to fear. We might want to say that his *fear* is "unfelt" in that case; but its affective component—"feeling" in the narrower sense—is felt. He simply fails to identify it *as* a feeling of fear, perhaps because his fear is masked by another emotion. Where there is reason for supposing that the unconscious danger-evaluation is one of the objects of his discomfort, then, we can still say that he feels *afraid*—not just that he *would* feel afraid under certain unrealized conditions, as with dispositional fear.

Consider fear of failure—an unconscious emotion whose evaluative component surfaced briefly in my preceding discussion of the coffee case, to be rejected as unnecessary to an explanation of coffee-induced anxiety about some task. Now suppose there are reasons for thinking that an unconscious fear of failure does motivate the agent's behavior in general and is something he would take pains to deny. He abhors such signs of weakness, say, but his behavior indicates a tendency to drop major projects just at the point where they become difficult enough to pose a threat. What he feels at the time when he drops them is not anxiety, though, but boredom. He does genuinely *feel* boredom, let us grant. His discomfort has fixed upon another evaluation, of the project as uninteresting—a persistent thought that he may or may not believe. But we can also say that he is uncomfortable *about* the threat of failure, even though he has hidden this object from himself and with it a belief that failure is likely, or likely to prove injurious. We may need to say this in order to explain his conscious feelings—why he becomes restless rather than simply indifferent at just the point when he does—and it may be borne out by the emergence of anxiety after long-term introspection. If so, on my account, his boredom may mask a kind of fear—an occurrent state of fear, not just a disposition to exhibit fear symptoms with the appropriate sort of introspective prodding, and certainly not just a disposition towards strategies of risk-avoidance.

Why not limit ourselves to the weaker claim that an unconscious danger-evaluation *caused* the agent's discomfort and *would become* an object of discomfort and hence an internal object of fear with enough prodding? We could then stick closer to the agent's own view of his emotional life, it seems, counting only objects of attention as objects of occurrent feeling. But the analysis of his past reactions may lead the agent to see in retrospect that he was *acting out of* anxiety, while working to distract attention from the threatening features of his situation. Indeed, he may even acknowledge that his attention really was directed towards those features and was so because they were threatening, though he was not then aware of them as such. Nor need analysis be painful enough to suggest that he was browbeaten into a *change* of emotion, along with delusion about his past reactions. Indeed, it may not be *psycho*analysis that is in question here, but just the sort of rational analysis that we naturally engage in when an emotion ascription does not seem to make sense of the agent's situation or of some action that he introduces the emotion to explain. Since the alternative explanation involves positing unconscious "contents" of conscious states of feeling—a notion that may seem paradoxical itself—I shall pause to illustrate it in some detail, with an everyday sort of case I once observed.

A Case of Unconscious Jealousy. The "analytic work" here consisted in long conversation with a student—someone whose inclination to terminate a love affair immediately, apparently out of fear that it might absorb too much time, seemed to serve no rational purpose if I accepted her explanation of it. On the other hand, it did exhibit at least "basic" rationality once it was linked to some reasons for fearing loss of attention—the sort of fear that I take to be involved in *jealousy*.[4] The worry about becoming overcommitted was *felt*, clearly, but its object did not bear scrutiny—the affair was quite easily contained, if that was what was wanted—as the agent granted without hesitation each time the question was raised. But the worry persisted; and with overcommitment as its object it did not seem to account for her decision to cut things off immediately—before an anticipated absence over summer vacation. On the other hand, there were some grounds for uncertainty about the permanence of the relationship, and after being made to go over these in some detail, she eventually acknowledged *loss* as the real focus of her fear.

Coming to see the operative emotion here as a not so obviously unfounded fear of loss had an immediate and dramatic effect on the agent's behavior. She suddenly was able to pinpoint a number of causes of the emotion in her recent experience and began to construct reasonable plans for dealing with it, taking steps to strengthen the relationship. My guess is that no deep conflict was involved in this case but simply a kind of self-deception, perhaps out of moral or other objections to jealousy, or to jealousy in a relationship that *was* to be kept within tight bounds. That the agent's conscious discomfort was also, and more fundamentally, directed towards an unconscious object seems to me to be the simplest way of explaining, on the assumption of basic rationality, why the emotion did not evaporate when its surface object was agreed not to be her problem. During the intermediate stage of searching for its deeper object, her discomfort both persisted and seemed clearly to be *about* something—something specific, though not yet specified, not just something-or-other.

During the intermediate stage, moreover, her discomfort still seemed to function motivationally as an overriding reason for terminating the relationship—even though on her account its intensity was outweighed by the *pleasures* of the relationship. Presumably, if it had amounted merely to objectless discomfort or even to "objectless" *anxiety*, its rational bearing on escape behavior would have depended solely on its positive or negative assessment as a state of experience. Here, however, the content of the evaluation that caused the discomfort apparently influenced the weight the agent assigned to it as a reason against continuing the relationship. This suggests that the evaluation amounted to an *object* of discomfort even while it was unconscious. It would be odd, at best, to take its motivational role as depending on unconscious knowledge of a causal generalization—one spelling out its connection to "objectless" anxiety—or as only incidentally converging with a role played by objectless discomfort. Where an evaluation that makes better sense of motivation is found among those that an agent has on hand and its discovery alters behavior in emotional terms, it seems more plausible to count it as an unconscious internal object of emotion.

We may grant, then, that the agent in this case unconsciously *felt* jealous as long as her discomfort persisted. She did not feel jealousy—whether a particular characteristic sensation or an awareness of the emotion as such. I take that to make sense only on the conscious level, but not to pose a problem, if we include cases of tamped-down fear, where the agent feels afraid though he does not feel fear, as cases of occurrent emotion, in accordance with my earlier suggestion. In this case our rec-

ognition of an unconscious object of discomfort yields a reasonable explanation of the agent's motivation; and her own recognition of the object
yielded reasonable changes in both her motivation and various surrounding behaviors. I would also lay some weight on her after-the-fact
report of motivation. It would only complicate matters, after all, to suppose that the evaluation characteristic of jealousy *became* the emotion
only when it became a conscious object of discomfort. For even before
then, it apparently produced motivational effects typical of the emotion—
of *discomfort at* the evaluation of loss as a danger.

Of course, I am in no position here to settle detailed questions of
unconscious motivation. What I mean to do is mainly to make a case for
the claim that we sometimes have multiple propositional objects of the
same feeling, one of them unrecognized but causally operative, the other
wrongly identified as the feeling's cause. The former amounts to the
internal object of an unconscious emotion, on a view that is independent
of the details of Freudian doctrine—and that also will keep our notion
of an object from fitting neatly into philosophers' standard explanatory
categories. I have picked out objects here intuitively—just by reference
to "about"-phrases in common language—taking it as a "brute" fact (not
to be explained in this essay, at any rate) that a feeling of comfort or
discomfort may be about an evaluative proposition. Philosophers have
often tried to explain direction towards an object in terms of *causation*
by it.[5] But in cases like the coffee case, the causal relation seems to run
in reverse: a feeling seems to give rise to an evaluative proposition, as
something that would explain it intentionally in terms of current objects
of attention. This might suggest that emotional object-directedness can
at least be explained in terms of objects of *attention*. But in cases like the
case of unconscious jealousy at least one object of feeling is *not* an object
of attention. At most, we can say that attention *would* be directed towards
it if it were not "masked" by another evaluative proposition. When we
speak of the affective component of emotion, then, as "serving to hold
an evaluation in mind," we must mean something similarly hypothetical,
allowing for barriers to the natural tendency to focus on objects of feeling.
    My account of unconscious emotions is also meant to allow for the
possibility of long-term occurrent emotions: "abiding fears," for instance,
such as fear of failure and of loss, usually conscious at times, but not at
all times when they are activated. Their influence on motivation makes
it odd to take them, when they are unconscious, just as *dispositions* to
feel—or to behave in certain ways or to entertain certain thoughts. It is
surely not obvious, in any case, that they involve dispositions to feel *fear,*

as on the standard interpretation of dispositional emotions. On the verge of loss, say, an agent who fears loss deeply might just feel deeply despondent, without agitation or any urge to guard against the threat. Someone who acts out of a long-term occurrent fear of loss, moreover, is not simply timid about risking loss—likely to avoid it or to feel fear when he contemplates it—in the way that I am timid about driving in the snow. Nor is he simply acting in light of his emotional dispositions— in the way that I now might head off future fear by making arrangements to ride in to work with someone else next winter. On my view he is also attempting to alleviate his present discomfort *at* a danger-evaluation— in the first instance, by acting to falsify the evaluation. He is motivated *by* emotion, not simply by dispassionate judgment and desire.

It might be objected that abiding fears and other long-term occurrent emotions are more naturally thought of as *moods*. Moods, though somewhat transient, usually seem to be less so than emotions; and they usually seem to be directed towards less specific objects. However, the categories of emotion and mood exhibit a good deal of overlap, particularly with respect to "objectless" emotions. Although I have made occasional reference to "objectless" anxiety in this chapter, my general discussion of such emotions will await the treatment in my next chapter of some cases that are less commonly dismissed as irrational. It should already be clear, however, that I take them to be full-fledged cases of emotion, but with indefinite evaluations as internal objects. Fear of failure and similar examples may be said to be *semi*-"objectless," just insofar as their evaluative components are semi-indefinite: They pick out a particular *sort* of likely injury but not a specific *source*. Indeed, the main evidence for their long-term motivational influence is a tendency to *look for* the latter— and to find it everywhere. Since the notion of an unconscious object of discomfort necessarily leaves open many questions of verification, it is tempting to avoid them by treating such cases just as combinations of moods and dispositions. But assuming that "objectlessness" does not rule out their inclusion among occurrent emotions as well, we can defend their inclusion, at least in principle, by exhibiting its plausibility for cases with fairly definite evaluative components.

Consider, first, someone living in an area under siege, constantly on the lookout for bombs, but managing to suppress the conscious manifestations of her fear—perhaps by masking it with another fear. She mainly worries about her children, say, though she knows they have managed to escape to comparative safety; and she contemplates the danger to herself only rarely, with apparent dispassion. But once the war is over—possibly much later—she may acknowledge that she was in a constant state of tension at the time *about* the likelihood of injury in an explosion. Here we seem to have tamped-down fear, masked by fear with an invented object; and the result is a fairly broad temporal extension of the scope of occurrent fear. For if we trust the agent's own after-the-fact account in this case—and we seem to have no reason not to—what she was experiencing, besides concern for her children, was more than an anxious *mood*, accompanied by a tendency to look out for unexploded bombs. It was also long-term *fear*, with discomfort directed towards a fairly specific object.

Apart from problems of verification, I see no reason for a different treatment of cases where the suppressed emotion is irrational. These may not always be so readily understood by imaginative appeal to the reactions of a basically rational agent; but sometimes they are understandable enough. Consider a shorter-term emotion, but one that persists beyond its relevant temporal context. Perhaps the agent finds himself wondering, at some point during the day, why it is that he has spent the whole day feeling anxious. After some searching, he may conclude that the feeling he has been carrying around is not just "objectless" anxiety but more fundamentally *anger*: A clerk insulted him that morning, say, and there was no way he could respond. Revenge is even less achievable now, of course; but his anger has sustained itself by going underground— as he recognizes immediately when he manages to locate the cause of his discomfort. "Abiding fears" are really no more questionable in principle than the emotions in these examples; but they are longer-term and less susceptible to rational explanation in light of the agent's perceptual situation, even broadly construed.

(iv) Comfort and Discomfort

So far, I have attempted to interpret the unconscious manifestations of long-term occurrent fear as involving felt discomfort at a danger-evaluation, where the agent is unaware of the evaluation or perhaps just of the fact that it is an object of discomfort. But there may even be some cases where discomfort itself is something the agent does not recognize as such, at least at the time when he feels it. He might later come to realize, say, that he has been acting out of unconscious anxiety, though at the time he thought he felt extremely good. We need not deny that he did feel good; but we may have grounds for positing some negative affect as well. For instance, after probing into states of manic activity, during which he felt a heady thrill, he might come to see that his aroused state also had a *feverish* quality, unpleasant at the time, though he was then unaware of its unpleasant aspect. I want to allow, in fact, that emotional states, including conscious states, often involve affective mixture: comfort laced with, or layered over, discomfort. For even many genuinely pleasurable emotions, such as thrilled anticipation, do not amount to pure states of comfort, construed as states in which one rests content.

My claim here is not just a claim about the terminological oddity of describing pleasurable emotional arousal as "comfortable." I do grant that point, though, I should note. My comfort/discomfort opposition is intended to capture a first-person motivational assessment of affect, corresponding to whether an agent would naturally seek or avoid a given affective state. States of extreme intensity, however, even where they are properly classified as positive or negative by this criterion, may fit more idiomatically into the familiar pleasure/pain contrast. It seems lame, at best, to describe a state of ecstasy as comfortable—or of horror, for that matter, as *un*comfortable. But there are familiar pitfalls associated with the terms "pleasure" and "pain"—in particular, a tendency to take them as standing for isolable episodes of objectless experience. A related grammatical deficiency, moreover, would interfere with my main purposes here: The terms seem to lack adjectival forms for persons *undergoing* pleasure or pain *about* some proposition. The closest parallel to "I am comfortable," for instance, would seem to be "I am pleased"—an expression ascribing approval, rather than pleasure, to the agent. Similarly, "I am pained" apparently substitutes disapproval for pain—besides departing from idiom when applied to a propositional object. I have accepted another kind of artificiality, then, for the sake of grammatical uniformity, in adopting canonical expressions for the positive and negative affective qualities contrasted here. I use the term "comfort," most notably, to cover states of contented exhilaration—pure ecstasy and the like—despite their deviation from its usual "relaxed" connotations. But even taking note of this convention, I think we have to grant that pleasurable emotional arousal, to the extent that it involves some *striving*, involves *both* comfort and discomfort.

Discomfort is here construed as a state that an agent would naturally want to escape from—not itself a desire, but a source of desires, under appropriate circumstances. By detaching it from particular sensations as well as from conscious thought I have allowed for a broader range of occurrent emotions than those commonly recognized. But I do insist on an "extrajudgmental" component of some sort. A mental state like uncertainty, for instance, may or may not count as an emotion, depending on whether the agent *feels* bad about the negative evaluation of his current state of knowledge. My account should not be expected, then, to yield a neat ordering of emotions or one that corresponds neatly to our ordinary emotion terms. By allowing for the mixture of emotional comfort and discomfort, most notably, it rules out an easy division of emotions into "positive" and "negative." It does require that a positive or negative affective component be directed towards a corresponding evaluative component in the analysis of a given emotion; but some emotions may break down into several such pairs of components, opposing each other in affective quality. An enjoyable state like active curiosity, for instance, mixes pleasurable wonder with uncertainty and with a desire for action to *resolve* uncertainty. On my account, the latter amounts to discomfort that some such action is still called for.

Not all affective mixtures, however, are implied by the very analysis of an emotion. For cases of extrinsic mixture—cases whose explanation further undermines judgmentalism—let us consider some apparently pleasurable fear states. Fear experienced while watching a horror film was mentioned earlier as resembling my reflex-like reaction to the perception of a slight skid. But of course it is important that the horror reaction does not seem to involve a desire for action or a judgment of immediate danger to oneself.[6] Sometimes one is seeing the film from the point of view of some character or characters in it or possibly just an invented character—an anonymous member of the fleeing crowd, perhaps—on whose behalf one reacts to a perceived threat. Sometimes the horror reaction is not simple *fear* but a peculiar sort of repugnance compounded with fear. When Dracula ages centuries and disintegrates in the light, say, what one feels does not depend on identifying with Dracula—or for that matter, with the characters who have tracked him down, since they are now out of danger. Rather, the sight is a hideous thing *to see*, even as merely depicted on a screen. It is an object of more than disgust, though, because of its link with more general objects of fear: our own slower death and decay. But for much the same reason it yields pleasure. We seek it out, or some of us do, at least partly because such fears are seldom faced squarely—indeed, it is not clear how they could be—in real life. This fearful horror is grounded in *dread*—the fear of something inescapable—made comfortable here by its focus on an exaggerated symbol, and one that will soon fade from sight.

We should note, though, that even in a case of straightforward fear at a horror film—at the point when someone leaps out at the heroine with a knife, say—it is not the release of fear itself that is pleasurable, at least in immediate terms, but the fact that one is soon released *from* it. The overall feeling is discomfort yielding to comfort—a kind of "roller coaster" sensation that is pleasurable on the whole. One would not want to stay at the top, I take it—even without a belief that danger is at hand, but just the corresponding evaluation. Those adults I know who leave horror films or avoid them entirely because of excessive reactions apparently do so not because they are deluded by events on the screen but because they cannot *shake off* the danger-evaluation. The rest of us find the experience enjoyable in a way that may involve evaluating events on the screen from the standpoint of a character in the situation depicted but does not involve believing that we are in that situation ourselves. Our pleasure depends on unwavering belief in a more distant evaluation, of ourselves as relatively safe, so that we do not have to spend much time reassuring ourselves that our momentary danger-evaluation is false. Though we may be *emotionally* ambivalent, then, it is important that we do not hold contrary *judgments* in such cases. Our enjoyment of the overall experience can be explained without supposing that fear is itself enjoyable here; but the explanation seems to rest in part on detaching emotional evaluation from belief.

Even if certain fear *sensations* would be pleasurable when felt in isolation, moreover—as "pure" feelings, not directed towards a danger-evaluation—I take it that they would not be pleasurable in the manner of fear at a horror film. Of course, there is a certain enjoyment for some of us in brooding on invented or exaggerated objects of fear outside of films—sometimes even in making them real if only to overcome them, as in the daredevil's quest for danger. But I still would resist a claim that fear is ever pleasurable in itself. For one thing, we need to be able to distinguish the daredevil who seeks out *fear* from one who merely feels *thrilled* by the thought of danger or the thought of overcoming danger. In some such cases fear may be essential to an overall experience that is pleasurable: the experience of fear followed by relief or accompanied by a sense of immunity to danger gained by facing danger repeatedly in imagination or in real life. Even where the object of fear is known to be at least semi-imaginary, such experiences amount to real episodes of fear, though the symptoms may be somewhat mitigated in intensity, or intensity compounded by duration, as compared with fears directed towards *objects* taken as real. They all involve discomfort at the thought that some danger is at hand—at its seeming to be at hand, even if one also takes comfort in the thought that it is not or that it can easily be conquered.

I shall later make out certain emotions as *intrinsically* involving mixed affect since their analyses involve both positive and negative evaluations. This would seem to be the case for all emotions that essentially involve *desire*, on my account, along with comfort—including comfort at anticipating the satisfaction of desire—since I make out emotional, or "motivating," desire in terms of discomfort. But fearful dread does not seem to involve desire in this sense and thus may be thought of as passive. Moreover, those more typical varieties of fear that do give rise in context to a motivating desire seldom leave much room for the pleasures of anticipation. The daredevil's confident fear may be *a*typical in this respect; but where it actually involves a desire to flee, his mixture of emotions would seem to amount to a case of ambivalence. His confidence is *layered over* fear, that is, retaining its distinctness rather than being *blended into* the emotion. His fear might be said to heighten the pleasure of the mixture, if only by sharpening his perceptions, in advance of any pleasure he feels when fear yields to relief; but that is not to say that the emotion imports some advance pleasure of its own.

The daredevil example also indicates, though, that claims about the intrinsic or extrinsic features of a given emotion must be applied with some caution to particular emotion instances. Indeed, even emotions picked out by the same general term will exhibit a kind of classificatory variability, on my account. Some of the cases treated here as varieties of fear, for example, may be expected to fall into different categories on different occurrences. Suspicion and jealousy may often be manifested in *anger*, say, either mixed with fear or standing on its own, but at any rate involving some anticipatory pleasure at revenge. I might be suspiciously on the lookout for signs of untrustworthiness from X, for instance, not out of a desire to protect myself but because I want to get back at him and need some specific reason for blame. And cases of jealousy quite often involve blame, of both the person whose favor is in question and a putative rival for it. The agent may feel that the other parties have failed to respect his right to exclusive favor and that they therefore deserve punishment of some sort. Here we may have *both* fear and anger and both as occurrent states, though probably the agent's conscious feelings would mainly be feelings of anger—more readily dischargeable through action and hence a source of greater anticipatory comfort.

Such overlaps and shifts in our uses of emotion terms provide a reason against assigning emotions classificatory "essences"; but there are more telling reasons. Even to pick out cases of fear as such, we may sometimes have to appeal beyond the very general pattern of analysis I have proposed. With dread counted as a variety of fear, for instance, we cannot take fear as necessarily a "pressuring" emotion, involving a desire for action, just by virtue of its negative affect and evaluative content. But then we might need to say something more specific about the agitated affective quality of fearful dread in order to distinguish it from other future-oriented negative emotions. Gloom, for instance, where it amounts to deep despondency at all envisioned future possibilities, is passive in affective quality as well as motivationally; so it does not amount to a fear state, though it fits my general pattern for analyzing fears. The features that mark off fears, though, cannot be the same for all cases, it seems, if the notion is to cover the full range of occurrent fears, as mapped out in this chapter. Although discomfort at a certain evaluation is taken as a necessary condition of fear, that is, and in that sense as essential *to* it, some fears may have to be picked out as such by further specification of the discomfort and some by further specification of its evaluative object or objects. In particular, some tamped-down fears involve a more *brooding* form of discomfort, though unlike dread they also involve the typical desire to escape an object of fear since the discomfort takes on an action requirement as a further object in context.

My analysis, then, is not designed to give necessary and sufficient conditions for inclusion in a given emotion category, though it *is* meant to provide them for inclusion in the class of emotions. But despite its limitations—or perhaps just because of them—it should prove useful as a way of structuring our explanation of particular cases. We may approach the more complex emotions by linking them to a few that are fairly basic and then further specifying their affective and evaluative components, with the latter taken as explaining something, but not everything, about the quality of the former. It should be clear, though, that I have nothing in mind here—since I think that nothing is achievable—resembling the tight definitions of emotions by category that one finds in some authors. Seventeenth-century philosophers constructed all emotions out of a short list of "primary" states; and both Aristotle and Hume take emotion categories to be much more uniformly specified than I do here.[7] But my general account is not far from these—or from judgmentalist (and other evaluative) theories—except for the insistence on positive or negative feeling *tone*, with a corresponding propositional *object*, as a substitute for traditional talk of sensations of pleasure or pain.

I think that our ordinary emotion concepts are too disorderly, moreover, for linguistic analysis to yield much of interest without supplementation—and sometimes revision—in light of both careful introspection and a not-too-literal sense of what words mean. Fear provides a particularly vivid example of the discrimination needed to sift through emotion locutions for those that actually ascribe the relevant emotions; for "I am afraid that" is often used in English to mean "I regret to say that." When a doctor says to his patient, for instance, "I'm afraid you're dying of cancer," he is not claiming to be in a fear state. Fear is in many ways an odd example, in fact; but it is the standard initial example in treatments of the emotions—perhaps because, when it is fully activated, its symptoms are the most clear-cut (and the least helpful) in adult human life. Also, as I noted at the beginning of this chapter, it is relatively easily characterized in affective and propositional terms as involving discomfort at a danger-evaluation of one sort or another. At this point, however, we would do well to explore some further sorts of cases both to test out, clarify, and expand the suggestions made so far and to bring in a few sources of emotional pleasure.

I shall begin my next chapter by providing a kind of unifying theme for this wider-ranging discussion, picking out some common elements of the cases to be explored in relation to the question of the *moral* significance of the emotions. But quite a number of diverse issues will emerge in that discussion, and one result of it will, in effect, be to undermine my order of inquiry in this essay, ending Part I by anticipating many of the issues of Part II. In approaching questions of emotional justification, it seems obvious that one ought to begin with a treatment of the nature of emotion. I grant, indeed, that one first ought to settle on a workable analysis of emotion, if only in order to formulate the justificatory questions intelligibly; so I have retained the standard order of inquiry here, at least in main outline. But I also think that any adequate defense of a view on what emotions are must appeal to answers to some of the "later" questions. In fact, we have already glimpsed this intertwining of topics in my defense of unconscious jealousy in the present chapter. One main piece of evidence for the unconscious emotion, and hence for the general account of emotions that would allow for it, was its role in yielding a rational explanation of the agent's motivation. This sort of motivational influence is needed even to understand the notion of an unconscious emotion, on my account—to give sense to my talk of affect as "holding in mind" an evaluative thought in cases where it is not an object of attention. Just as judgments are picked out as such by their logical connections, then, so the nature of emotions will turn on our answers to questions of emotional justification.

3
Some Morally Significant Emotions: Rewards and Punishments

Some recent approaches to moral philosophy, focusing particularly on altruistic emotions, have maintained that we have a legitimate interest in what others *feel* as well as in their detached judgments and desires.[1] Others' compassion, for instance, is valued beyond the mere belief that our sufferings ought to be alleviated and whether or not any action on their part would help to alleviate our sufferings. I think this is true and important to note for the sake of *both* our understanding of morality and our understanding of the emotions. But I also think that it ought to be extended beyond altruistic emotions—eventually to the full range of emotions, brought together by a form of compassion that I shall call "identificatory love." This is not a single emotion but a tendency to take on various identificatory emotions, in response to others' emotional pleasures and pains—to fear "for" them when they are threatened, say. On my brief account of identificatory fear in response to films in my last chapter, it should be obvious that this cannot always involve a judgment. Instead, it may involve feeling as though one is in a situation of danger oneself—or, as I shall suggest in what follows, as though one is specially *responsible for action* on behalf of those who are.

I shall later deal with some questions about how this sort of identificatory evaluation can count as rational. For the moment, however, I shall simply accept it as a possible imaginative response to the perception of another's standpoint—something not limited to films. In this chapter I want eventually to contrast it with the evaluative standpoint involved in emotions that preserve the sense of one's own real-life situation, including more distant forms of compassion, directed *towards* the other person. First, though, I want, in effect, to expand our conception of the possible contents of identificatory love by examining some "personal" emotions that are *not* based on evaluations of another person's perceived sufferings but that may themselves be morally significant as rewards or punishments. I shall consider pride (i), anger (ii), and what I shall call attachment-love (iii). Like fear, as we shall see, these also pose problems for a unitary account of "an" emotion—though partly because of their greater cognitive complexity—and I shall not attempt a complete treatment of any of them. My aim is rather to look closely at variants of a few central cases, initially in order to add to the defense of my view of emotions as "propositional feelings," showing how this view may be further specified in application to emotion instances. For the view is meant to cover all emotions, including some whose evaluative content is hard to pin down and whose affective content may be equally elusive even in clear-cut cases of the emotion.

As my exploration of the cases proceeds, however, it will yield some more particular results. In fact, it will indicate that moral or quasi-moral considerations often stand behind our grouping of the emotions into descriptive categories. For despite their variable manifestations in thought and feeling—and in desire, interpreted in terms of thought and feeling—the "personal" cases under discussion here seem to be united by a connection to ascriptions of *responsibility*. The connection is a normative one, imposed by social learning on earlier manifestations of the emotions in question. To the extent that we see these as amounting to rewards or punishments for others, in short, we see the emotions' affective components as properly directed towards evaluations *of* those persons, by virtue of which our responses to them might be said to be deserved. In their more developed forms, that is, the emotions must have evaluative content of a sort that would tend to justify their affective consequences. But since their simpler forms also survive in adult human life, they yield a kind of "double standard" for certain emotion categories: a distinction between "full-fledged" and "deficient" instances, the latter requiring less in the way of structure and support. For present purposes the distinction serves to widen the class of morally significant emotions beyond those standardly considered *moral*—whether in terms of content, as with guilt, moral indignation, and the like, or in terms of value, as with identificatory love.

When I do turn to the question of the moral value of identificatory love (iv), my discussion should provide us with stronger support for the view of emotions whose defense, in Chapter 2, began with cases of irrational "spillover." For my argument in this chapter will eventually extend my comments on fantasy-emotions to cases of quite central moral significance. The social importance of *identificatory* emotions, I shall argue, depends on their interpretation as "propositional feelings"—states of comfort or discomfort directed towards evaluative propositions that may well part from belief. Indeed, I shall argue that the interpretation must apply specifically to their components of motivating *desire*—with the agent seen as ascribing to himself responsibility for action on behalf of others—in order to cover the full range of identificatory emotions. My argument here will bring out one way of establishing my overall point in this essay: that emotions play an important role in practical reasoning as supplements to warranted belief. But before attempting to unpack these abstract claims, we need to do some further work *in concretu*, looking into detailed questions raised by particular cases. I shall continue to let variants of the cases influence the direction of my discussion, with some of the points extracted from them to be put to use only later. Although I shall have to make increasing reference to justificatory issues, my extended treatment of them will be postponed until Part II. Here, at least in the first instance, I want to show how my view of the nature of emotion applies to cases with different connections to feeling, judgment, and desire—different from each other and from the fear cases stressed up to this point in Part I.

(i) Pride

Let us first consider pride, an example familiar from Hume, and currently interpreted by a number of philosophers as involving a positive evaluation of oneself.[2] Sometimes it seems to involve no more than this, since ascriptions of pride apply (contra Hume) where the agent undergoes no particular characteristic sensation. But we need to pick out genuine ascriptions of the *emotion* of pride. I might grant, first of all, that I am proud of my fine house, meaning only that I take it as reflecting well on me and that I take myself as praiseworthy for owning it. But this ascription of pride does not clearly attribute an emotion to me. My pride may manifest itself, say, largely in dispositions to sidestep sources of shame. "Out of pride," for instance, I insist on making repairs; but this does not mean that I feel proud before making them or even that I anticipate feeling proud as a result of making them. My response to someone's later admiration of the house need not be occurrent pride. Rather, I have avoided "compromising my pride"—with pride understood as a character trait, or a trait of temperament, not necessarily an emotion.

In fact, we might imagine a case in which I am such a perfectionist that there are no conditions under which I would allow myself the reward of occurrent pride. As long as my action of fixing up the house rests partly on a view of myself as praiseworthy for owning it, the statement "I am proud of my fine house" may be used to explain it. However, while agreeing that a characteristic sensation of pride need not be involved in the emotion, I think we do need something besides a positive self-evaluation, even one with motivational effects. In the present case we might suppose that I am so strongly motivated by pride as a general trait that I never let myself rest content with *any* achievement. I rush on to the next task, acutely aware of the defects in the last, or perhaps just too "driven" to find time to dwell on its perfections. I do recognize that I am praiseworthy for my accomplishment; but without some sort of comfort at that thought—a relaxed survey of the house, say, with an air of self-congratulation for a job well done—I do not feel proud. The urge to make out *all* affective elements as unnecessary to the emotion results, I think, from conflating feeling proud with feeling *pride*—an error retained in judgmentalists' reactions to the traditional identification of emotion with sensation. We can insist on some element of feeling *tone*—exhibited, say, in the *way* I entertain the thought that owning such a fine house counts as an achievement—without narrowing occurrent emotion to cases of full-blown emotion *symptoms*. Unlike fear, if my own experience is indicative, pride only rarely manifests itself in a particular characteristic sensation. But we need to discriminate among pride locutions to pick out those that ascribe to an agent an ongoing state of feeling as opposed to other sorts of properties, including dispositions to act, to think, or to feel.

The word "pride" has multiple functions, in short: It and its derivatives are often applied to traits and tendencies generally linked to the emotion but not necessarily backed up by it at the time in question. For occurrent pride, even without a characteristic sensation, it is not enough that I would include my house if asked to make a list of things of which I am proud. And there are more extreme examples of the application of the word without ascription of the emotion. The emotion of pride is just one manifestation of a cluster of traits and tendencies called by the same name; and it is by no means equally central to all of them. If we say that I am "houseproud," for instance, we may mean only that I have an enlarged conception of what would constitute grounds for "house-shame"—a slight smudge on my dining room table, perhaps—and not that there are many circumstances under which I actually feel proud of my fine house. If we say that I am "a proud person," moreover, we may mean just that I often act to avoid grounds for shame, seeing an unusual number of things as beneath my ideal self. Whether my reaction is or includes occurrent pride depends on whether it currently involves comfort at a positive self-evaluation—besides, though perhaps based on, my determination to *become* a more suitable object of the emotion.

On the other hand, the view of my current self as praiseworthy need not involve a belief that I am so now, in order to give rise to occurrent pride. I may undergo the emotion as a result of fantasy, imagining an achievement so vividly that I feel as though I were already praiseworthy for it even though it is not something I have accomplished. It need not even be something I think I *can* accomplish. While walking down a certain street, for instance, I used to imagine climbing a tree, performing a handstand on one of the branches, and similar acrobatics that are beyond me. Although not deluded about the likelihood of such achievements, I would feel proud—of myself, of course, but apparently *for* achievements I would not attribute to myself—as a result of imagining them. My evaluation here would seem to be a fictional one, like that involved in fear felt at a horror film, where the projection of oneself into the imagined situation is at least momentarily vivid enough to yield evaluations from the standpoint of a character in it. But since it persists beyond my moment of vivid imagination, we might want to say that my pride in this case also resembles "objectless" anxiety, where fear has only an indefinite internal object. For pride the evaluative object of comfort may fail to pick out a specific reason for praising me. I might have come to see myself as praiseworthy for some *unspecified* achievements, not particularly those whose rehearsal in imagination produced the feeling. At any rate, my feeling here is more than a "pure" feeling of elation, objectless in the strict sense, like my edginess in the initial version of the coffee case in Chapter 2, since it clearly involves comfort *at* a positive evaluation.

Unlike simple joy, moreover, my emotion clearly involves a positive evaluation of *myself*—and is therefore especially rewarding to me, even with a basis in fantasy. Consider the pleasure taken in anticipating the achievement of some very uncertain goal or in watching someone else's achievement in a role one appreciates but does not covet—as an Olympics gymnast, say. With enough imagination, this sometimes amounts to fantasy-pride—pride *in* one's current self but nicely independent of any judgments about it. Its self-direction is important, moreover; for it supports a view of oneself as *responsible* for an object of joy and thus as *deserving* pleasure. Pride symptoms alone or another emotion—eagerness or admiration as well as simple joy—would be significantly less rewarding, without the leap of fantasy-pride to a future time or a different "persona," while retaining the element of present self-content. Pride, in such cases, amounts to a modification of joy, with a positive evaluation of some state of affairs seen as reflecting on oneself. Where the evaluation is indefinite, moreover, pride might be thought of as joy with the self as its sole external object—in the sense of something viewed as standing outside the emotion, as the object of its evaluative component. In standard cases pride has the self as its primary external object, with reasons for praise given as secondary objects. But sometimes we may have only the former—and a basis in fantasy that should now let us see how emotions can part even from factual beliefs in a more radical move away from judgmentalism.

"Objectless" Emotions and Indefinite Evaluations. Let us first pause for some more extended comments on "objectless" emotions, in contrast with nonintentional feeling states, but still without attempting to explain

their intentionality except by reducing it to that of their components. In cases of pride in an achievement, actual or imagined, I would say that the emotion also has a proposition as its external object—the fact that I fixed up my house, say, or that I (supposedly) performed some acrobatics. But in the less-than-vivid fantasy cases and indeed in some real-life cases there may be no factual proposition to back up the emotion. Sometimes I may just be proud *of myself*, as if I were praiseworthy in some respect or other but without even an indefinite reason for praise— a proposition linking me to some-*achievement*-or-other, without specifying which. My pride still has an internal object—namely, the evaluative proposition that I am praiseworthy—and this may be said to "exist" as an object of thought, even where it is not thought to be *true*. To yield pride, it need only be positive and self-directed, however indefinite it may be, but assuming that positive affect is directed towards it.

The external objects of emotion may sometimes be said to exist in a similarly undemanding sense, as long as they are objects of its evaluative component. But since a problem for standard causal accounts of object-directedness turns on emotions with *nonexistent* objects, we would do best to distinguish these from emotions that *have* no *definite* objects. For pride there is at least one external object whose existence in the usual sense seems to be guaranteed, assuming that anyone undergoes the emotion. However, for other fantasy-emotions, such as fear at a horror film, there may sometimes be nothing real that an emotion is about; and in certain cases, there may be nothing at all—real or unreal—depending on how vivid my imagination is. I discussed such cases in Chapter 2 on the assumption that my imagination was fairly vivid, at least for a moment: As the knife descends on the movie heroine, I feel fear "for" her, as if I were in her place. This is fear *of* being stabbed, presumably—or at any rate, it is fear that *she* will be stabbed—but without the belief that stabbing is a real threat. Still, if I imagine stabbing as a threat, however briefly, my fear *has* a definite external object, though one that does not exist. The same point applies to real-life fears that are based on a mistaken but specific *belief*—for instance, a belief that the dog who attacked the agent in the made-up Fido case in Chapter 2 is on the loose and likely to attack me next.

In other cases, however, "objectless" fear may result from either imagination or mistaken belief. Indeed, it may even be warranted—as where others' behavioral responses indicate that a situation is somehow dangerous but without specifying the danger. Here I want to say that fear *lacks* a definite external object rather than being directed towards a nonexistent object. It has an *internal* object; hence my insistence on quotation marks around "objectless," in contrast with the case of a pure sensation of edginess induced by drinking too much coffee. For the emotion amounts to a state of discomfort directed towards a highly indefinite evaluative proposition: that *some* danger looms, but "I know not what." Fearful suspense at a horror film, induced by the background music, often seems to be like this. Since it has an internal object, it does amount to an emotion, on my view; and the reference to future danger is enough to make it fear. Similarly for indefinite pride—but with future danger replaced by self-directed praise, so that its "objectlessness" is qualified by reference to the self, as something that already exists, though it may not be taken to exhibit any grounds for praise. I may or may not feel proud of myself *for* some fantasized achievement, then, in the case where my imagination is less than vivid. But as long as my fantasy yields comfort at the thought that I am praiseworthy in some-respect-or-other, I do feel proud as a result of it. And my pride has as much of an object as it needs.

I am taking the external objects of emotion, here and elsewhere, to be picked out by their role in "about"-phrases in common language— as what I am afraid or proud *of*, in the first instance. But "about"-phrases may also apply to the reasons for the emotion in question and thus bring in some further external objects, including propositions, as we have seen. I may be afraid or proud *that* something will happen or has happened to me. We should bear in mind that this factual proposition is not the same as the evaluative proposition that constitutes the internal object of emotion, on my analysis. Rather, like any external object it will be specified by the internal object, at least if the latter is spelled out sufficiently fully. We might say, for instance, that I am proud of *someone else's* achievements, or that *he* has accomplished something, leaving it unstated that I take the other person to be related to me in some way that lets me share the credit. If it is pride that I feel, though, it involves the thought that *I* am praiseworthy by virtue of the relationship—as a member of some group on which the other's achievements reflect, say. Once again, this evaluative thought need not be backed up by the corresponding belief. Indeed, we can now see that it need not even be backed up by a factual belief—by belief in any propositional external object of emotion as a basis for the evaluation that constitutes its internal object. In the case just sketched, for instance, I may not really think that my relationship to the other person yields grounds for praising *me* just because I do not really think it is close enough to support a claim of common membership in some significant group.

We can now extend this line of argument to show that some emotions involve hardly any belief content. The case is easiest to make for an "objectless" variant of pride; for its internal object may be so indefinite as to bring in no factual proposition beyond one acknowledging the agent's own existence. My earlier arguments against judgmentalism, in

Chapter 2, were concerned only to detach emotions from their "corresponding" beliefs—those corresponding to their evaluative components, that is. But now consider another case of fantasy-pride—one that arose in discussion of the question whether music induces emotions: feelings with objects, even if indefinitely specified.[3] As I listen to *Alexander Nevsky*, my reaction to the turning of the tide in favor of the Russians seems clearly to involve more than a set of pleasant sensations, even supplemented by emotions of aesthetic appreciation, though these occur as well. It seems to involve something like a feeling of martial pride—joy at military triumph, with myself as vicarious participant but without a belief that I played a role in the battle or that I am related to anyone who did. I need not even believe that the battle occurred or that it would have reflected well on its participants if it had. My reaction may well be influenced by past associations with the music—in this case including the film for which it was written—or to military music generally. But it amounts to an emotion directed towards something in my present (imagined) situation.

Do I feel pride, or simply joy, at Nevsky's triumph? My emotion may sometimes be too indefinite even to allow for a specific classification. But to make it out as an emotion, we need only grant that I feel good *about* something—something besides the quality of the music or the fact that I am listening to it or any other objects independent of imagination. It is not as though the music simply brings on a positive mood without even an indefinitely specified object. The distinction between moods and emotions is not sharp, as I have noted; and philosophers' attempts to sharpen it—sometimes by insisting that emotions have a clearly defined object—do not seem to capture all the states we recognize as emotions. But even granting the distinction, my responses to religious music— quite without belief, as I would say—might be used to provide some examples of fantasy-emotions with relatively clear-cut objects. Without some element of imagination, of the sort involved in acting, my reaction to the liturgical content of the music would in most cases be negative.

In the *Alexander Nevsky* case my elation may or may not last beyond the music. But while I am absorbed in the music, it is elation *about* something seen as depicted or suggested by the music—perhaps along with real-life objects, past or present associations with the music, but not in competition with them. When the music stops, moreover, any generalized mood it gives rise to is distinguishable in quality from what I felt while listening—from the *range* of emotions I went through at different stages of the music. And something similar—but with even less clearly specified emotions—seems to be true of nonprogrammatic music or at any rate certain instances of it. I think particularly of romantic violin concerti, where the music is sometimes said to depict emotions themselves, without embedding them in a story. Instead, it seems to imitate some of their features: valleys and peaks, a "crying" tone, extreme arousal and release. I take the result—ecstasy when a peak is finally achieved, say—to be *both* a short-term mood and an emotion, but one that has only an indefinite internal object: that something-or-other is overpoweringly good—not *just* the music, though that too. One comes to feel something *like* what the music expresses, something with intentional content, but with little or no foundation in belief.

I shall have more to say later in this chapter about the importance of imagination in generating emotional states. But lest emotions with the end of enjoyment seem to exhaust the category of propositional feelings without assent, I ought to say something about confidence. I take confidence, in some instances, to involve a long-term variety of occurrent pride, of a sort that may be valuable to the agent even where it is not adequately grounded. It may sometimes be built up through imagination, via fantasy-pride of the sort I have been considering. But alternatively, we might suppose that I just have a general tendency to "proceed on the assumption" that I am up to any task. This is my "outlook," let us say. It is not necessarily, as so far described, an emotion; but it may, along with other general attitudes—optimism, for instance, or the feeling that things will work out for the best—provide further cases of evaluations not necessarily involving genuine assent. If I am asked or ask myself whether I think my attitude is warranted by the facts, I may immediately (and sincerely) say "no." To maintain confidence, I have to ignore some of the facts; and I know this, though I keep myself from attending to it. For the attitude serves me well, and a relatively enduring feeling of comfort at it—which does yield an emotion, on my view— serves me even better. Or let us suppose that it does, since it can sometimes make such an outlook self-fulfilling.

Maintaining confidence here depends on not raising the question whether it is justified or not inquiring into it too closely. I take a positive self-evaluation for granted, that is, leaving it indefinite rather than making up some specific reasons for it. Some would object, though, that I must at least believe it *at those times* when I avoid inquiring into its grounds. But a further use of the Principle of Logical Charity, as defended in Chapter 2, seems to be in order here: we should resist attributing to me beliefs in logical conflict with my beliefs about their *grounds*, whether or not I am attending to the latter. I take it that, in so far as I am "basically" rational, I cannot believe that a full inquiry into the grounds for one of my beliefs would uncover decisive evidence for its contrary. Assent to the content of a thought, in fact, entails an implicit claim about its relation to the total body of evidence. I need not take it to be supported by the evidence now in my possession—or even by any evidence that I *could* gather myself. Indeed, let us grant that I might believe it without thinking that there is adequate evidence *for* it, even evidence available only hypothetically or to hypothetically ideal observers. If it amounts to more than an assumption, though—borne in mind just for practical purposes, or to see what theoretical consequences it yields—then I must at least hold that the total body of evidence would not cut *against* it.[4] But I need not hold anything of the sort when I feel confident, any more that when I feel optimistic. My verbal behavior may suggest that I even hold the contrary judgment—recognizing, but looking away from, what I take to be decisive evidence against my general self-evaluation.

Perhaps there would be no "judgmentalists" if proponents of judgmentalism were held to a strict conception of belief, as distinguished from other predicative propositional attitudes, such as assumption, along the lines just sketched. However, there is still a point in isolating and questioning this straightforward interpretation of the view that emotions essentially involve evaluative judgments. For one thing, the weaker propositional attitudes that some authors might happily conflate with beliefs would seem to yield a different account of the justification of emotions and of their role in the justification of action. In the case just sketched, for instance, neither pride itself nor the sorts of self-displaying actions that typically arise from it would be based on evidence for a *belief* that I am up to any task. Their justification would have to involve a "forward-looking" reference to their effects—in generating future achievements, say, by making me more likely to take risks. Whether this reference to adaptiveness is enough to justify holding in mind an *assumption* of general competence—to justify it in "backward-looking" terms, that is, but without the corresponding belief—is a question of emotional appropriateness of the sort I shall examine in Part II.

If we do drop the insistence on belief, though, why should we take emotions as involving propositional attitudes at all? What happens in the case of confidence-without-belief, it might be said, is just that my attention is focused on features of my past performance that suggest that I am generally able to cope.[5] This is part of what goes on, let us grant; but is it sufficient for a feeling of confidence? I *could* pay attention to the same features of the situation while feeling insecure, for instance—raising a host of uncertain questions about whether my past performance will be borne out this time or attempting to work up confidence, but in vain. For my strategy to succeed, I must manage to work up comfort *at the thought* that I can cope, in a way that is likely to make future performance bear it out. I must do so, moreover, by attributing to myself prior abilities, vaguely specified, that I know I do not possess or possess to the requisite degree, independently of that feeling. That is, I must interpret the objects of my attention in a certain way—as clear evidence of competence. I take this to involve *predicating* something of myself, along with other objects of attention, whether or not I do so explicitly.

My confidence here, on the view I shall examine in Part II, involves a prima facie evaluation that I hold *as if* it were "all things considered" but without believing that it is. Even at this earlier stage in my argument, though, it should be clear that I share with judgmentalists the view that some belief-like structures are needed to distinguish among emotional states. Feeling quality seems to be necessary too, especially for fine distinctions—between pride as a relaxed attitude, say, and mental *bluster*, or the aggressive eagerness to display my abilities by mastering the task at hand. But feeling quality is clearly not sufficient—to distinguish pride from joy, for instance. Nor is pride picked out as such by reference to a characteristic motivating desire. The desire for self-display may well be absent from cases of pride of the more relaxed sort: "contented" or "quiet" pride. I shall go on to consider some cases, though, in which emotions do seem to be identified by an essential connection to desire. What sorts of emotions they are, that is, depends on their orientation towards action; but I shall attempt to account for this in terms of affect and evaluation.

For the moment, let us note that pride, insofar as it involves a positive evaluation of *oneself*, can be picked out from joy only if we assume a fair degree of cognitive sophistication. It would seem to require at least a causal notion of responsibility for occasions of joy—seeing oneself, at a minimum, as partly responsible for praise that yields joy, where pride is based on features of the self that do not result from voluntary action. So its identification as the emotion it is depends on more than reference to the physiological bases of affect that we share with animals and infants. We can expect this to be true of emotions generally and to raise some questions about emotions picked out by the *same* term, but at different stages of cognitive development—and, for that matter, of social development. For the same physiological factors may produce different emotions with different evaluations of an agent's situation; and evaluative discriminations are modified by social interaction.[6] Emotions at different stages of development, then, may not always embody the distinctions that apply to human adults. I shall go on to argue that other "personal" emotions—those that rest on a notion of responsibility for *desire*—exhibit a variable evaluative content, even in human adults, just because we use the same term for them at different stages.

(ii) Anger

It seems quite obvious, first of all, that animals have emotions, even in the face of doubts about whether they have beliefs. But it is not at all clear that their emotions have objects like our own—or in what sense they could be directed towards *any* objects, without animals having the capacity to make some evaluative distinctions. Consider the emotional behavior of a cat: When a larger cat comes to the window, the cat inside exhibits the standard attack posture, hissing and snarling, with one paw lashing out. This is the behavioral prototype of what we call *anger*, and we may assume that the physiological symptoms are similar. But does the cat feel anger, or fear, or some mixture of the two? I have heard fear brought in as an explanation of some bizarre behavior on the part of a former cat of my own, which turned on me as I tried to shoo the other cat away. But how could we tell? The two postures cannot be mixed; nor did one yield to the other in the case I have in mind. For that matter, why should we say that the cat felt angry at its *initial* target (the cat outside) rather than simply *hating* and fearing it, or undergoing a "pure" feeling of arousal, with attack as the automatic response? The orientation of anger towards future action is supposed to be based on a negative evaluation of its object's past or present actions, a view of them as deserving some sort of punishment. Did my cat then see the other cat as the source of some injury or offense for which a kind of punishment was warranted? Perhaps the intrusion on her territory might be seen as something like a deep insult. To the extent that we can make out a cat's views in such terms, we are attributing to it anger—rather than simply "negative arousal" or the like—along with the propositional attitude.

Even with the propositional attitude, though, but assuming that its notion of *responsibility* is limited, we would have to say that a cat's anger is only roughly like our own—not just in quality of experience but more fundamentally in degree of differentiation from other emotional states. At most, perhaps, my cat just evaluates certain *situations* as "threateningly bad," say, and reacts with the attack posture where the other cat provides a safe target for aggressive action. We need not attribute to it even a very clear distinction between past and future harms, of the sort that is needed to distinguish anger from fear in this case. But unless we attribute to it at least some evaluation of the situation—however indefinite or foreign to human ears—why should we say that it experiences *any* emotion? Perhaps it simply undergoes a pure feeling of arousal, whose modification by human categories, in light of its perceptual causes and behavioral effects, yields anger. Unless it evaluates the other *cat*, moreover—as a moving target but also a (re)movable *source* of "badness"—why should we attribute to it *personal* anger, on the model of my anger at an intruder? Since I never have seen a cat exhibit anger of a diffuse sort, not directed towards an animate target, I would in fact be inclined to say that it does have this limited notion of "agent-responsibility."

The question applies more forcefully to human infants, though, since simple physical restraint apparently produces the earliest occurrences of anger in humans.[7] When the rattle falls out of its crib, say, and turns out to be beyond reach, the infant's initial whimpers may give way to a scream of rage, with arms flailing about and a distinctive facial expression. Does its reaction amount to "fretful" sadness plus a primitive kind of *blame* for the situation of confinement—with a negative evaluation of the outside world *as if* it contained a cause of injury? Or is this just an alternative, "active" response to certain causes of sadness, a response that *becomes* anger when it is selectively reinforced by adults on the basis of adult conceptions of its appropriateness? I would suppose that the infant's initial "emotional" behavior often involves screaming out of hunger or some other state of physical discomfort—not itself an emotion, unless it has an evaluative object. Discomfort takes on an object resembling the internal object of adult anger, I should think, as the infant learns that the aggressive behavioral reaction gets the attention of adults, who sometimes remove barriers to satisfaction. But at the earliest stage, before adult notions of appropriate occasions for anger are learned, the external object of infant anger is probably something like "frustration of immediate needs," without any definite personal target of aggression. It involves a notion of injury, perhaps, but only the most rudimentary concept of responsibility for injury, of the sort that distinguishes full-fledged adult anger from the infant's impersonal rage.

If these speculations on the development of anger are at all reasonable, it seems that the very *nature* of the emotion is modified by changes in adult acceptance of its characteristic behavioral reaction. We might say that this is so because the reaction is itself a kind of punishment for others, or others in the infant's vicinity. It is accepted without much discrimination as long as others think themselves responsible for attending to the infant's needs and as long as nothing else serves the infant better as a way of communicating those needs. But its acceptance eventually narrows to situations where others may be seen as *sources* of frustration—or are not around at all. The result of the latter alternative seems to be a carry-over of infantile rage to some situations where the blame involved in full-fledged adult anger would not have a *chance* of counting as appropriate since it lacks the appropriate *sort* of object. By the same token, though, the standards for appropriate anger seem to be less demanding in such cases. I bump into an unexpected wall, say, and react to pain with fury, emitting a curse. This is such a widely accepted reaction that it seems odd to call it inappropriate; but its easy justification depends on taking it as a "deficient" case of anger, one that does not involve blame. Am I angry at the wall, the situation, or what? An urge to punish the object of anger would seem to be inappropriate in such cases, to say the least.

Note that while I refer to anger of this sort as "impersonal"—since it involves no notion of personal responsibility—it may be incidentally directed towards persons or towards situations that include persons, as in a case where I bump into someone else. Conversely, personal anger may sometimes be directed, though usually inappropriately, towards situations *not* including persons—most reasonably in cases where the emotion is semi-"objectless." Even in the case where I am angry about bumping into an inanimate object, I might sometimes be said to feel *as though* someone-or-other (besides myself) ought to be held responsible for the event. I would then be angry in the sense that does involve blame but without a specific target for the aggressive urge that makes my emotion count as anger. However, unless it involves a propositional attitude that would justify at least a *hunt* for some target, as a suitable object of blame, my anger would seem to be deficient.

Deficient anger amounts to something like hatred of a state of affairs, without all the distinguishing features of full-fledged adult anger. We still call it "anger" because of its resemblance to the infantile prototype; but by now the latter has been refined in a way that gives the term a normative force, requiring a suitable evaluative basis for the characteristic urge to attack. On the assumption that infants and animals are at least capable of evaluating the environment in relation to their immediate needs, then, I would take them to have emotions, in addition to objectless feelings. Their evaluations may or may not exhibit the distinctions characteristic of beliefs; but an emotion, to have *some* content, requires only an indefinite (internal) object. Whether their anger has a content like our own, though, is a further question, which depends on whether the emotion has a *personal* (external) object. But even our own anger may sometimes take a "deficient" form, by dropping its usual element of blame—yielding a "double standard" of anger in adult human life since the criteria for the appropriateness of deficient anger are less demanding.

I have been assuming that the urge to *attack*—to lash out at something, appropriately or not—is what unites animal, infantile, and full-fledged adult anger. This urge is often valuable as an "energizing" response to a perceived injury, even where no one is to blame. So it may sometimes be justified in forward-looking terms in cases where it is not grounded in a suitable evaluation or is grounded in one that is not appropriate—just as confidence may be rational to cultivate in ourselves in some cases where it rests on fantasy-pride. Even impersonal anger, or what might be called "frustration-anger," seems to be essentially connected to desire, in a way that sadness at a perceived injury is not. It involves not just a wish that things were otherwise, that is, but also an urge to act to change them somehow. Its link to action, of at least this rather indefinite sort, is also tighter than that of the other emotions discussed so far. As I noted briefly in my last section, pride often involves a desire for self-display; but it need not do so in order to be pride. And cases of fear of something viewed as inescapable may simply involve a state of passive dread, agitated in feeling tone but without the typical urge to escape the object of fear, as discussed in Chapter 2.

Adult anger *that* some state of affairs obtains—that my car has broken down again, say—would normally be made out, on my account, as involving discomfort at an indefinite action requirement: the thought that I ought to take some sort of aggressive action in response. "Ought" should not be interpreted in a narrowly moral sense, of course; my thought here amounts to an evaluation of aggressive action as somehow "called for" by the situation, with all alternatives ruled out. My anger will be deficient, though, unless it grounds the action requirement on a suitable personal evaluation: one that assigns "agent-responsibility"—responsibility for the bad state of affairs by way of wrongful *action*—to some target of aggression. But full-fledged anger need not be appropriate, even where the personal evaluation is left indefinite. Whether or not blame is justified in backward-looking terms, I might feel as though my car breakdown warrants some sort of punishment—as though I ought to get back at someone, perhaps just someone-or-other, for the harm done, once again, to my finances and my schedule. As an object of discomfort, this action requirement yields a *felt need* to take revenge: an urge of the sort that involves emotional "pressure" towards action, now focused on a personal target of aggression.

This squares with Aristotle's definition of anger, though Aristotle makes out the "impulse" towards revenge as "accompanied by pain," along with pleasure at the expectation that revenge will be accomplished.[8] He also makes out the object of anger in somewhat moralistic terms—as "a conspicuous slight directed without justification towards what concerns oneself or towards what concerns one's friends." But this may be broadened to include any offense or injury for which another agent is viewed as responsible; and "pleasure" and "pain" may be replaced by reference to intentional states of comfort and discomfort. The latter may then be taken as accounting for the impulse that constitutes anger—or the urge, let us say, in order to cancel out the suggestion of suddenness and allow for cases of "slow burn." The definition should apply to cases of *personal* anger, that is—the standard cases in adult human life, where anger seems to demand some action in revenge.

Broadly construed, as "injury" is for fear, revenge might be called the "proper aim" of anger: As a refinement of the urge to attack, grounding it on a personal evaluation, the urge towards revenge may be taken as definitive of full-fledged anger. The thought of revenge may itself be a source of some comfort, let us note, even where it is not achievable—where I know I cannot get back at X, say, except in fantasy or by some sort of indirect action, such as muttering a curse. I may have to content myself with a kind of symbolic revenge on X, which does not in fact get back at him but still provides at least partial relief for me. But if anger intrinsically involves some element of comfort for the agent—as I shall grant, following Aristotle—its primary desire component must involve discomfort to the extent that it exerts pressure towards action rather than being fully satisfiable without postponement. A cat, when it confronts an intruder on its territory, knows no limitations except those imposed by physical barriers and by fear; but full-fledged human anger cannot so easily be vented on its object. Its spillover to more manageable objects and the sorts of behavior that emerge when it does spill over—kicking the dog, say, or something inanimate—suggest that it still involves an urge to attack. Although the urge is capable of indirect satisfaction, it involves an element of discomfort as long as it remains unsatisfied.

A brief look at an example should begin to make clear the complex relation between anger, revenge, and discomfort. X has "slighted" me, let us say, with an insult. Under ordinary circumstances the most extreme form of revenge that would occur to me would be a rebuke that somehow humiliates him. In escaping social discomfort, this is by now more effective than physical attack if only because it is considered socially acceptable. It also is more comfortably conjoined with life in a society that will still include X, perhaps as someone I shall have to deal with again. But the point is not just that rebuking someone for an insult would in fact serve my interests better than physical attack. Rather, this has been so obvious to me for so long that challenging X to a duel or the like would not *achieve* revenge, even in fantasy. By now it is something that I have no urge to do when angry—unlike rebuking X, even in situations where *this* would not serve my interests. On the other hand, my anger now might also be satisfied without actually satisfying the urge towards aggressive action that seems to characterize even deficient anger. Calmly extracting an apology from X, say, involves obtaining a kind of submission, on his part; and this might seem sufficiently humiliating to count as adequate revenge. In short, the very notion of revenge is a product of the social development that makes it part of the definition of full-fledged human anger.

With this understood, we may say, following Aristotle, that anger intrinsically involves discomfort at a thought of revenge as something the agent should arrange for. The claim may be extended even to cases where the desire for revenge turns out to be satisfied independently of the agent's action. My discomfort at the need to get back at X may in fact be alleviated by something that happens to him or something he does himself, such as offering an apology spontaneously. But while I am angry, I *feel as though* some action on my part is needed for revenge on X; and I feel as though I shall continue to be uncomfortable at that thought until I act on it. My thought need not be true, however; nor need it always be believed. For one thing, even if X's situation remains unchanged, anger can sometimes fade, rather than fester, with time; and I may be aware of this but still remain uncomfortable at the thought that I ought to secure my revenge. If I take steps to secure it, moreover, I act at least partly *in order to* discharge my discomfort. It is the only thing that *I* can do, at any rate, to improve my present state of feeling; or so it seems to me, insofar as I am angry and my anger exerts pressure towards action. "Pressuring" anger thus involves discomfort, even where it is comfortable on the whole. X may be "the man I love to hate," and his insult may have given me a welcome opportunity for the perfect squelch, say; but if my reaction is joy mixed with *anger*, it must involve discomfort as long as the urge towards revenge remains unsatisfied.

The discomfort of anger need not have the explosive quality of *rage*, though, except to the extent that the agent has to control a tendency to lash out immediately when a well-planned squelch would be more effective. I shall postpone until my last chapter a sustained treatment of the pressure exerted by anger towards *immediate* discharge in action. In any case, whether the agent goes red in the face or feels as though he is about to is neither here nor there. Once anger has developed into indignation, resentment, and other moral or quasi-moral reactions, the standard case is no longer the case of full-blown anger symptoms. What distinguishes it from "churning" sadness or simply feeling injured or offended by the insult is its orientation towards action, with a kind of mental arousal or sharp focus often replacing the characteristic physical sensations. Even this may sometimes be "tamped down," or masked by an overlay of inhibiting feeling, however. To find out whether someone who claims only to be *hurt* is really angry, for instance, we raise questions about his underlying evaluation of the situation and what role his denial of anger might play in achieving his ends—in supporting a certain image of himself, say. We need not deny that he accurately describes the quality of his feeling.

It is the feeling *that* one must get back, then, even if more brooding than aroused, that makes the full-fledged adult case a case of pressuring anger. Sharp displeasure at the insult alone or at some state of affairs that is seen as no one's fault, without any urge to take revenge—even on "something-or-other"—still would be *called* "anger" if it involved an urge to attack and resembled anger in felt quality. But this "deficient" case would also resemble the first version of the case of coffee-induced edginess in Chapter 2, before my feeling took on an object. Here, however, my feeling would have an object, though it would have no *suitable* object—one that allows us at least to raise the question whether anger is deserved. It would still count as an emotion—unlike objectless edginess—but it would not count as the paradigm case of anger. In the paradigm case, which is based on socially inculcated norms, what we have is the sort of pleasure/pain mix described by Aristotle, with discomfort at the insult, comfort at revenge, and discomfort at the need to make up for the former with the latter. It is the propositional content of these feelings that makes them add up to anger—as opposed, say, to churning sadness at X's insult, or at having to punish X, in the case just sketched.

At any rate, the goal of this sort of analysis, shared with judgmentalism, is to differentiate among emotions, as far as possible, on the basis of their evaluative components. Once again, I take this to work only up to a point: Feeling quality needs to be brought in when we attempt to make finer distinctions—between rage and resentment, say, which may have the same internal object. But for anger, in contrast with fear and pride, we presuppose a fairly complex evaluative *structure*. A desire is taken as essential to the emotion, with normative constraints imposed on "full-fledged" cases, requiring a basis in personal evaluation, of a sort that would tend to *justify* the desire. If I am angry *at X* in response to his insult, that is—not simply hurt, or angry about his role in something unintended—I must view his insult as a wrong that I ought to repay. I must "feel as though" I ought to repay it at least partly *because* he is to blame for it—and because I am uncomfortable at that thought.

Note that what is required here is a structured set of evaluations, not necessarily of beliefs. We might extend our coffee-case analogy for a case of full-fledged anger that is known to be inappropriately *personal*: Although I know that X was not really to blame for a remark that embarrassed me, say, my anger at the remark comes to focus specifically on *him*. It takes on a personal object, we may suppose, in a way designed to explain my urge to attack as aimed towards revenge. This is achieved at the cost of appropriateness but with the benefits attaching to outwardly-directed anger that sets up a suitable target for aggressive action. However, the double standard imposed on anger by our recognition of deficient cases gives the agent an alternative here: an emotion appropriately directed towards a proposition that *includes* a personal target, though not as personally *responsible*, and thus only incidentally. My later defense, in Chapter 5, of a compound of anger and envy will trade on this possibility, in fact. For the moment, though, we may conclude, in general terms, that the "nature" of anger is one imposed on it by norms governing its component of desire—just because action on it is generally unpleasant for others, even where anger is pleasant, overall, for the agent. Anger, in short, is essentially an emotion one would not want to be the object of; and some of the initially clearest cases, such as animal and infantile rage, turn out to be deficient once social constraints are built in.

(iii) Attachment-Love

A similar selection for evaluations that would justify natural manifestations of feeling goes on for *love*—but with multiple standards, resulting in a kind of fractioning of the notion. Even that sort of love that involves attachment to an individual will make different demands, for example, if it is impersonal—amounting to loyalty, say, as in love of country, as distinct from the love of friends. Attachment-love may also sometimes be said to be directed only incidentally towards a person, but with important differences from the corresponding form of anger. Instances of the emotion may be dismissed by the object as "deficient," that is, where they fail to come up to the standard of the sort of love he *would* want to be the object of in a relationship of mutual personal closeness. But they may still be quite firmly focused on *him*—and far from deficient as measured by other standards. As with anger, though, "full-fledged" attachment-love is picked out as such by the justificatory completeness of its analysis, with personal evaluations taken as needed to support its characteristic desire: the desire to *be with* another person. As with pride, on the other hand, its feeling component may often be hard to pin down, even on our assumption that it does involve occurrent feeling, and not merely a disposition to feel, or to act to achieve or maintain closeness to the love-object.

With its unique combination of affect and evaluation attachment-love provides a particularly clear-cut example of the distinction between internal and external objects of emotion, since it normally has no propositional external object. It need not be backed up, that is, by *love* directed towards a proposition, including the evaluative propositions that come into its analysis: that one ought to act to achieve closeness or even that the object displays certain positive qualities. Although love of the fact that one *is* in love may be possible, one might say, it is hardly a necessary concomitant of love. However, taken as an occurrent emotion, full-fledged attachment-love must involve at least ambivalent *comfort* directed towards a positive view of the love-object as a basis for the desire for closeness—and a possible basis for its acceptance *by* the object. Briefly, the evaluation must be "personal" in a way that tends to *justify* the desire, particularly as something that promises mutual rewards. Its requisite element of positive affect and evaluation separates the most complete form of attachment-love from a range of other emotional and nonemotional states, such as affectless admiration or the simple desire to possess the love-object. Because of it, we count love as a positive emotion, though it often involves greater intrinsic *dis*comfort—at a negative evaluation of *distance* from the love-object and the need for action to bridge that distance. This last evaluation, of a sort inapplicable to self-oriented pride, is what links the emotion to desire—but with normative constraints imposed on full-fledged cases. For as with animal and infantile anger, the earliest occurrences of attachment-love may rest on only the most rudimentary personal evaluation, of a sort that yields deficient cases in adult life.

I shall defend this complex view of the evaluative structure of love in opposition to a recent *reaction* to judgmentalism, exploring a case of "nonjudgmental" maternal love, whose object seems to be *simply* a person, namely Lisa.[9] Lisa questions her mother's love for her on the grounds that her mother does not "know" her. She would have no complaint, it seems, if personal love required only that a certain feeling or desire be directed firmly towards *her*—even if not for reasons that reflect her personal traits. But love-for-all-the-wrong-reasons may be taken as a deficient case of love—falling short of the standard of full-fledged personal love, as opposed, say, to the love of one's fans or admirers—even where it does not "alter when it alteration finds." Lisa's mother's *attachment* to her is not in question; but without some reasons, this is no more love than was my attachment to a particular car, which I stuck with through all sorts of misadventures but without any special regard. Lisa is criticizing the *reasons* for her mother's attachment and is declining to call it "love," we may suppose, because the reasons misrepresent her central personal traits, whether by omission or by distortion. We might even suppose that her emotion would be *undermined* by any real knowledge of Lisa.

Lisa's mother does *feel* something for her, let us grant; but what might this be? There are several possibilities, depending on the sort of love that is in question. Concern for her offspring's welfare might be thought to be sufficient for maternal love; but if this is *all* her mother feels, Lisa has a right to dismiss it as in one sense impersonal. In any case, her mother's unwillingness to see what Lisa is like might deprive this of any current value for Lisa—if, for instance, it leads her mother to want things for Lisa that are not really in her interests and to worry over things that are. To make her case as strong as possible, we might also suppose that Lisa's mother exhibits tender feelings in her presence and distress in her absence—manifestations more typical of romantic love, perhaps, but possible here as well. These might just be a nuisance, though, an indication of "blind" possessiveness, rather than love, if they have no basis in a positive evaluation of Lisa for traits she could reasonably be expected to see as central to her personality. What Lisa's mother feels tender *about*, say, is Lisa's former childlike sweetness or what a fine reflection on her parents she is or simply that she has returned, however briefly, to the "nest." Or perhaps she just feels tender in response to the thought of *Lisa*, in a way that depends on seeing Lisa merely as her offspring. Even if she can manage not to see more, the constancy of her feelings and their particular felt quality may be thought insufficient to support a claim that they are directed more than incidentally towards Lisa—that her emotion attaches to *the person* who is her child.

It is personal love that Lisa takes as the standard—a standard most clearly exemplified by the love of friends, though applied to parental and romantic love as well. Lisa is *not* asking that her mother relate to her *as* a friend or that she strive to learn everything about her, on this version of the case. She is questioning the value, as an emotion, of her mother's feeling for her by questioning its internal object. That she is the external object of some emotion often called "love" is not in question, any more than it is when John Hinckley's love-object, Jodie Foster, denies that he could possibly love her—at that distance and with that effort to please. That he knows *who she is*, in the sense of being able to pick her out, is clear enough but hardly a help. Despite the obvious dissimilarities between these cases, Lisa too may prefer that her mother not know her any better than she does. As I interpret the case, she is simply unwilling to dignify a shallow or impersonal feeling with the name "love," even granting that it is directed unshakably towards her—and that unshakability, in this case, has its uses. Her mother's *loyalty* may still be valued— perhaps even more so, on the model of patriotism independent of one's view of the nation's worth.

We might be tempted to say instead that her mother's loyalty is based on personal love, or is itself a form of it, but that it simply falls short of ideal love, or love of the sort that Lisa values, where its internal object is impersonal, or lacks any personal depth. Lisa's mother sees her as "my child" and evaluates her positively under that description, as something of irreplaceable importance to her. This is enough for love of an infant, one might grant, where the object's personal traits are as yet undeveloped or unknown—or where impersonal love may be valued as a more reliable motive for maternal care. But should we make the same judgment of maternal love where the feeling *remains* shallow and its manifestations become either empty or annoying—much as with infatuation from a distance? The persistence of love in this case depends on "maintaining one's illusions" about the object; and of course the same might be said of some forms of love that *are* considered ideal. But the "blindness" involved in this case presumably requires blocking out the central traits of the object, not just winking an eye at peripheral failings or retaining the positive evaluation despite recognized changes in its initial grounds. And it requires blocking out the object's central traits *because* the agent does not value them highly—or value the object highly from her own standpoint, one might say.

Why should the object care about this? The enduring nature of personal love is supposed to be grounded in more than the fact that one has "fixed upon" a particular object, as John has fixed upon Jodie, either for no reason or for reasons that obviously misrepresent its worth. It is supposed to be potentially *mutual* in its rewards, offering a reason for its acceptance and even for love in return. This is the source of the normative constraints on love, I take it, analogous to those imposed on anger by its role as a kind of punishment for its object. Like infantile rage, love may at first be accepted without adequate grounds, with the object seen merely as "source of my food supply and reassurance"—or, perhaps, as "the only girl who would go out with me at age sixteen." If a feeling of tender attachment emerges, we might date the *onset* of love at this early point, but only where it does turn into something deeper, by taking on another internal object.

This personal evaluation need not be easy for the agent to articulate, if only because it may be left indefinite; but it must at least be *open* to the object's central self-evaluations. A persistent desire for closeness, even though essential to personal attachment-love, is not enough for love of the sort that supports mutuality—mutual *intrinsic* rewards, that is, with value placed on the emotion itself, not just some extrinsic uses to which it may be put, as with loyalty-love. It must attach to the object for the appropriate sorts of reasons—on the basis of a personal evaluation, for traits whose importance the object could reasonably be expected to acknowledge. Otherwise, though the desire may not be *diffuse* in the manner of deficient anger, its focus on a particular object would seem to be equally incidental. To grow into full-fledged personal love, the desire must come to be grounded in a relatively deep and *therefore* enduring positive view of the love-object—if only as the participant in an ongoing personal relationship valued over time.

This last, "historical," evaluation may or may not apply to Lisa's mother's love for her. A relationship will provide sufficient grounds for full-fledged love only if it does go on and retains its value for the object. But Lisa's complaint suggests that without some deeper knowledge on her mother's part, of a sort that would support a positive evaluation of her for herself, any earlier relationship would by now have lost its value. Her mother's current feelings for her amount, at most, to a mixture of loyalty and fondness. The past relationship, though it may itself be called "love," still may not be enough for a full-fledged case of the occurrent emotion—even though it *has* been more useful than John's love for Jodie and calls for something like gratitude from her. Is Lisa measuring parental love against an unreasonably high standard? Perhaps loyalty and fondness are all one can expect in many cases—though surely something deeper is not impossible. But if, as seems likely, the issue of her mother's love arose as part of a request for love in return—or at least for acceptance of the closeness that a claim of love tends to justify—Lisa's comment is quite appropriate. It is not love of *that* sort and does not warrant that sort of response—supposing that more than gratitude is expected.

If fondness begets fondness, that is a happy accident. But the standard of love appealed to here, in attempting to explain Lisa's remark, is one that provides a reason for love in return—if only on the basis of a positive evaluation of the agent for the depth of *his* love. It obviously does not *require* mutuality or even acceptance of closeness; but its role as a prima facie reason seems to be presupposed by "protestations" of love. That it constitutes a distinct standard is suggested by the fact that an agent feels cheated, and reasonably so, if the response to full-fledged personal love is represented as a feeling of the same sort but turns out to be deficient. We can see this and broaden our treatment of Lisa's case by examining a variant of the familiar "John loves Mary": John does love Mary and enjoys a long and rewarding marital relationship. But he finds out, after her death, that Mary's tender feelings towards him were entirely attributable to gratitude for his financial support and comfort in his company. Their enduring quality was based on the knowledge that an equally comfortable adjustment to another, wealthier partner would no longer have been possible by the time he introduced her to one. We may suppose that this knowledge kept Mary from feeling anything for those other men she did meet; the limitations on her view of John are revealed by entries in a diary, say. But John, if he offered something more personal, could reasonably complain that any talk of mutual *love* was based on an equivocation.

If what he offered was grounded in a positive evaluation of Mary, did *his* love then amount to no more than a feeling of personal *admiration*—something easily transferable to another object, if one had come along, and hence something equally deficient, if we hold to the standard suggested by Lisa's remark? No—as we can readily see if we consider the different sorts of evaluations involved in personal attachment-love. For one thing, these may well include some that are indefinite and best left so. Love of someone for her *"je ne sais quoi,"* whatever its defects as an explanation of *why* one loves her, may adjust most readily to likely changes in the object's personal traits. At least in combination with a tendency to *seek out* more specific grounds, it may yield personal love, on the view proposed here. But in any case, a positive evaluation of someone for relatively basic traits, such as kindness, would be equally unlikely to be shaken by superficial personality changes, of the sort that "nonjudgmental" love is supposed to endure. If kindness does change to unkindness, loyalty may well yield an obligation to continue one's *concern* for the object on the basis of a deeper love once shared. But there is no obligation to continue the *love*, or to wish to *be with* the object for its own sake.

I take the desire for closeness to the object to be essential to personal attachment-love in the way that the desire to attack is essential to anger. Here the desire is supposed to be grounded in a relatively central evaluation of the object, for a "full-fledged" instance of the emotion, on the normative conception of its evaluative structure that my talk of potential mutuality is meant to explain. However, this does *not* mean that personal attachment-love is directed towards its object only *as* the bearer of certain traits, whose other bearers would have equal claim on the emotion—or greater claim, if they exhibit the same traits to a greater degree. For among the evaluations associated with mutual attachment-love, there are also likely, as I just noted, to be some concerning one's particular history of interaction with that object. To see the object as irreplaceably valuable, one need not have a list of presumably unsurpassable traits—even very general traits, such as kindness, of a sort that make comparison with other objects unlikely or unlikely to undermine love. This basis in "historical" traits is typically what gives attachment-love its *exclusivity*, in fact; for assuming that the traits are nontrivial, they may be very unlikely to apply (or to be rivaled by equally significant traits that apply) to another object. John's love for Mary, then, may have been as resistant to competing objects as one could expect.

As with anger, full-fledged personal attachment-love may be said to assign its object a kind of responsibility as the bearer of traits that would tend to justify its characteristic desire. Its direction towards a particular object *would* be incidental if the desire were grounded only in trivial or peripheral traits—in traits shared by many objects or not plausibly taken as central to its own. As with pride, though, the object's responsibility here may be merely causal, not a result of voluntary action. The object may not be aware of the emotion's evaluative basis; but the emotion clearly cannot be reduced to a "pure" feeling, analogous to coffee-induced edginess, with a basis only in perception. John might experience a feeling of tenderness in response to the sight of Sue, for instance, only because she reminds him of her sister Mary—now dead, her diary rifled through, no longer the object of his love. This is not love *for Sue*, though, unless it involves an urge to be with *her*, for its own sake—perhaps because of some traits she shares with Mary but not just because she calls up memories of his better days with Mary. Without an evaluation of Sue, John's feeling would not be personally ascribable to her even if it resulted quite reliably from her presence.

Unless the evaluation of Sue, moreover, is based on traits that are reasonably seen as central to her personality, she could easily shrug off more than incidental responsibility for the feeling. John would have no right, by virtue of his love, to expect anything in return—even any special attempt to soothe his unwelcome feelings of attachment—where the attachment is based on a superficial evaluation, either recognized as such or so obvious that it ought to be. This is not to say, let us note, that the evaluation involved in personal love must be *believed*. It may sometimes amount to "wishful thinking," acknowledged as such by the agent and supporting a kind of fantasy-love with a basis in the perception of some real-life object. But to count as personal love *of that object* it must be reasonably thought to be relatively central, in a sense that requires plausibility to *both* the agent and the object. Otherwise, the feeling would have no real claim on its presumed object's regard, where the object's responsibility for it is assumed to be merely causal. Sue could simply dismiss a love that depended completely on fantasy as essentially impersonal, even though it claimed her as its object. Such a love would really be directed towards a fantasy-object, using her only as a springboard to imagination, in much the way that anger directed towards some frustrating state of affairs may include a person viewed as a barrier to satisfaction.

"Love is not love," then—or at any rate, full-fledged personal love—unless, like the corresponding form of anger, it involves a certain configuration of internal objects. Its evaluative structure and the ways in which its structure differs from that of anger, can be seen to depend on justificatory questions—in this case questions of adaptiveness, of a sort that will be addressed only later. For the present, let us note that the other emotions discussed so far could also be said to have more than one internal object, if only more specific versions of their characteristic objects: that Fido is likely to *bite* me, for instance. But for love, as well as for anger, the multiplicity results from social norms imposed on the infantile prototype of the emotion. Fear and pride may also be said to be norm-based; for they require evaluations—of something as dangerous, or oneself as praiseworthy—that may not be distinguished in the earliest reactions to which the terms are applied: certain cases of shock, say, or of joy. But anger and love, in their most developed forms, seem to be picked out by reference to norms of social acceptance. I have tried to explain these in terms of the punishing nature of anger for the object and the mutually rewarding nature of personal love. Love is more complex than anger, though, partly because it is measured against multiple standards. There are impersonal forms of love, such as loyalty, that may be no less morally significant than personal attachment-love. Some, in fact, may not even be forms of attachment-love at all, but may surpass it in moral significance, just because they extend more readily to multiple *external* objects. I now turn to an alternative standard of love, ideal but in some sense impersonal.

(iv) Identificatory Love

Love for others, as a source of general benevolence, is sometimes called "fellow feeling." I shall call it "identificatory love," though it needs to be distinguished from love of the sort that attaches to particular persons, on the basis of positive evaluations of them. Identificatory love is not a single emotion, but it is something we care about in others' reactions to us, beyond their tendency to act in our interests. It reinforces the motives for benevolent action with various identificatory emotions, such as fear "for" another person, that are not specifically *moral* emotions but serve important moral ends. Even ignoring its motivational influence, though, we value emotional identification for providing a kind of communal *reflection* of our individual standpoints. There is something reassuring in knowing that the sources of our own reactions "register" on others—more deeply than the dispassionate evaluation of our welfare plus a wish for its continuation or improvement. But this sort of love, in contrast to personal attachment-love, need not involve a personal evaluation of any particular depth or a desire for closeness except on the level of mutual support or communal feeling. That is what makes it less exclusive; it is limited by our capacity to take on different imaginative standpoints but not by "historical" attachment to certain objects.

Still, unlike the neutral sorts of regard for others' welfare that are commonly associated with "the moral standpoint," identificatory love, as an *emotional* tie to others, is naturally slanted towards objects of attachment. For personal attachment-love gives rise to identificatory love. Its characteristic desire for closeness to the object of attachment includes a demand for psychological closeness, of a sort that standardly involves preferential regard for the feelings of the object, seen as potentially *shared* feelings. Our particular personal identificatory attachments may be extended in imagination, sometimes by appeal to the nonemotional features we share with others, including simple humanity. But it is not clear that they can or should be extended equally to everyone in the interests of moral neutrality. We ought to have some minimal *compassion* for everyone, perhaps—even the justly condemned man, say, or the man whose vicious character is a product of bad psychological luck. But identificatory love, on the notion I mean to defend here, amounts to more than compassion—or sympathy or even empathy—at least as these notions are commonly understood. Although philosophers may sometimes hark back to the broader meaning of *pathos*, a dictionary limits these notions to sorrow at others' sufferings and hence to relatively passive states of negative emotion, taken as identificatory variants of *pity*. Identificatory love, by contrast, is meant to cover active and positive emotions as well.

It also involves emotions based on evaluations *from* another standpoint—in contrast to the more "distant" variants of pity, involving other-directed sorrow, along with some similar forms of *concern*. This basis in imagination means that its rationality may be called into question, since an identificatory evaluation may seem to be unwarranted from the agent's own standpoint, most clearly in cases of conflicting emotions. If I feel sorrow, for instance, on behalf of someone who has failed to attain some goal I was competing with him for—a goal whose attainment by him would not have promoted any other end of mine—we might be tempted to deny that my reaction is appropriate. From my standpoint there may be no reason to think that his failure was anything but a boon. I may recognize, of course, that it was bad *for him*; but negative feelings in response to this judgment, though they may sometimes rest on imagination, need not involve an imaginative *evaluation*—of the situation as somehow bad *for me*. Identificatory sorrow, by contrast, would conflict with the joy that I feel on my own behalf.

Such cases can be defended, I think, by reference to my view of emotions as involving states of comfort or discomfort directed towards evaluative thoughts that they serve to hold in mind—whether or not their corresponding beliefs are seen as warranted. I shall postpone their defense, however, until I have outlined a general account of emotional appropriateness, in contrast to belief warrant, in my next chapter. I assume, of course, that they *can* be defended—that questions about their rationality are properly framed as Kantian inquiries into the possibility of something that must be thought to obtain. For present purposes we need only grant that identificatory emotions may often be adaptive, or instrumentally valuable, even where their appropriateness is in doubt—on the model, say, of the case discussed towards the end of my treatment of pride. Even where pride is based on imagination, perhaps of some next-to-impossible feat of skill, it may be useful to an agent in generating confidence.

Here, however, the relevant notion of adaptiveness is *social*, with "instrumental value" taken as covering the promotion of ends besides those of the agent. What I want to argue at this point is just that certain fantasy-emotions—those we experience on another person's behalf—are often best suited to the social functions of emotion and in that sense have a special moral significance. As reasons for action other-directed emotions may in some ways be more *altruistic*; but they are not therefore more *valuable* to others, considered either in isolation or in light of their motivational consequences. In what follows, then, I hope eventually to pin down some of the defects of "distant" pity, interpreted in contrast to identificatory love. My argument will proceed by reference to examples—of emotions other than *love*, since identificatory love is really a tendency to take on various different occurrent emotions in a way that seems to reflect the standpoint of its object.

In fact, I shall pay particular attention to *anger* and to other emotions whose evaluative content differs sharply from that of attachment-love— and even from the identificatory variants of pity, as these are usually conceived. For my exploration of cases will suggest that somewhat less tender-hearted emotions are often more helpful. It will also lead, via a side-discussion of moral *offense*, to a notion of identification as involving imaginary attachment in some cases, instead of simple self-projection into the other person's situation. If the main thrust of my argument succeeds, though, I take it to indicate that the conflict between emotion and belief that is involved in fantasy-emotion is not limited to private flights of fancy with occasional uses in pursuit of an agent's own interests. On the assumption that community of feeling is of basic ethical and evolutionary importance, so is the tendency of emotional evaluations to spill over to situations that do not warrant their corresponding beliefs.

For a concrete example, or set of examples, let us consider my reaction to a slight by X to someone other than myself. This may just involve feeling sorry for the target of the insult, taking it as a wrong done to him, whether or not he recognizes it as such. But it may also involve feeling uncomfortably *as though* I had been wronged by X myself and therefore ought to take some action in revenge on him—whether or not I really think so. Before we accept this departure from belief, though, let us note that a range of intermediate responses might also come into play and might seem to serve the target's interests no less than my identificatory anger. These include less "personal" forms of anger— in several senses, though I shall limit the term to that sense that makes out the emotion as person-directed *blame*. Let us suppose that the insult is some sort of racist "put-down," directed towards a race other than my own and limited in a way that also keeps it from posing any indirect threat to me.[10] It is a drawn-out compliment, say, for abilities that should be treated as standard and that X would clearly take for granted in me. X's intent is to humiliate—as others may or may not know. One possible *non*identificatory response is *impersonal* anger, involving a kind of frustration directed at the situation as a whole. I may be angry *that* an instance of racism has occurred or that the target has been insulted—or even that X has insulted him. But here we assume that my urge to attack—

the motivating desire characteristic of anger—is focused on X only incidentally, as part of a hated state of affairs.

Anger may *sometimes* be identificatory in such cases: I may think, rightly or wrongly, that the target of the insult should not blame X himself, so that my anger "on his behalf" should also be "impersonal," in the sense just sketched. But whether it is identificatory or not, my impersonal anger might also involve seeing *myself* as the one who has been injured—and hence in some sense "taking the insult personally," perhaps without any conflict with belief. Suppose I have reason to think, for instance, that X comes out with racist remarks to attempt to get at *me*. For he knows that they violate my moral principles—but that my moral principles also force me to limit myself to impersonal anger at a cost in self-control that he finds amusing. If I do manage not to blame him, I still may be angry about the situation in a way that is nontrivially *self-involved*—though it is not "personal," in my sense here. The affective component of my anger of course applies to me; but this is true of any emotion. It is I who am uncomfortable, that is; but more to the point, my discomfort has an evaluative object that makes reference to myself. By contrast to such cases, however, the evaluative component of "personal" anger, in the case I began with, links it to my action against X. It involves the view that X is *responsible* for the hated state of affairs and that I therefore ought to take action against him.

The ascription of responsibility to X thus gives focus to the urge to attack that I take to be characteristic of "pressuring" anger; and in the case at hand we may assume that this focus serves the target's interests. I see X's remark as intentionally humiliating and therefore as warranting my taking revenge on him—at least in a broad sense, including (among other things) my aiding the target in taking revenge and thus in warding off future insults. But the insult's relevance to my action, on this view of things, does not seem to depend on whether I see it as humiliating *me*—on whether my anger is "self-involved" in any further sense, even in imagination. Its offensiveness to me can apparently be understood just in general moral terms, without reference to some imaginatively enlarged picture of myself as somehow in the position of the target. But if so, it might seem that *offense-without-injury* provides us with a "distant" variant of *personal* anger. Where it does involve blame, as it clearly may, it would not seem to require a departure from belief in order to yield action on behalf of the target, of the sort that arises from identificatory anger. However, just because it is more "high-minded," it may be less reliable as a way of satisfying our interest in emotional community. I shall return to it later; but at this point I shall take the low road and provide an initial critique of the variants of pity, in contrast to identificatory anger.

Pity is commonly thought of as a somewhat unsatisfying response, largely because it is often humiliating in itself. Or at any rate, this is the common view of some of the more distant forms of pity, or pity unmixed with empathy. Despite the common regard for empathy, however, it is not clear that its identificatory content would make up for all the short-comings of distant pity. In the situation just sketched, *self*-pity would also be a humiliating response on the part of the *target*. On my part, then, we might say that identificatory pity would be less than fully satisfying not because it places me on a higher plane of estimation but because it places both of us on a low plane, relative to X. It lacks the active force of an angry response—one that lowers X (if only by protesting his self-elevation) rather than simply acknowledging our low status as his victims. The "sting" of distant pity—and its tendency to turn grounds for grat-itude into causes of anger—is not explained solely by the assumption that it involves an invidious comparison. Even in response to some natural disaster, feeling sorry for oneself often compounds the problem—amounts to a kind of collaboration with the natural forces of oppression. But the same point would seem to apply to the identificatory variants of pity. Just insofar as it is *passive*, then, pity may be a less than helpful response.

The point is not just that pity lacks the aroused affective quality of anger; it also lacks anger's orientation towards change. Its negative eval-uative content, let us note, is compatible with a kind of acceptance of the target's situation that is not compatible with anger. If in response to X's insult I feel sorry for the target, I need not view the insult as un-justified. Indeed, my discomfort may be directed towards an evaluative proposition that acknowledges grounds for the insult: that it is a shame to belong to an inferior race, say, and thus to be subject to the occasional, quite reasonable put-down. Compassion and sympathy also allow for "identification with the aggressor," in evaluative terms, though they may be more sensitive to the target's feelings. Even concern, which may some-times involve a desire for action on the target's behalf, may also rest on acceptance of the target's humiliation, as something he *has* to undergo at least to some extent, though its effect on his feelings might be mitigated. X, the aggressor, might himself feel any of these emotions of tender-hearted regard for the target, in fact. He need not have regrets about coming out with his (relatively mild) insult in order to regret its aptness, say, or even to feel sad about the hurt it causes X.

In general, passive states of negative emotion, since they take for granted the other party's misfortune, may yield a kind of after-the-fact compensatory benevolence, at best. Even their identificatory variants need not involve identification with the other party's *aims*, with an urge to act in advance of their frustration, canceling out the cause of misfor-tune, as well as simply limiting its effects. Thus, when I compete suc-cessfully with someone for a prize we cannot share, I may feel "sorry for" him when he loses without having any qualms about my victory. I may be sorry that he *has* to be the one to lose—given that *someone* has to—but take no action on his behalf beyond (at most) an attempt to cheer him up about the loss. My identification with him may extend only to those of his aims that do not conflict with my own. My benevolent promotion of his good, then, may involve only an attempt to keep him from suffering any more than is required by *my* good—with my compassion as compensation for what he *must* suffer.

Note that feeling sorry *for* someone ordinarily just means feeling sorry *about* his situation—not feeling *his* sorrow, or the sorrow that I would feel (or think that I should feel) if I were in his situation. It is thus unlike, say, *embarrassment* "for" someone, which is essentially identificatory and contrasts with the embarrassment one might feel on one's own behalf in response to the same situation. The example of embarrassment may be used, for a moment, to provide a nice illustration of the social value of even passive identificatory emotion—and of its limitations. Suppose it turned out, for instance, that my argument here did little but repeat some points that were made in a widely read article I managed to miss. After reading my own effort to a group that was aware of the overlap, I might be somewhat consoled to hear that a friend in the audience was embarrassed *for* me. But I would not be much consoled to hear that he was embarrassed *to see* such a thing. He might also report that he was embarrassed "as my friend"; but much depends on whether he meant that our friendship led him to take my failures as his own, or that he expected *others* to link them to him.

Even the identificatory embarrassment, however, would be valuable to me in isolation only on the assumption that nothing more active was possible—that he could think of no minor point of difference from the article, say, that might be stressed in discussion to help conceal the extent of overlap. Like fear, which may also be "for" someone in the sense that implies identification, embarrassment is typically linked to a characteristic desire: to hide the object of embarrassment. The content of the desire has to be left somewhat indefinite, though, in order to allow for a reasonable response in cases of identificatory emotion. My friend has no serious urge, for instance, to interrupt the paper and extemporize on the subject—as he might if he really put himself in my place. But at any rate, even the indefinite desire, taken as a desire for action, may be absent in cases where the agent thinks that its satisfaction is impossible. Just as fear may sometimes amount to a passive state of dread, that is, so embarrassment may involve no more than discomfort at the thought that its object is and must remain in plain and devastating view.

How is anger different? There certainly are situations where the desire to get back at someone is unsatisfiable. Yet anger seems to be essentially active, in a way that sorrow, fear, and embarrassment are not.

As I analyze the emotion, it essentially involves a desire for action, interpreted as discomfort at an unfulfilled action requirement. But why should this remain in force when action of the relevant sort is viewed as impossible and therefore as something that *cannot* be required? Impersonal anger provides a more readily satisfiable option here; but I would look for the full explanation in the fact that the expression of personal anger, even if limited to identificatory thought, normally goes at least some way towards achieving the emotion's "proper aim." Unless the object of my anger has complete contempt for me (and even in some cases where he does), my viewing him with anger is normally itself a kind of punishment for him, whether or not I can punish him overtly. In general, our interest in others' emotional reactions to us includes a *negative* interest in those based on negative evaluations *of* us, such as personal anger. Although this may be compounded when the emotions in question increase the likelihood of *action* against our interests, it need not be canceled out when they do not—or even when they increase the likelihood of action *in* our interests, including acts of thought. I may actually relish being feared, say, if I think that some of my Machiavellian aims are served by others' flight from my presence—or just that their fearful attention "registers" my power. Certain cases of anger may be like this too, of course; but since blame involves assigning fault, personal anger itself counts as a kind of punishment for its object, whether or not he is aware of it as such and whether or not on balance it yields a reward.

Personal anger remains "active," then, where overt action on its characteristic desire is blocked; for mental action on the desire provides at least prima facie satisfaction of it, even as an identificatory response. Identificatory anger therefore provides some aid as well as comfort to the other party. By contrast, in the case of identificatory embarrassment, a friend's attempt to conceal my problem simply by looking away from it in thought—something *I* might do, if I were aware of it—would not help me in dealing with questions from the audience. Mental escape from an object of identificatory dread may be equally useless to the other party, moreover—for instance, in a case where one might instead minimize the threat by helping him prepare himself for it. Similarly for cases of sorrow, I would say—but with a twist. Looking away from one's own suffering may sometimes help to alleviate it: Perhaps the target of X's insult would be able to avoid "hurt feelings," say, just by ignoring the insult. As in the cases just cited, however, this would not normally be helpful as an identificatory response. But neither would it seem to count as a way of satisfying some desire characteristic of sorrow for oneself, in contrast to the cases just cited. Here, in fact, it seems questionable whether there *is* such a *motivating* desire, even one that depends on a standard situational context. It is not at all obvious, in particular, that sorrow typically involves a desire to improve matters—as opposed to a desire for some form of *expression*, a desire linked to emotions in general and sometimes encouraging action of a sort that preserves the status quo.

Anger is sometimes viewed as *built on* sorrow, in the sense of "hurt feelings," understood as a passive reaction that is transformed into active anger by its attribution to some cause. This is a bit too simple, however, to capture anger's direction towards revenge. Also, sorrow includes some forms of distress that are at any rate mentally active, or aroused in affective quality, such as *anguish*. Still, the main "activity" in question here might just involve *dwelling on* sorrow, or on its object. Similar expressions of identificatory sorrow—offering the other a kind of emotional succor—might be likely, then, to increase the tendency of sorrow to sustain itself. This is what seems to stand behind the passivity of identificatory pity; but in fact, I shall later have a few kinder words to say about *some* identificatory variants of pity, at least in contrast with distant pity. For the moment, I want to return to the case of identificatory anger, since I think I can extract from it a notion of identification that will eventually allow for more active variants of pity as responses to others' passive or self-sustaining sorrow.

The case of anger should make it clear that identificatory emotions need not be limited to those one would or should experience *in* another person's place. For instance, since X presumably does not care about the fault assigned him by the target of his insult—except positively, perhaps, as a sign that the insult hit its mark—angry thoughts on the part of the target could achieve only a self-defeating sort of revenge. What should I feel on the target's behalf, then? Where a passive response more accurately reflects his *actual* standpoint, it might seem that anger would not do at all as a way of satisfying his interest in "community of feeling," strictly construed. If this is understood to mean that "misery loves company," the best response would seem to be *commiseration*. Should we say instead that the target's interest in community of feeling is an interest in others' reflection of his *ideal* emotional standpoint? Even this is inadequate, I think, to handle cases like the one just sketched, at least if "reflection" is interpreted narrowly. For it may sometimes happen that an identificatory emotion accomplishes something for another person that the same emotion on his part could not. In my central case, as outlined so far, anger on the part of the target of the insult would have no negative emotional impact on X and might in fact compound the target's humiliation, to the extent that his response is self-involved. Anger on his behalf, by contrast, might be more effective as a means of revenge, assuming that it comes from someone not subject to X's contempt. Ideally, perhaps, the target ought to limit himself to a distant and somewhat scornful form of sorrow, without particular focus on himself—sorrow that the world contains racists, say—while relying on others for revenge on any particular racist.

One might be tempted to say something similar of my identificatory emotion, however, particularly if X has some positive interest in my anger—as in a case of impersonal but self-involved anger that was outlined earlier. My personal anger, in the present case, does count as prima facie punishment, on our assumptions; but we might also suppose that X is willing to put up with some punishment for the reward he gets out of baiting me on moral issues. The reward is not simply attention, let us grant, but rather attention *as* a source of anguished frustration, say; so he does want an *angry* response on my part. But before retreating to distant sorrow, in order to deny him what he wants, I might try the distant form of personal anger that was introduced but quickly bypassed at the beginning of this section. *Im*personal anger would *not* be helpful here: Simply lashing out at the surrounding situation would not normally amount to action against X's interests, except where it serves to "energize" the target of his insult; and on my part in this case it might give X exactly what he wants. But offense-without-injury is "personal," in my sense, if it rests on a view of X as responsible for the situation; and it might seem not to require a basis in self-involved distress. However, I now want to argue that it does require a kind of identification, at least if it is to be widely applicable to cases of the sort just sketched.

Offense and Identification. Let us note, first, that not all grounds for anger are grounds for *moral* offense and, secondly, that an active response even to those that do amount to moral wrongs may depend on placing extramoral *stress* on the emotional standpoint of the injured party. Suppose, for instance, that someone misspelled your name in a citation that was important to you. Your anger at him for his carelessness might be warranted, even if moral offense would be quite unreasonable. In any case, there would be no real reason for me to share your anger—though I might if I happened to share your standpoint, as someone who might be in the same position someday or merely because I can imagine how I would probably feel if I were. Or perhaps I am just a stickler for correct spelling, reacting to a lapse with something like *aesthetic* offense. But my general thoughts on the subject, though they might be particularly welcome to you at the moment, might also be *too* general to reflect your reaction to the actual injury you think was done to you. Further, if we add to the case some reasons for moral offense—reasons, perhaps, for thinking that your interests were wantonly disregarded—these need not be seen as terribly important. They would be important to *you*, of course; and I ought to recognize that fact. But without some form of identification—with you as a fellow academic, say—their significance from my own standpoint or from a neutral standpoint need not be enough to yield a requirement of action on your behalf.

Similarly, in the case of X's insult to someone else, the wrong actually done by the remark may be relatively trivial. We may assume that in extraemotional terms the unavenged insult would have no negative effects in this case and that in emotional terms, apart from identification, it would affect only the target. Suppose I know, for instance, that ignoring X's behavior on this one occasion would pose no real threat to the functioning of our professional group, or the like, even by encouraging similar remarks in the future. For in fact X is quite impervious to social disapproval on this subject; and everyone but the target has learned to dismiss his occasional remarks. Perhaps, then, the insult should be taken, from my own real-life standpoint, as something that is overshadowed by X's many good deeds in relation to myself and others and hence as insufficient to yield more than prima facie warrant for a judgment that I ought to punish X. Indeed, this may be true from the *moral* standpoint, thought of as one that blends emotional standpoints of evaluation, so that wrongs done by X may be canceled out by reasons for gratitude to him.

It is only from the standpoint of the target of the insult, let us say, that X's lapse into mild racism properly looms large, as an overriding reason for action in this case. Still, it may be better for the target—and better *as judged from* the moral standpoint—that someone else be prompted to act on his behalf. But without some special connection to the target, why should I be the one? In contrast to the preceding case, I am not a member of the group of potential targets of such insults. Even if I were, though—or if appeal were made to common membership in the *human* race, say—that would not be enough to shift full responsibility for action onto me.[11] The insult was hardly so vicious as to call for action on the part of all mankind; nor am I in a special position to avenge it, we may grant. If I do avenge it with offense, then—taken as a form of personal *anger*—I shall have to be "imagining things" at least to the extent of viewing some action on my part as required.

I need not imagine anything further, however. Indeed, if I did, my response might be too ludicrous to be helpful. "How dare you insult my race!" would just leave X befuddled; so a tendency to come out with that response or something similar would undermine the social adaptiveness of the identificatory emotion. As in the earlier case of embarrassment on behalf of a friend, my desire for action might have to be rather indefinite, here prescribing revenge of some sort or other but with room left for a choice among particular actions in light of my actual situation. In any case, the wrong attributed to X, on this notion of identification, must itself be somewhat indefinite, insofar as my identificatory anger involves thinking of it as a wrong done to me. I need not see X as having insulted me, as I would if I identified with the target of his insult in the sense of putting myself in his place. But nor need I see him as having insulted a member of some specific group that includes me—putting myself in the place of a potential target, say. Rather than putting myself in his or a similar place, I may just actively "take the part" of the target. I may see us as connected by membership in some unspecified group, in a way that makes wrongs to him *count as* wrongs to me. Instead of adopting his own actual or ideal emotional standpoint, that is, I may adopt something like the emotional standpoint of a friend—ideal, and at least semi-imaginary, to the extent that it involves the thought that I am responsible for action on his behalf.

This looser notion of identificatory emotion should yield a more plausible account of what goes on in our private flights of fancy, as well as those of moral significance. When I feel fear "for" the movie heroine who is about to be stabbed, for instance, I need not be under the impression that I am about to be stabbed. Rather, I am uncomfortable "at the thought" that I am in some-danger-or-other—whether of being stabbed or of losing a friend to that or some other misfortune, but in any case, in a way that rests on imagination. The sight of the knife may be taken as bearing on my own fate not because I view it as intended for me but because I see my fate as bound up with the fate of the one for whom it *is* intended. The desire linked to identificatory fear is not always the desire to flee, then, but a desire to escape the danger, often unspecified, that is envisioned as applying to oneself. Where this is the danger of losing a friend, one might escape it by warning the other party, say, at least in real-life cases. Here, too, identification—and its potential social value—depends on an imaginary extension of one's circle of attachments, on putting oneself in the place of a friend of the person with whom one identifies, rather than simply putting oneself in *his* place.

There is a looser notion of identification, then, that involves imaginary *attachment* to others, at least in the sense of taking special responsibility for their welfare or assuming an obligation to act on their behalf. It is "looser" in the sense of tying the agent less tightly to the person with whom he identifies, though its link to action is meant to be more direct. We might understand the latter in terms of our natural desire to benefit an object of attachment-love, whose feelings we potentially share; but identificatory love, on the looser notion, still does not amount to a single emotion, including attachment-love. Besides making out offense as identificatory, this notion may now help us to exhibit a kernel of truth in some of the value distinctions commonly made between distant and identificatory pity—despite my many criticisms of identificatory pity earlier. The word "pity" is often used in a particularly pejorative sense, in restriction to the *most* distant forms of the emotion. The suggestion is that pity unmixed with empathy is somehow smug or aloof, perhaps even scornful, and hence unreliable in generating active concern for the welfare of others, as well as being unsatisfying to others in itself. I now want to say that this is so because the emotion's evaluative component in such cases involves mainly positive self-reference, of a sort that depends on seeing the other as outside one's circle of attachments and the other's welfare as outside one's sphere of practical responsibility.

The agent's predominant emotion in such cases may well be a variant of *pride*, based on comfort at a positive evaluation of the comparison between the other's suffering and his own good fortune. This invidious comparison must be the only recognized link to the other, if pride is to stand unqualified as a source of self-content. Even in certain distant but tender-hearted forms of pity, though, whether the emotion gives rise to a desire to aid the other will depend on whether its element of discomfort comes to focus on a negative evaluation of failure to aid him. Initially directed towards a negative evaluation of his plight, discomfort might come to focus instead on a negative evaluation of *attention* to his plight— viewed with revulsion, perhaps, or perhaps just faint-heartedness—where it does not simply remain in place. As an alternative to corrective action, at least as effective in overcoming discomfort, one might look away from the other's sufferings, stressing one's own good fortune—in this case with *relief*, but with comfort again augmented by the contrast. Corrective action may still be taken—as it may even in the prideful cases—but even this form of distant pity will be unreliable as a motive towards action. Nor will misery be reliably supplied with company—except, perhaps, as a stage on the way to its opposite—when distant pity takes this tender-hearted form.

By contrast, compassion and sympathy, interpreted as identificatory forms of pity, would seem to involve discomfort at a negative evaluation of *one's own* (imagined) plight—now taken as including, in some cases, the plight of passive acceptance of the other's situation. One sees oneself as essentially "in the same boat" as the other party—as subject, if not to the same misfortunes, at least to the misfortune of standing by while one's fellows are subjected to them. Identificatory pity may still sometimes be passive, of course, as in the cases I considered earlier. But where it rests on the looser notion of identification, it typically involves taking responsibility for alleviating the other party's sufferings rather than simply taking them as one's own and perhaps just dwelling on them. Even other-directed *concern* may involve an element of identification, in this sense, we should note, to the extent that it places a stress on others' sufferings that exceeds their actual importance to oneself or to others for whom one actually bears responsibility. In its active forms, along with compassion and sympathy, it need not be limited to identificatory *sorrow*— or something more active in affective quality, such as sorrowful *anguish*— even if that is what the other party feels and should feel. Another possibility is some variant of *fear*—worry, anxiety, or the like—to provide us with a future-directed, and typically an active, alternative to anger, useful particularly in cases where no one is to blame.

On the looser notion, then, identificatory pity focuses more directly on the need for action to alleviate the other party's suffering—as distinguished from one's own emotional discomfort, though aiding the other is seen as a means to relieving one's own discomfort. It is always *possible* to look away from others' suffering, of course, in order to avoid discomfort. But identificatory pity at least ensures that the agent cannot look *at* it without "registering" it in discomfort of his own, with an identificatory evaluation as its object. Since the looser notion of identification standardly involves the assumption of practical responsibility for others, identificatory pity, as now interpreted, supplies the agent more reliably with a reason for corrective action. It may now be said to "reflect" the other's standpoint *actively*, even where it is not quite the same emotion as his or as the one that the agent would have (or should have) in his place. Where corrective action is not in question, moreover, this sort of identificatory emotion will be more valuable to others than distant pity, just in so far as it involves a sense of attachment to others at possible variance with belief.

This view of the value of identificatory emotion is not meant to suggest that it is always preferable to dispassionate judgment. There clearly are cases where dispassionate judgment would reliably give rise to action, perhaps without some of the pitfalls of emotional response. Identificatory emotion may not be adequate on its own, for that matter, in cases where it is needed as a *supplement* to judgment. My claim here is simply that it *is* sometimes needed as a supplement, particularly where it supplies a reason for action on behalf of others. But the judgment that it supplements—the only judgment that is warranted in a given case—may sometimes be weaker than the one corresponding to the emotion's evaluative component. As we saw in the case of offense-without-injury, there may be nothing to pick out the agent, in particular, as responsible for action to aid the other party. If so, identificatory emotion may be seen as supplementing judgment, in some cases, by strengthening it in evaluative terms for a genuine break from judgmentalist accounts of emotional justification. Let me therefore turn to two judgmentalist lines of objection to my treatment of identificatory pity: one that, though worth consideration, may be answered fairly easily in light of my preceding discussion; and one whose more complex answer requires a separate subsection.[12] Both focus on my attempt to explain motivation by the emotion as prompted by an urge to escape discomfort; and my answers to both will anticipate my treatment of justificatory issues in Part II.

First, it might be said, the account removes any *altruistic* significance from what I have called the emotional counterpart of benevolence. Distant pity—or for that matter, simple benevolence, without any element of affect—at least involves an evaluation of *the other's* state of misfortune. But identificatory pity, on my account, might seem to amount to a kind of *self*-pity, even if occasioned by someone else's misfortune. As such, one might wonder how it can be either valuable as a source of altruistic motivation or satisfying to the other party in itself. However, the superiority of identificatory pity, on the view defended here, is not supposed to be a matter of motivational altruism. In general, the point of my account of emotional motivation is to reinforce altruistic with self-interested reasons for action on behalf of others—and to exhibit the special role emotions play in providing the latter. As long as weakness of will is possible, the urge to relieve one's own identificatory emotional discomfort may be extremely *useful* to others, just insofar as it serves to advance their interests. Whether or not its motivational role should be counted as altruistic, then, its role may have altruistic significance.

However, let us consider the suggestion that identificatory pity has no altruistic significance "in itself." What one feels is often subject to voluntary control, at least indirectly, via control over what one attends to. But in that case, paying attention to others' sufferings, when it means subjecting oneself to discomfort, will often be altruistic even if action to alleviate the discomfort is not. It will be valuable to others, moreover, to the extent that it reflects their own emotional standpoints. Identificatory pity, resulting from imaginative openness to others' *reasons* for sorrow, should not be confused with self-pity merely "occasioned by" others' misfortunes. In response to the news that someone else's article has been rejected, say, one might might remember one's own bad luck in similar past situations, or imagine a similar future situation as applying to oneself, and feel *self*-pity. But this is not *identificatory* pity, of the sort that might provide the other party with a kind of emotional support. Although it does embody the recognition that the other's fate could be one's own, it focuses attention entirely on one's own fate, real or imagined.

Identificatory pity thus amounts to more than other-occasioned self-pity—and not just because of its basis in imagination. This is brought out most clearly by the looser notion of identification, which lets the emotion retain its sense of the pitiable fate as someone else's despite its imagined bearing on oneself. I may see myself as "sharing" your fate just insofar as I am related to you in some way that yields responsibility, that is—not necessarily by subjection to the same misfortunes. Identificatory emotions in the standard sense may of course be exhibited as well; and so may distant pity or affectless benevolence, along with self-regarding emotions based on the perception of my own situation. Imagination, I take it, allows for a few gestalt shifts (or even, for that matter, some simultaneous equivalents) to let us explain how motivation by an identificatory emotion may be conjoined with judgment, as it clearly must be to allow for a reasonable choice of action. In the case of pity, the looser notion of identification, by combining imagined attachment with the perception of one's difference from the other, also encourages a less passive form of response than is typical of sorrow for oneself. Indeed, it even allows for an element of altruism in motivation by identificatory pity. Although that motivation rests, on my account, on the need to alleviate one's own discomfort, it is important to my general view of emotions that the discomfort is *about* something; and here it is important that its object concerns something besides oneself. Still, in the sense in which helping a friend is standardly not a *pure* case of altruism, neither is action from identificatory pity.

Another objection might be raised, though, to my view of action on behalf of others as more reliably motivated by identificatory than by distant pity. For it might seem that, on my account, only the affective component of identificatory pity has a role to play—or at any rate, a rational role—in motivating action on behalf of others. The emotion itself motivates such action only *indirectly*, one might say, as a way of improving its accompanying affective state. But to the extent that this amounts to a distinct objection from the one just answered, it seems to assume a standard judgmentalist account of emotional motivation. Motivation by identificatory emotion might seem to come out as indirect, that is, just in so far as it rests on something besides the evaluative judgment that the objection apparently equates with "the emotion itself." For the objection assumes that the act of aiding the unfortunate other cannot be motivated by the imaginary object of emotional discomfort: the negative evaluation of one's own state. However, discomfort with that object still should not be conflated with objectless discomfort—as it would have to be to yield the conclusion that affect operates *alone* as a reason for action, on my view. Rather, my view maintains that object-directed discomfort supplements evaluative judgment with an imagined link to the other that makes the agent feel specially responsible for action on his behalf.

If this reinforcement of judgment with affect makes motivation indirect in judgmentalist terms, I am not sure why that should concern us—any more than purity of altruistic motivation, as in the first objection—unless it threatens the emotion's link to action. Directness would indeed be provided by affectless benevolence—or by its emotional counterpart, distant pity of the sort I have called "tender-hearted," involving discomfort at a negative evaluation of the other's unfortunate state. But the sources of altruistic motivation here—judgment supplemented by affectless desire or by other-directed emotion—may often need to be strengthened. My claim is just that they *can* be strengthened by identification—at the easily affordable cost of some purity and directness. As to rationality, I would also claim that emotions whose evaluative components are not warranted as judgments can still be seen as supported by reasons and as yielding reasons for action. There may be reasons for holding certain generally valuable thoughts in mind, that is—by making them objects of comfort or discomfort— even where the evidence runs against their corresponding beliefs, perhaps decisively. This is the claim that stands behind the defense of the appropriateness of conflicting emotions that was sketched earlier but whose full discussion was postponed until Part II. For the moment, I have presented only an argument concerning the *adaptiveness*, in social terms, of identificatory emotions. Even on this point, however, another interpretation of the second line of objection may be used to question the motivational role of identificatory pity, if we anticipate some of the results of Part II, at least to the extent of allowing for emotional conflict.

Identification, Ambivalence, and Desire. Consider my earlier suggestion that looking away from others' misfortune, in response to distant pity, provides an alternative to corrective action since it serves just as well to alleviate discomfort. I granted that this was also possible in response to identificatory pity. Identificatory emotion does not guarantee action since it does not guarantee its own survival. But my claim was that identificatory pity is more directly oriented towards action, assuming the looser notion of identification; so it at least guarantees an active emotional response to others' misfortunes while one does attend to them. As long as the emotion does survive, that is, it guarantees an urge towards action on behalf of others. But more needs to be said in defense of this claim; for ambivalence would seem to be possible here—and indeed to be likely where the agent has the information needed for a reasonable choice of action, including information that may serve as the basis for self-regarding emotions. Ambivalence would seem to undercut the motivational force of the identificatory emotion. Along with identificatory pity, that is, as a response to someone's perceived misfortune, an agent might undergo a contrary emotion with the same (external) object—namely, his own state—such as relief that his own state is not really bad and does not involve any real attachment to the other. Simply by shifting his attention, then, by vacillating between identificatory pity and the perception of his own state, he could achieve a kind of reassurance and alleviate his discomfort to some extent without taking action.

On my view, however, where identificatory pity does survive the interruption of attention, it will retain its connection to motivating *desire*. By contrast, even tender-hearted distant pity may be mixed with a comfortable self-regarding emotion in a way that preserves its essential content without a desire to act to aid the other. The agent's attention may be fixed upon his own comparatively good fortune, that is, even though he still would be said to feel sorry for the other. His compound emotion may amount to an overall state of comfort: relief heightened by its comparative basis, including a "mingled" element of passive *dis*comfort. I take this result to be analogous to some of the pleasurable fear-based experiences—those not involving ambivalence—that one might have at a horror film or in facing the challenge of some real-life danger, confident that no harm will befall oneself. Fear in such cases may survive as a state of discomfort—at the thought that harm is likely—but it will be blended with anticipatory comfort, yielding an overall sense of immunity to danger. The resultant state is pleasurable on the whole, retaining the arousal of fear, but without the typical urge to flee its object, which in this case is canceled out by confidence. Similarly, distant pity, mixed with self-content, may not involve a desire to aid the other party. It may still remain in force—*as* a state of discomfort *at* the other party's plight—but its component of discomfort may no longer be directed towards an action requirement.

Now what about identificatory pity? If we allow for the possibility of ambivalence—as in other cases of pleasurable fear—the emotion may remain in force along with its contrary. But we will not get quite the same result here, I think. The contrary evaluative components of these conflicting emotions will not so readily combine to yield a single emotion with a comparative (internal) object, as opposed to an unblended mixture of distinct emotions, with one layered over the other. While feeling uncomfortable about my own (imagined) state, say, as I identify with someone else, I might also feel comfortable at the recognition that I am not really in such a state, that the identificatory evaluation *is* just a product of imagination. Here my discomfort may be balanced by comfort—perhaps even *over*balanced by it. But their evaluative objects are contraries and not of a sort that can be reconciled by qualification ("bad-for-him" versus "good-for-me" or imaginary versus real) unless I *cease* to identify. So my opposing affects will not blend into comfort at a comparative evaluation, as with distant pity, but at most will alternate in occupying my attention while my identificatory emotion remains in force. If my discomfort is directed towards a view of myself as responsible for aiding the other party, then, as on the looser notion of identification, it will still be directed towards a requirement of action, yielding a desire to give assistance, despite my ambivalence.

If my discomfort is overbalanced by comfort, however, might it not also be overridden as a reason, even granting that it does provide a prima facie reason? Indeed, yes—though it has to be overridden in combination with discomfort from the other-directed sources that it supplements. I have attempted to make out identificatory pity as motivationally more reliable than distant pity; but it is important to my argument here that both lack the essentially active force of identificatory anger. Where anger is a source of overall comfort, it is so at least partly because it involves a thought of acting on its characteristic desire and achieving its "proper aim," namely revenge. This thought, however, normally goes some way towards *satisfying* the desire. Ambivalence might allow the agent to achieve a similar kind of comfort from identificatory pity; but here his mental action would in no way benefit the other party. It may indeed be rewarding, on the whole, to identify with the unfortunate, just in order to experience a sense of relief—at calling to mind their distinction from oneself. We should note, however, that *lasting* relief here would seem to depend on *ceasing* to identify. The alternative would involve at least a layer of discomfort, perhaps emerging into consciousness only off-and-on, but retaining even while unconscious its direction towards an unfulfilled requirement of action on behalf of others. On the looser notion of identification, then, identificatory pity would seem to remain active as long as it remains in force. It is distant pity, even if tender-hearted, that is apt to involve the passive relief that responsibility for others' welfare may be assigned to "the grace of God."

I shall eventually argue that ambivalence is often rationally appropriate, even in some surprising sorts of cases. My detailed discussion of the topic in Chapter 5 will fall in between an attempt to work out a general account of appropriateness in Chapter 4 and its application to the distinction between appropriate and merely understandable emotions in the initial argument of Chapter 6. The issue will surface where it does, in the middle of Part II, because it raises questions about the breadth of the notion of appropriateness that need to be answered before I apply it to my final argument, on the full rational justification of emotions. On my view, emotions may be rationally required, by virtue of their role as reasons for action, in cases where they are both appropriate and adaptive. My explanation of such cases will turn on an account of practical reasoning from emotion, with emotions seen as supplements to judgment, in the way that I have anticipated in this chapter.

My main aim in this chapter, and in Part I as a whole, has been to exhibit the breadth of the category of emotion in order to allow for a genuine alternative to judgmentalist accounts of its justificatory role. Besides broadening its two components beyond judgment and sensation, I have pointed up some complexities in their relation to motivating desire—and some cases where emotion yields a motivating desire even though the corresponding judgment requiring action is not warranted. If the emotion in such cases can be made out as appropriate, then, on some defensible notion of appropriateness, it would seem to give us an "extrajudgmental" reason for action, as promised in my introductory chapter. Although I shall leave the sustained treatment of emotional motivation until the notion of appropriateness has been pinned down further, I think we have seen enough if it at this point to use it to sum up the nature of emotions, very briefly, in terms of their justificatory role. Emotions serve as rewards or punishments for their agents, their objects, and others, we may say, by "registering" evaluations in positive or negative affect. Our interest in them and their motivational influence depends on the way they record evaluative information in good or bad states of the agent. In certain cases, where the bad state amounts to discomfort at an action requirement, they punish a failure to act with continuing discomfort, thus exerting pressure towards action beyond what judgment strictly requires. Emotion may be thought of as strengthening a weaker judgment motivationally, bringing a general recommendation of action to bear, as a requirement, on the agent in the particular case at hand. This is the view I shall attempt to defend in my treatment of justificatory issues in Part II.

II
EMOTIONAL APPROPRIATENESS AND ADAPTIVENESS

4
Perceptual Warrant:
Suspicion Revisited

Let us now begin to work towards an explanation of the notion of emotional appropriateness, taken as capturing our first-level rational assessment of emotions, by analogy to belief warrant. Up to this point, I have relied on an intuitive understanding of the notion, applying it to emotions that are rationally justified in "backward-looking" terms. On this use, it is to be distinguished both from moral worth and from instrumental value—the "forward-looking" justificatory category referred to as "adaptiveness" and taken as implying another sort of rational assessment. But a deeper account of appropriateness will exhibit its dependence on *general* adaptiveness. My inquiry into emotional justification—an attempt to extend the limited analogy between emotion and belief that was set up in my treatment of the nature of emotion—will therefore lead me to qualify some of its starting points. From the outset, moreover, it will lead me beyond the attempt to capture preexisting intuitions to some stipulative uses of the analogy needed in applying the justificatory standpoint to emotion.

For instance, ordinary language does not confine the word "appropriate" to a single univocal use, even in nonmoral and noninstrumental assessments of emotion. Thus, we might sometimes say that an emotion "turned out" to be appropriate where it turned out, quite by chance, to represent the agent's actual circumstances—where it happened to "fit the facts." Appropriateness, conceived as a kind of *representational* rationality, is naturally interpreted, on the model of belief, as amounting to the "truth" of the emotions.[1] But assuming that this means "truth to the facts," we had better mark it off with another term—"applicability," say—understood as referring to the truth of the evaluative component of a given emotion. For it does not capture appropriateness as a *rational* value of emotions, in the justificatory sense presupposed by my discussion. Thus, a fear of being hit by a falling rock might seem to be appropriate, in ordinary terms, just as long as I am actually in a "falling rock zone" on the turnpike (ignoring questions of affective strength, at this point). But suppose I have no inkling that I *am* in a falling rock zone, having failed to see the sign. I am reacting instead to a sudden delusion that rocks seek out my head. Whatever limited sort of appropriateness we might be inclined to ascribe to my fear in this case, it clearly does not involve *rational* fitness to the facts. It would seem to be analogous to the accidental truth of an unjustified belief. But the notion of appropriateness was introduced to cover emotions that are justified by the situations in which they arise. So it seems to require truth to the *perceived* facts: "perceptual" warrant, one might say, of a sort that makes truth to the facts nonaccidental, though it may still fall short of full evidential warrant, of the sort that we require for beliefs.

This last qualification is needed if we are to allow for cases of "intuitive" emotional appropriateness, without adequate warrant for belief, as illustrated by the suspicion case in Chapter 1. In Chapter 1 the suspicion case was introduced to illustrate several of my argumentative aims in this essay, including the possible dissociation of emotion from belief—from the belief corresponding to the emotion's evaluative component, that is. The belief in question was taken as corresponding to a fear-evaluation: that a certain salesman, X, is untrustworthy, in a sense that makes him likely to act in ways injurious to my interests. As the case was set up, though, the little evidence I have, from the testimony of others, gives me reason to believe that X is trustworthy. Since I cannot identify any grounds for thinking X a threat to me, I withhold assent from the judgment that he is. But I still feel edgy at the *thought* that he is, which arises in response to some unrecognized perceptual cues—eye movements were suggested—that in fact are reliably linked to untrustworthiness, though I am unaware of the connection.

I shall now assume that the cluster of cases discussed in Chapters 2 and 3 was sufficiently persuasive against "judgmentalism," understood as the view that emotions necessarily involve their corresponding beliefs. But I shall continue to work with the suspicion case, answering objections and considering possible variant cases, in an attempt to see what can be said about the distinction between emotional and judgmental *warrant*. Most of my early cases of fear-without-belief in Chapter 2 were cases of *irrational* fear; and later, especially in Chapter 3, my discussion focused on fantasy-emotions, whose rationality raises questions too complex to allow them to serve as the basis for my treatment of emotional justification. Here, then, I want to return to the case of fearful suspicion and show how my emotion may be rationally appropriate as a real-life response even if the corresponding belief is unjustified—and whether or not I accept the corresponding belief.

I shall attempt to defend this possibility, in what follows, while sketching and refining an account of the notion of appropriateness that would explain it. Juggling these two tasks will require re-addressing certain questions as they re-arise in application to variants of my initial case; so my discussion will therefore occur in overlapping stages, with complementary approaches to the limited analogy between emotions and beliefs. First I shall focus on the appeal to nonevidential "standards of significance" in assessing warrant for emotion (i). Next, I shall examine the role still played by the evidential standard (ii). I shall end by attempting to bring together both sorts of standards in a nonquantitative criterion of appropriateness, framed in terms of belief warrant but allowing for a practical *weight* on the evidence for the evaluative component of emotion (iii). The criterion will leave some questions unanswered; but it should serve as a compact summary of my results in this chapter for application to a wider range of cases in my next.

(i) "Fitness to Significant Perception"

Let me begin by stipulating that the claim that suspicion is warranted, in any of the cases to be examined, is *not* to be interpreted just as a claim that the emotion in question happens to fit the facts, as in the falling rock case. If my suspicion of X rested on a delusion—or on no grounds whatever, even perceptual grounds that I cannot identify—the fact that X is indeed attempting to deceive me would be insufficient to justify the emotion. Rather, our assumption here is that an attempt to deceive someone, unlike the tendency of rocks to fall, is commonly manifested in perceptible behavior, in ways that an agent may sometimes sense, even without awareness, or any special experience or ability. Where suspicion is appropriate, that is, its "fitness to the facts" must be based on some sort of subliminal connection to perception. We may also grant, however, that my success on a single occasion, in the case now under discussion, is indeed accidental in some sense. The case assumes that I am not a "reliable indicator" of untrustworthiness—a good barometer of its presence in light of my general reaction patterns. I am inexperienced in business transactions, and, we may add, I am not particularly attuned to "body language" even in more familiar situations. That my suspicion is right this time is nonaccidental, then, just to the extent that it *is* backed up by something in perception—but not enough, or so one would think, to yield a warranted belief.

There are weaker accounts of belief warrant, of course, though they are more often applied to *knowledge* than to warrant and other explicitly justificatory notions, whose relation to knowledge they call into question.[2] However, our case may be set up so that it fails to satisfy even accounts that do not require the ability to *state* a justification, but simply some generally reliable way of arriving at belief, for belief to count as warranted. Let us suppose that my perceptiveness on this occasion, besides resting on cues I cannot identify, would not extend to similar situations, even with the same cues on hand. Perhaps I usually fail to look at people's eyes, say— and shall continue to fail in the future—thus lacking even "subliminal" awareness of the relevant eye movements in other situations. But in this case something about the lighting in the room changes my usual focus; and the intensity of X's focus or the way it varies with changes in my own behavior (something less obvious than a "shifty" look) makes me uncomfortably edgy about his intentions. I do not know *why* I am edgy, however. The most I can say is that there seems to be *something* about X or about X's manner when addressing me that makes me uncomfortable. But I also am inclined to say that I may very well be attributing to X something more properly located in myself—in my own insecurity in business transactions, here masked by feelings of suspicion.

Still, we assume that my suspicion here does rest on some particular external perception, something I might at least look for in the future, as itself a reliable indicator of deception, even if my emotional reactions are not yet reliably connected to it. In that case, however, someone might suggest that the subliminal connection set up on *this* occasion is enough to warrant a belief, no less than an emotion, on the basis of an account of belief warrant that appeals to the community of scientific experts as an independent justificatory standard. We cannot say that I am reacting here in a way that accords with the reactions of some actual community of experts on "body language" interpretation or the like, since there is no such paradigm of accuracy in this area. But perhaps it is enough to claim that a *hypothetical* paradigm interpreter *would* have the same reaction here and on the basis of the same cues. No doubt he would also have something approaching an understanding of their relevance—at a minimum, the ability to identify them—as well as reliable attunement to them in those situations where they *are* relevant. But I need not come up to this standard myself for my beliefs to be warranted by their conformity to it—or so this alternative account maintains.

The account is too weak, however. It may or may not be enough for a belief that simply reports what is perceived, a belief of the sort taken as "noninferential." But here we are dealing with a complex evaluation of someone's character or intentions as likely to prove harmful—something with a distinct perceptual basis. Although perhaps not "inferred" from the agent's immediate perceptions, if that implies an actual *process* of inference, it is supposed to be "keyed" to them in a way that *would support* an inference to the corresponding belief from a justificatory standpoint like that of the paradigm. But here, even ignoring my inability to identify the causes of my response in X's eye movements, we might have a causal connection that is itself too crude to support such an inference. There *is* a connection, let us grant: I would not have the same reaction in the absence of the relevant eye movements if the situation were otherwise unchanged. But we might still suppose that I *would* have the same reaction in their *presence*—or wherever I perceived them, if only subliminally—even if the situation contained some further features that undercut their role as evidence of untrustworthiness. A developed science of body language, or its paradigm practitioners, would take X's eye movements as evidence of untrustworthiness, say, only where there was no reason to think that he had just been given an eye medication for "refraction." His intense and changing focus here does suggest an attempt to manipulate, or so the case assumes; but other explanations are possible as well: perhaps he is simply having trouble focusing. For my own mistrust to be grounded in perception, then, in a way sufficient to yield warrant for belief, it must at least be responsive to evidence that would *undercut* the evidence for it.

Where my mistrust is not thus responsive to counterevidence, as on our present version of the case, then the evidence for it may justify an *indefinitely qualified* judgment: that X exhibits *some signs* of untrustworthiness, say, with the signs left unspecified. Even this rather weak judgment would be justified, however, only if I did know enough to attribute my reaction to something-or-other I notice *about X.* Here, perhaps, I should limit myself to a judgment that my reaction itself amounts to a sign that X is untrustworthy or gives me prima facie reason to think him untrustworthy, leaving unspecified its link to subliminal perceptual cues.[3] At any rate, if we grant that an appropriate emotion here need *not* be similarly qualified, it seems that it may be stronger in content than a warranted belief. Nor should this be so surprising. The pull towards forming an "all things considered" evaluation, with evidence weighed on both sides and one's initial impressions modified in light of the results, is surely an essential part of the notion of belief warrant. Where the evidence cannot be identified and assessed adequately, this must be reflected in the qualified content of a judgment that is to count as warranted. But it need not be reflected in the content of an emotion—its evaluative component need not be qualified—for the emotion to count as appropriate. My appropriate feelings of suspicion towards X, in the initial suspicion case, may still amount to discomfort at the thought that he *is* untrustworthy—that he is likely (in the sense of "apt") to mislead me. They need not be limited to feelings that he *might* be untrustworthy—that he is likely to mislead me for all I know—even where only this is warranted as a belief.

To expect emotions to be more sensitive to evidential considerations would be unreasonable. It is important to their motivational role, in fact, even where their perceptual sources are clear, that they resist qualification in light of the total body of evidence. They are typically "all-out" reactions to *portions* of the evidence—"all-out" in the sense of "unqualified" rather than "extreme"—registering evaluative information that may not be fully digested in justificatory terms. Where their perceptual sources are *not* clear, rough reliability, of the sort exhibited in the present case, without the ability to state even a partial justification, will not yield adequate warrant for the corresponding belief. But I do want to say that it allows for appropriate emotion, in view of the limitations—and, as we shall later see, the value of the limitations—on emotional focus and control. In short, emotions are properly less *malleable* than beliefs in response to further evidence or to the recognition that further evidence is needed.

On my view, then, an emotion will count as appropriate where it is keyed to a *significant subset* of the perceptual evidence available—whether or not the agent understands its significance and can offer more than an indefinitely qualified version of its corresponding belief. Emotional appropriateness amounts to "fitness to significant perception," we may say—rather than fitness to the facts or even to the total body of perceptual evidence. This gives us a kind of slogan to work with, easily borne in mind, but requiring a good deal of qualification itself. It is based on a view of emotions as reactions to perception; but we should note that "perception" is here construed broadly, as a substitute for "nonevaluative apprehension," since we need a term that has an adjective form. Perception, in this sense, is taken as necessarily veridical; but it is meant to cover nonsensory information from memory and self-awareness: the knowledge of others' past testimony and one's own present ends, for instance. On the view suggested here, various such pieces of sensory *or* reflective information may stand out at various times against the overall background of perception—whether by coming to mind overtly or simply by generating an emotional reaction, as in the present case. Emotional appropriateness depends on whether this "figure-ground" relationship represents things more or less in proportion. An appropriate emotion fits *some* significant perception of the facts, that is to say; for there are multiple standards of significance, as we shall later see, in contrast to the single "evidential" standard, the standard of importance *as* evidence, that properly figures in assessments of belief warrant.

The "Hard Sell" Broker and Prima Facie Warrant. Towards the end of this chapter I shall attempt to replace this initial characterization of the notion of appropriateness with a brief criterion for the appropriateness of the evaluative component framed in terms of hypothetical belief warrant. First, though, it needs to be tested out—and filled out—by comparison of variant cases. In the present case, it allows us to say that suspicion may be appropriate even where the emotion conflicts with warranted belief. But we can also use it to exhibit the possibility of appropriate suspicion in conflict with *true* belief. Consider a case where my feelings of suspicion do have identifiable sources. A broker phones me in response to a letter to his firm and exhibits an insistently friendly manner that strikes me as overeager—as suspiciously "hard sell." My suspicion might, for all I know, be called into question by further, less prominent features of the situation: I can tell from his voice that he is young, say; and there are other reasons for thinking that he is not comfortable with a phone contact. But this does not make the emotion inappropriate, even if it means that I should avoid "rushing to judgment." We might suppose, too, that a later check on the broker's recommendations reveals him to be perfectly trustworthy. I think we would still want to say, though, that my suspicion, at the time of our phone conversation, is appropriate—rationally warranted *as* an initial reaction *by* what I hear on the phone. It is not just an *understandable* emotional reaction; it is one that fits "significant perception," even if not "the facts." Nor is it just appropriate relative to some belief I hold—a criterion that would allow for emotions based on delusion, as in the falling rock case, while ruling out our original case of suspicion.

If this treatment of the "hard sell" broker case is correct, emotional appropriateness does not even *entail* the truth of the emotions, taken to mean the truth of their evaluative components, or what I have termed "applicability." In this case, the evaluation in question is my view of the broker as apt to talk me into something ill-considered and unwise. I am uncomfortable at the thought that dealing with this broker is likely to cause me injury—to use the somewhat overblown terms fitting my general pattern for analyzing fears. But let us grant that injury is *not* particularly likely here, in fact: The man is quite competent and responsible, knows his obligations to his customers, but gives a misleading impression over the phone. So a belief that he is untrustworthy would be *false*, even though the corresponding emotion is appropriate since my experience of the man is limited but significant—important enough to be worth "registering" affectively. Just because of its limited evidential basis, moreover, the belief would be *unjustified*, in the sense I have in mind here: On the basis of one phone conversation, I would have only prima facie warrant for it. So I should try to limit myself, intellectually speaking, to the belief that there are some reasons for mistrust, while suspending definite judgment.

In practice, of course, given the usefulness of a firm belief in protecting my interests and the relative unimportance of my judgment of the man, we might say that *I* am warranted in jumping to a conclusion, rather than simply entertaining the thought that the broker is untrust-

worthy, but without commitment. However, if evidence is in question—
as it properly is in assessments of belief warrant—an "all things considered" judgment would not itself be justified here, even if my act of
forming it is.[4] As we saw in my last chapter—and will have cause to
remember in my next—there are practical reasons, concerning the effective choice of action, for retaining the distinct justificatory standpoint
of judgment, even in a case where emotional evaluation plays the central
role in motivation. In any case, "jumping to a conclusion" here *means*
adopting a belief that is not really, or not yet, justified. I am not in
possession of overriding evidence *against* it, as I was in our original case,
of "intuitive" suspicion in conflict with others' testimony. But assuming
that I am in possession of evidence that calls into question the evidence
for it—undercuts its force as evidence of untrustworthiness but without
yielding reasons for trust—I do not have adequate warrant for it. There
are reasons for thinking that the broker's overeager approach might just
be a result of job pressure, awkwardness on the phone, or the like—
reasons that cancel out its force, or some of its force, as evidence of
untrustworthiness. They do so not strictly by overriding it but rather by
providing an alternative explanation for it. However, either sort of "coun-
tervailing" reason is reason for taking the belief as prima facie warranted,
at most.

Is this just to say that my emotion here amounts to a "prima facie
judgment"? Adopting this expression might seem to yield a version of
judgmentalism, after all. However, I think that the expression is ambiguous—and sufficiently misleading on either interpretation to be worth
avoiding. On one interpretation, it might just fail to apply.[5] It might be
used to describe a *qualified* judgment, even if one that is held "all things
considered": that the broker exhibits some signs of untrustworthiness
or that he is untrustworthy (apt to talk me into something unwise) *insofar
as* he uses "hard sell" tactics. But then the expression may misdescribe
the internal object of my emotion, in the case at hand. On at least some
plausible versions of the case, my suspicion amounts to discomfort at the
thought that the broker *is* untrustworthy, not just that there are signs
that he is, or the like. Further, my discomfort may still be directed towards
that *un*qualified, or "all-out," propositional object when I question the
grounds for the corresponding belief— even if the feeling also may be
said to take on a more qualified object, reflecting my reasons for withholding full assent. So at any rate, not *every* internal object of my emotion
would correspond to a prima facie judgment in the sense of one that is
unqualified.

On the other hand, the expression "prima facie judgment" might
be meant to describe an evaluation that is *not* held "all things considered,"
perhaps just because it is left unqualified. On this use, however, the

expression would apply to variants of the case at hand only if "judgment" is interpreted to cover an evaluation that is not really "held" but is entertained without full assent and taken as supported by certain incomplete pieces of evidence. But then the expression cannot always be understood as referring to a *belief*, as a literal reading suggests. It apparently would extend to evaluations falling short of belief, whose corresponding judgments may be thought of as prima facie *warranted*. On the view I sketched in the preceding chapter, assuming the agent's basic rationality, a belief the agent holds in mind must at least be thought by him to stand in light of a full review of the evidence, even if only hypothetically. In the present case, however, I might suspend judgment on this issue—on whether, for instance, my reasons for mistrust would be overturned by the later testimony of others who deal with this broker.

At any rate, to the extent that it goes beyond the denial of full assent, and hence beyond my own view, the expression "prima facie judgment" would seem to require distinctions whose application to the content of my emotion is questionable. On an emotional level I am not just uncertain or entertaining doubts about the broker's trustworthiness—though this is surely possible, on another version of the case. At least one of the objects of my discomfort here is the thought that the broker is untrustworthy, *simpliciter*. In cognitive terms this is held in mind as prima facie warranted; but its warrant as the evaluative component of emotion may not depend solely on its degree of evidential backing, which is rather slight. It need not vary in "strength," say—whether we take this as intensity of associated affect or the tendency to dominate consciousness or something more directly motivational—with my conception of the strength of the evidence. A disparity here need not be seen as making my suspicion inappropriate, that is, even in the sense of "disproportionate." For the strength of an emotion is quite properly influenced by nonevidential reasons affecting the *significance* of the evidence for it— most notably, its general adaptiveness, or the importance in general terms of holding in mind its evaluative component before more evidence is available.

The preceding case suggests that the notion of emotional appropriateness combines prima facie judgmental warrant with reference to adaptiveness. It was initially set up in contrast to adaptiveness, as a noninstrumental rational value; and I shall go on to give a number of cases that indicate that the notion does not just collapse into that of adaptiveness. I do expect emotional warrant to exhibit a closer connection to practical concerns than we allow to influence similar assessments of belief. But the relevant connection is to *general* adaptiveness, or the instrumental value of the emotion *tendency*, not necessarily the adaptiveness of the particular instance of emotion in question. Thus far, I have sketched a view of emotional appropriateness as requiring warrant by a "significant" subset of the evidence and of significance as measured by more than one standard. The obvious candidate for a nonevidential standard, though—allowing for a greater weight on evidence that would otherwise be thought inadequate—is surely the importance of the emotion tendency in question to the promotion of the agent's ends. Its adaptiveness, in this sense, may make it appropriate for the agent to hold its evaluative component in mind, that is—*by* feeling comfortable or uncomfortable about it, if that serves the purpose—even where he has only prima facie warrant for the corresponding judgment.

This is not to say that he *must* hold it in mind. I shall argue in Chapter 6 for a more particular connection to adaptiveness, where any rational requirements on emotion are concerned; and my argument there should provide us with a more detailed conception of the general notion of adaptiveness. But I shall also take some pains in Chapter 6 to distinguish appropriate from merely understandable emotions. For it should be clear that a claim of appropriateness is meant as more than a claim that an emotion is rationally permissible, or "acceptable" in the sense of being *allowed for* by the available evidence, perhaps just because there is no decisive counterevidence. Rather, it is meant as a claim that something reinforces the available evidence to make the emotion a rationally *justified* response—acceptably *grounded in* the evidence, one might say. On this view, appropriateness does require an evidential basis of some sort, as suggested by the notion of "significant perception." In fact, the evidence may have to be substantial—in a sense that does not reduce to quantitative strength—even where it is not adequate to warrant the emotion on its own. In the "hard sell" broker case, for instance, my suspicion seems to come out as appropriate because I am assumed to have some slight, but direct, evidence as to X's trustworthiness, in particular. Not just any bit of prima facie evidence only indirectly bearing on X would combine with considerations of general adaptiveness to justify my emotion in its situational context.

We might suppose, for instance, that I once had a disastrous experience with a broker. Given the "spillover" tendencies of emotion, as illustrated initially by the Fido case in Chapter 2, it might be understandable if I reacted with suspicion the minute a broker got in touch with me without knowing anything about him besides the fact that he *was* a broker. My emotion would be inappropriate, however, even granting that the fact that someone is a broker—and hence is in a business that can net him money whether or not he advances a client's interests—has some slight weight as a reason for thinking him untrustworthy. His profession gives him a motive for deception, that is, just as Fido's species membership makes him susceptible to rabies. But though this may yield a reason for initial caution, it is a reason independent of my previous experience with a broker. My experience may lead me to attend to this general reason for mistrust but does not lend it any greater evidential weight. As evidence for an evaluation of X as untrustworthy, its weight is rather slight; and it is not reinforced by accidental features of my history, in view of the *mal*adaptiveness of bringing these to bear on each new situation. My suspicion here would be rather like a fear of falling rocks, at every point on the turnpike, after one bad experience when I failed to notice the "falling rock zone" sign. Indeed, even several bad experiences with brokers might not be sufficient to warrant suspicion with X as its object—as opposed to *self*-suspicion, say, or suspicion with a relational object, centering on my own inability to work with a broker, or to choose a broker wisely.

An emotion is not warranted, then, by just any prima facie reason for the truth of its "all-out" evaluative component. Emotional warrant still does not require reason sufficient for believing the latter, with sufficiency measured in evidential terms, if I am right. But despite the role assigned to adaptiveness, the notion of appropriateness applies to emotions in something like a cognitive sense, on my view. It provides an assessment of their representational rationality—as distinct from their instrumental value for the agent or others as well as from appropriateness in a moral or quasi-moral sense. In the case just considered, for instance, we might suppose that my suspicion will have good effects, given that it is directed towards a broker, since it serves as a check on my tendency to invest impulsively. It still comes out as inappropriate, however. Or we might consider another sort of case, where suspicion is likely to have bad effects—incapacitating me for essential interpersonal relations, say— though the evidence clearly supports it. Here we might decide that I would do best to block out the emotion, allowing myself to trust someone in the face of the likelihood of some relatively minor injury to my interests. Perhaps I ought to loan some money to an unreliable friend or relative and then expect him to "forget it," in more senses than one. Suspicion would still come out as appropriate, though, to the extent that it accurately represents my perceptual situation.

The weight we would place on *less* clear-cut evidence, however, is properly influenced by the general value of the emotion, in such cases, to the promotion of human ends—in this case, to avoiding injury in my business dealings with X by encouraging alertness, in the way sketched in Chapter 1. Suspicion registers information of a sort that, in many cases, has to be absorbed quickly, on the basis of a few perceptual cues, as a check on any tendency towards overhasty trust. It would not have quite the same force for action, moreover, if it were readily modified in light of further evidence. Something like this seems to be generally true of emotions: Their affective components serve to add force to "snap" evaluations, where the evidence at hand, even if not decisive, is significant enough to warrant holding them in mind. They have a basis in associative links that are useful in general and useful partly because of their responsiveness to more or less immediate perception. But the same responsiveness may make them spill over to insubstantial evidential cues and persist in light of decisive counterevidence, with maladaptive consequences in some cases.

(ii) Intuition and Inference

Now let us return to our initial case of "intuitive" suspicion, for it might seem to cast doubt on the claim that the evaluative component of an appropriate emotion must have an *evidential* basis, of a sort that could be used to construct an inference to it, independent of considerations of adaptiveness. How can a feeling be rationally grounded in something the agent fails to notice—something inadequate, for just that reason, to warrant the corresponding belief? I think we can answer this question by indicating how my appropriate suspicion here may rest on associative links to perception. For it cannot fit significant perception merely by chance—as in the falling rock case, but with unnoticed perceptual cues now replacing "the facts." Since I am unable to identify those features of X's behavior that make me feel suspicious, my reaction here is *not* rationally grounded in the sense of being rationally *derived* from its grounds, with variations in eye focus interpreted as evidence of untrustworthiness. But it still may exhibit a nonaccidental connection to perception—of a sort that implies causation, of course, but also what might be called causation "in accordance with" a rational derivation, conforming to the basic pattern of belief warrant.

In our initial suspicion case how is my reaction more than a "lucky shot," in this sense, even supposing that my attention to X's eye movements *is* accidental? Presumably, my reaction rests on some relevant, though fragmentary and unanalyzed, past experience—if not with people who have deceived *me* then with fictional portrayals or accounts of deception or with my own attempts to deceive others. I may have acquired a general tendency to react with suspicion to visible manifestations of untrustworthiness that were never *seen* by me, that is. But on our assumption, I lack sufficient evidence for any general beliefs about their relevance to untrustworthiness. Nor did I acquire any beliefs about them—

or any tendency to look for them, of a sort that might be relied upon to activate my reaction tendency in a future situation. In the present case, then, at any rate consciously, I simply react with suspicion, without the sort of inference from perceptual cues that would seem to be needed to warrant the corresponding judgment. In fact, without warrant for a supporting generalization, I lack even the raw materials for an inference. Nor am I in a position, with my limited experience, to provide materials for an inference from my past reactions. If my current reaction is appropriate, though, it must rest on some unconscious association to perception that *could* be set up in inferential terms by someone who knew enough about the relation between eye movements and untrustworthiness. "Intuitive" suspicion is rationally grounded in evidence, on this view, just in so far as it is causally generated by—and only by—inferentially relevant perceptual cues, from among those pertaining to the case.

In a contrasting variant case, we might suppose that my suspicion resulted from an attempt to "rationalize" feelings of edginess in an unfamiliar situation. Although rationalization might very well yield an "applicable" emotion—and indeed one that fits the *perceived* facts—the representational accuracy of my suspicion here would still be accidental. Even supposing that it was caused by X's eye movements—they were the particular features of the situation that made me edgy, say—it would not rest on any past association of those movements to untrustworthiness. The causal generation of my emotion would depend on something besides its perceptual grounds, something inferentially irrelevant to the corresponding evaluative judgment: a need to attribute my discomfort to some *personal* object, perhaps. As in the falling rock case, I would have jumped to a correct emotional conclusion—though here it would fit "significant perception" and indeed would be linked to it causally. Its causal "fitness" would still seem to be accidental, however, just insofar as a crucial link in its chain of causes was one that would standardly produce *un*fitness. Suspicion would be appropriate for a person in my perceptual situation; but *my* suspicion would be *in*appropriate unless it were rationally grounded in perception, in the sense just outlined.

Associative links like those sketched in defense of our original case of intuitive suspicion are commonly thought of as "nonrational," in part because they often omit steps that would be needed for an adequate inference. In the sense just outlined, however, they are rational to the extent that they *could* be filled out to yield an adequate inference to the corresponding belief. Qualifications, as well as steps, might have to be provided: exception clauses mentioning factors that would count *against* taking variations in eye focus as evidence of untrustworthiness, for instance. But an association that does allow for this sort of inferential expansion may be thought of as exhibiting a nonaccidental link to significant perception—"fitness" to it in a *rational* sense, reflecting the evidential reasons for its significance. Thus interpreted, "fitness to significant perception" requires more than truth to some body of facts, including psychological facts, in an extension of the notion applied to belief. Rather, it suggests something like what we have in mind when we speak of a "true likeness": an appropriate emotion "faithfully represents" its grounds, in terms of both proportionality to them and a certain kind of derivation from them. But by allowing for rational gaps in the latter, I do allow for a weak analogy between appropriateness and truth. As with a true belief, an emotion may be appropriate without being fully grounded in evidential terms.

A Case of Impersonal Suspicion. More needs to be said to explain emotional appropriateness in terms of belief warrant. At this point, however, I want to discuss a different sort of case, where the connection to belief seems to be as close as it can be. The case should help to illustrate a number of my claims about intuitive suspicion; but since it involves little or no affect, it should mainly serve to isolate the evaluative component of suspicion, as the belieflike element whose distinction from belief has been in question. For one might object, at this point, that my defense of intuitive suspicion could also be used to justify *belief* without awareness of its grounds, given that so little has been said about *feelings* of suspicion. My case here should eventually help to pinpoint the intended contrast; but first it should let us cancel some unfortunate associations with talk of appropriateness in the interpersonal realm, where it might be interpreted in something like a social sense. It will become evident in my next chapter that I do take general considerations of social *adaptiveness* to affect our assessment of emotions as rationally appropriate. But my use of "rational" in application to appropriateness is meant to rule out more particular reference to social norms, as opposed to norms of representational rationality. The latter should stand out more sharply if we look at a case whose evaluative content is impersonal, in a context somewhat removed from considerations of adaptiveness.

Philosophers, in confronting an argument, often have the preanalytic "sense" that it must contain an error. Discomfort at the thought that the argument is deceptive may precede the ability to identify the error—even ostensively, by indicating where in the argument it occurs. On a wide enough conception of "injury," it should be possible to squeeze such cases into my fear-based model of suspicion. They involve something stronger than suspension of judgment: One thinks, "This can't be right" and not just "I can't be sure of this" in the cases I have in mind. The author's intentions are not in question; but the argument is viewed as involving some unintended sleight-of-hand—as threatening a reader with the injury of unjustified persuasion, let us say. Fear *symptoms* are unlikely to exceed a kind of tamped-down worry, in such cases; and even this may be masked by a positive emotion, such as pride in spotting an error in someone else's work. In some cases, for that matter, the reaction may not count as an emotion at all—if it involves *no* affect, even generalized comfort or discomfort. But it still has in common with fearful suspicion a negative evaluation of some future possibility, viewed as a *real* possibility and to that extent viewed as a threat.

Persuasion by the argument is evaluated negatively simply because the argument "looks suspicious." At any rate, that is often all one can say to back up this sort of "snap" reaction. Even if some more particular perception stands behind it, moreover, the example provides a vivid illustration of the breadth of the term "perception," as I am using it here. It has to cover quite a lot—certainly more than the look of printed words on a page. "Significant perception" here no doubt includes fragmentary information from past experience, picked up bit by bit as one analyzed various arguments and hence not easily characterized in general terms. For that matter, it might also include memories indicating the reliability of one's own past "snap" reactions. But a similar reaction might still be appropriate—might have a kind of "perceptual" warrant, besides applying correctly to the argument—even where it did not result from the exercise, as in this case, of developed critical skills. On the view I have just outlined, though, it would have to be based on information that could be used to construct a general criticism of the argument.

Consider most beginning students' reactions to the ontological argument. The standard response from students, judging from comments and facial expressions, seems to be something like suspicion of a hoax. In a case where this rested merely on disbelief in the conclusion, the reaction would *not* be appropriate, in my terms, even supposing that it is on the mark in this instance, at least to the extent that it is impersonal. The student's reaction needs some sort of grounding in perception—in something he might have observed about the structure of the argument, something that could be refined and used to show that the argument contains an error. He might be reacting to the derivation of its conclusion from a definition, say, even if he cannot pick this out as his reason for suspecting a fallacy. We may count this as "perceptual" warrant—yielding adequate reason for his initial reaction and for its persistence in the face of his inability to formulate an objection—to the extent that it grounds his response upon information relevant to flaws in the argument.

The source of the student's reaction, however, would not seem to count as adequate warrant for a *belief* that the argument is flawed. Indeed, it would not even count as prima facie warrant, if all he can say is that the argument as a whole looks suspicious—if he cannot at least point to a problematic step in it, with or without the ability to explain the error. This claim rests on our assumption that the student has not had enough experience with philosophical arguments to base an inference on his past reactions to them—though he *has* gained some information from experience with arguments in ordinary discourse. I shall continue to leave open the question whether a belief could be warranted *solely* by reliability—an undiscovered talent of unusual proportions for spotting invalidity at a glance, say, on the model of a talent for "divining" the presence of water. In any case, I shall also assume that our student is not *all that* reliable, even in his reactions to definitional argument. Perhaps he would exhibit the same reaction to any philosophical argument from a definition to a *nontrivial* conclusion. If so—granting that some such arguments do go through, but only those whose conclusions make no positive claims about existence—the student would sometimes come out with "inapplicable" reactions, understood as those that fail to fit the facts about validity. But his reactions would still be appropriate—adequately warranted *as* "snap" reactions—in cases where they fit significant perception, in the sense I have outlined.

Even in the context of a philosophy class a particular standard of significance may be applied with varying degrees of exactitude—with higher or lower expectations of student performance, for instance. It will sometimes be natural, then, to speak of applying "different standards" here. But in this case, we seem to have a single *qualitative* standard—"the" evidential standard—in relatively sharp focus. In another version of the case, for instance, the student's suspicion might just be a reaction to Anselm's rather rhetorical style of exposition. Associations with rhetoric in political contexts—or with extraphilosophical approaches to nonbelief in Anselm's time—lead the student to feel that the argument must contain a trick, say. For a student without much experience of philosophical writing, such a reaction might be understandable. For that matter, it might be based on a way of sorting information that tends to yield adaptive reactions in more ordinary social contexts and hence in general. But it would not yield an appropriate reaction to the argument as such, as the target of philosophical criticism. And we *are* speaking of *rational* appropriateness when we make this judgment. In reacting to the argument as a piece of rhetoric on the basis of the author's style, the student is not simply deviating from some standard of "what is done" in a philosophy class. That is also true, of course; but our claim is, rather, that the argument's style of exposition has no significance as evidence, even as indirect evidence, of its flaws as an argument. The student's reaction here resembles an "overpersonal" interpretation of a remark made in a professional context. It *is* in some sense socially inappropriate; but it is so largely because it is based on a distorted view of the situation, carried over from other contexts of evaluation.

The issue of appropriateness, in this case, has been isolated from ordinary issues of adaptiveness. In applying the standard of evidential significance, however, we do make some reference to practical concerns of a sort. Persuasion by Anselm's argument, in the context of a philosophy class, may not be much of a personal threat. But impersonal suspicion, on grounds insufficient to warrant a belief, might still be justified as intellectually "energizing"—useful in generating a desire to locate the error, say. By contrast to Anselm's style, the fact that the argument derives a nontrivial conclusion from a definition does seem to give a reason for intellectual mistrust—without appealing beyond its role as evidence, but with its *weight* as evidence influenced by general adaptiveness. Although it needs to be narrowed down quite a bit to support an acceptable objection, it does give a rough indication of where the argument fails. I take it, then, to justify the student's initial "snap" reaction—but not a *belief* that the argument is fallacious, unless the student can exhibit the objection, at least by indicating that it turns on the definition.

In discussing the case of a beginning student's reaction to the ontological argument as an illustration of the contrast between belief warrant and warrant for the evaluative component of emotion, I have assigned an important role to the agent's past experience. My remarks on the case may now be used to handle more straightforward "perceptual" cases of intuition. First, let us see how the remarks apply to our initial case of suspicion. In the ontological argument case, I have been assuming that the perceptual factors controlling the student's response, though they do figure among its causes, are distinguished from his other perceptions bearing on the argument *only* in that respect. His inability to give a justification for his feeling that the argument must contain a trick is not based on lack of verbal fluency or the like but on lack of differentiation in perception as a result of his limited experience. The case thus resembles our initial suspicion case, where I may be said to *perceive* X's eye movements—among other things—but am aware of them only subliminally. They do not stand out against the background of perception except to the extent that they control my emotional response, that is; and it is only in that sense that I "pick up on" them. In the ontological argument case, similarly, the student lacks the ability even to locate the flaw in the argument ostensively, by pointing to its definitional step.

It seems, then, that the student's unnoticed perception of the error does not yield even prima facie warrant for a *judgment* that the argument is flawed—a rather sophisticated evaluative judgment, concerning truth-conferral by arguments of the same form. I take it that such a judgment *would* be warranted for someone with a history of reliable response to arguments or perhaps just an untested tendency towards *very* reliable response, but that the student in this case has neither. It might now be useful to compare the judgment with one that simply gives a report of what the agent perceives but also seems to be based on some unnoticed perceptual cues. Consider, for instance, a standard example of spatial intuition: the judgment that one object is nearer than another, as warranted by a perceived difference in size. Warrant for *this* judgment—even adequate warrant—may *not* depend on the ability to identify the relevant cues. But it does depend on experience with objects like those now perceived, surely—enough to indicate that they would appear to be the *same* size if placed at the same distance, say.

By contrast, our beginning student has not had enough experience with arguments and with the standards for evaluating them in a philosophical context for his reaction to be grounded in a warranted subliminal generalization relating use of definition to invalidity. In the case of spatial comparison, our reliable reactions to objects in space make it reasonable to suppose that we do have such general knowledge—here relating differences in apparent size to distance—even if only subliminally. But for all our beginning student knows and on whatever level, he *is* reacting to the argument's style or to disbelief in its conclusion or simply to discomfort at confronting an unfamiliar critical task. Similarly, in the case of suspicion towards *X*, despite our assumption that my reaction is based on *some* past experience, I am assumed to be inexperienced in business transactions and to be in no position to see that my wider experience has any bearing on them. For all I know, then, my reaction is an inappropriate spillover from fictional portrayals of deception in personal relations, say, where different behavioral norms apply; or perhaps I am simply "rationalizing" my own discomfort in the unfamiliar business situation. All I have is a tendency to feel suspicious under circumstances that in fact pick out untrustworthiness, at least roughly, but without adequate reason for thinking that they do—even a reason that I am unaware of.

If my reaction tendency were refined on the basis of further experience, surely the relevant perceptions would begin to stand out against their background. They would then be verbally identifiable *if* I were given the linguistic tools or the analytical prodding to describe them. But something like this is already true of our spatial judgments, it seems. We need no further experience to support an inference to a judgment of relative distance; what we need in order to *reconstruct* such an inference is a different way of sorting the experience we have on hand. I would suggest that we do recognize apparent size as relevant, but essentially refer to it in distance *terminology*, to the extent that it deviates from real size. Since its relevance was absorbed prelinguistically—and

since we have no ordinary use for an independent way of describing it—
the notion of apparent size now has to be disentangled from that of
distance. This may require further experience for purposes of illustration, but it does not require further experiential evidence.

To provide warrant for a judgment of untrustworthiness, by contrast, one needs to establish the relevance of certain perceptual cues to
some fairly sophisticated evaluative property: the tendency to mislead,
say, whether by deception or by fallacious argument. Even at an early
stage, this is unlikely to involve conflating the inferred property with
the one it is inferred from, on the model of the case just considered;
for here we have a link between factual and evaluative properties and
a move beyond immediate perception. Indeed, the link is unlikely to
be established before a stage at which fairly advanced discriminations
are standard—and at which they are presumably accessible to reflection, even if describing them sometimes depends on training in the use
of a new vocabulary. At any rate, in our case of ordinary suspicion, a
simple vocabulary seems to be sufficient to capture the distinctions underlying my reaction tendency. Something more advanced—medical
terminology ("refraction"), say, to capture a counterfactual that my reaction tendency ought to take into account—would be needed only to
describe a possible refinement of the tendency, to support an adequate inference. What I lack here is not so much vocabulary, then, as
differentiation in perception.

So the more basic cause of my inability to justify my suspicion in
this case would seem to be limited *experience*. In contrast to the "hard
sell" broker case, I am here unable to give even a prima facie justification
for believing X untrustworthy. To minimize the importance assigned to
verbal proficiency, particularly in application to the ontological argument case, my argument has allowed for a rather weak interpretation
of the ability to give a justification, covering a kind of justification by
ostension. But it still seems to bear out the stronger claim made in Chapter 1 with reference to our initial case of suspicion: that appropriate
emotion need not involve even prima facie justification for belief. In
both of our clusters of cases in this Chapter, adequate warrant for either
emotion or belief requires evidence of an inferential sort, grounding an
evaluation in perception, but with further evidence required for belief.
Even prima facie belief warrant, however, requires a kind of *explicit*
grounding—if only ostensive—that emotional appropriateness does not.

(iii) A Nonquantitative Criterion

Throughout my argument here, I have taken belief warrant as a
kind of paradigm for understanding emotional justification, with ap-

propriateness characterized mainly in terms of lesser demands of the same general sort. This approach was reasonable enough just as a way of using a more established philosophical field to provide us with questions—even granting, as my reference to reliability accounts should indicate, that it does not provide very firm answers. But the results of adopting this approach can now be seen to yield a further reason for it. The appeal to an evidential basis of some sort applies even to cases of "intuitive" emotional appropriateness. It is supplemented by appeal to practical considerations, of a sort not properly brought to bear on assessments of belief warrant, with its limitation to backward-looking justification. The ontological argument case suggested that this extraevidential appeal remains even when we minimize both affect and social significance. But that should not keep us from using the evidential basis to characterize emotional appropriateness in terms of hypothetical belief warrant.

Just because of their partly practical assessment, we would not want to treat emotions as *conferring* warrant on beliefs, except in so far as their bases do coincide.[6] An emotional response to the conclusion of the ontological argument, for instance—even as essential to one's system of beliefs—would no more justify a corresponding belief than does my need in the suspicion case to attribute my discomfort to something external. Yet we surely would not want to relegate emotions to a completely separate sphere of justificatory influence unless it proved impossible to explain them as connected—and connected in justificatory terms—to an agent's system of beliefs. I take the treatment of emotions as completely *sui generis* to be a last resort, that is, from the standpoint of rational explanation, given the mutual causal influence of emotions and beliefs. But my argument here may be used to show how we can avoid this while also avoiding the judgmentalist extreme of equating warrant for the evaluative component of emotion with belief warrant.

One way of seeing belief warrant as adding something to emotional appropriateness—something that might be used to construct a hypothetical criterion of appropriateness—arises naturally from my argument. In cases of intuitive suspicion, one might say, undifferentiated perception simply yields up a feeling keyed to a significant subset of the evidence. But since the agent lacks the ability to identify the relevant cues, the evidence does not warrant him, even prima facie, in thinking that the subset is significant or that his feeling is keyed to it in the requisite sense. To warrant a belief, that is, even prima facie, an emotion must be supplemented by warrant for some belief *about* emotion. The mere fact that one *is* responding to relevant features of the external situation, though it might be said to warrant *attention* to a proposition (if only as a possibility that ought to be borne in mind), does not warrant *assent* to it. Assent requires taking it as something that would not be overturned by a full review of the evidence, on the view outlined in Chapter 3. At a minimum, then, for prima facie warranted assent one needs a reason for thinking *that* one is responding to relevant features of the external situation—to signs of X's untrustworthiness in the initial suspicion case.

For *adequately* warranted assent, though, one would seem to need something further: reason for thinking that one is responding to a *substantial* subset of the evidence, with "substance" determined in relation to the total body of evidence, including evidence available only hypothetically. For reasons I shall pause, in just a moment, to explain, I shall not attempt a general account of substance in a quantitative sense—of the evidential *strength* required to justify the strength of the affective component of emotion. But presumably, in our case of suspicion, the evidence must be strong enough to justify applying to X some relevant generalization and hence to ground the evaluative component of emotion in a kind of subliminal inference. This means, I take it, that suspicion rests on the same sort of evidence as the corresponding belief but judged by more tolerant standards. There may be variable quantitative standards of belief warrant, of course. I have been assuming here that "adequate" warrant sets a high standard; but in any case, a lower standard would still be *evidential*. For emotions, by contrast, we need a broader *set* of standards. I take it that all the standards, however, are standards of significant perception. Some of them may weight the perceptual evidence according to the general adaptiveness of basing a certain emotion on it, but as with belief warrant this does involve an assessment of the evidence, as "substantial" at least in a qualitative sense.

Matters of Degree. In attempting to understand emotional appropriateness in qualitative terms, I have focused almost entirely on the evaluative component of emotion, as a propositional attitude held in mind by some unspecified degree of affect. The strength implicitly attributed to the affective component varied from the ontological argument case, where it was assumed to be minimal, to the more ordinary suspicion cases, where it was assumed to be enough to make the feeling generally adaptive. But this is not to say, of course, that feelings of suspicion are adaptive in all or most cases where their evaluative components are appropriate. I have ignored a whole range of cases of "disproportionate" emotional response, where the notion of fitness to significant perception might be interpreted to apply to *degrees* of affect, ruling out further instances of emotion as inappropriate. Suspicion with adequate grounds, for instance, may be "paranoid" in intensity, or the extent to which it dominates consciousness, or some other measure of strength. I see no hope, though, of providing a more informative *general* answer to justificatory questions of emotional quantity. As formulated for appropriateness, such questions are ambiguous. There are different measures of strength, as we shall see; and "fitness" may be taken to require different kinds of proportionality.

First, let us see some different possible measures of emotional strength. The analogous property for belief would seem to be strength of *conviction*—how strongly the belief is held, that is, whether or not it is often, or ever, held in mind. But this is generally inferred from behavioral evidence. Felt conviction does not provide a real parallel for belief to the felt intensity of emotions, with their fairly immediate basis in physiological sensations. The result is that emotions may be "strong" in more than one sense. In the suspicion case, besides the degree to which I *feel* suspicious—assuming that this is implicitly disjunctive, so that the different affective symptoms of emotions pose no problem—duration might also be taken as a measure of strength. A weak feeling of suspicion that stays with me might be taken as a strong *emotion*, that is. And there are other measures, behavioral in the broad sense or specifically intellectual. A strong emotion may make me incapable of performing certain acts, say—including acts of attention, most notably concentration—or it may have an effect on my choice of which acts to perform, at least partly by its influence on my thinking prior to action. The special motivational force of emotions is clearly something variable; and it has a place, along with intensity and duration, in our list of measures of emotional quantity.

Even if we decide to concentrate on a particular measure— affective intensity, let us say—there are other reasons why a quantitative criterion of appropriateness would seem to be beyond reach. The natural appeal to *proportionality*, in formulating a criterion, also leaves us with several possibilities; for the strength of a given emotion may be said to be proportional *to* other things besides the strength of the evidence for its evaluative component, on the model of belief. The warranted strength of the evaluation supported by the evidence may also play a distinct role. In determining how much suspicion of X is warranted, for instance, we may consider *how* untrustworthy he is thought to be in addition to how well grounded the thought is. If the evidence suggests that he poses an *extreme* threat to my interests, that may be enough to justify a stronger feeling without any further evidence. The strength of the evaluative component may itself be estimated differently, moreover—most notably, by applying measures of probability or measures of importance, corresponding to its factual and evaluative aspects, for fear cases. Perhaps we should simply say, then, that the affective component of emotion is appropriate, in quantitative terms, as long as it fits at least one of these several measures in degree.

A more clear-cut notion of appropriate emotional quantity would have to rest on more particular reference to adaptiveness. We might be inclined to say, for instance, that an emotion is appropriately strong as long as its affective component is no stronger than is needed to hold its evaluative component in mind. But the appeal to *general* adaptiveness that would stand behind this suggestion, as an extension of my account of appropriateness, has no clear quantitative interpretation that would work here. If the requisite amount of affective intensity is taken as that which *usually* is needed to hold a certain evaluation in mind, this may be too weak for its particular circumstances in a given case. But if so, our criterion would seem to rule out as *in*appropriate any emotion that would actually fulfill its adaptive function in the particular case at hand. A consideration of cases suggests, in fact, that we blur over the distinction between appropriateness and adaptiveness, in application to the particular case, when considering matters of degree. If *some* suspicion of X is appropriate, say, in a case where the counterevidence is weighty enough to make watchfulness depend on a *strong* feeling, we may allow for the latter, even though it is not needed, in general terms, in order to fix attention on an evaluation of someone as untrustworthy. However, if we allowed for an equally strong feeling across-the-board, some intuitively inappropriate cases of "disproportionate" suspicion might come out as appropriate. For similar reasons I take it that other versions of the suggested criterion will fail unless they are applied case-by-case.

It seems that we must content ourselves, then, with a necessary condition of appropriate emotion. This should give us all we need, though, to support my main argument in this essay for the special motivational role of emotions as supplements to judgment. The emotions whose appropriateness the argument calls into question, as indicated in my last chapter, would seem to be those whose evaluative components are themselves stronger in qualitative terms than the closest available warranted beliefs. So it will be enough to offer a condition of appropriateness formulated in terms of the evaluative component, on the assumption that the affective component is *at least* as strong as is needed to hold that proposition in mind. Weaker or stronger affect may or may not be accepted as appropriate in a given case, depending on further appeal to considerations of adaptiveness, considerations even more variable than those that apply to the evaluative component. In my next chapter we shall see more clearly how much variation may come in just with reference to the evaluative component, in particular cases. My aim here is to suggest a kind of *general* rational justification of emotion; but when I claim that emotions are adaptive "in general," I have in mind no particular view about how often some sort of forward-looking justification is possible.[7] Nor, for that matter, shall I attempt to estimate how often the pitfalls of emotional response make it more trouble than it is worth. I take it, rather, that a general justification of emotions will be one that exhibits the general *importance* of their role in rational motivation—indeed, if I am right, its *irreplaceable* importance—and explains irrational cases as side-effects of something valuable. But to achieve this limited aim, it is enough to justify the evaluative component of emotion, as an object of *some* degree of affect.

In this chapter, working with a case of rational conflict between emotion and belief, I have defended a notion of appropriateness set up to justify the evaluative component as a generally adaptive reaction to a significant subset of the evidence. By allowing reference to other standards besides that of evidential significance, the notion allows for the assessment of emotions in relation to *different* subsets of the evidence. As we shall see in detail in my next chapter, it therefore leaves room for conflicting *emotions*. The claim that a certain emotion is appropriate, that is, will not imply that a contrary emotion is not. I take this endorsement of "rationally appropriate ambivalence" to be a confirming consequence of my view of emotional appropriateness.[8] But a full defense of either the view or this consequence of it will require applying it to some further sorts of cases. Before attempting this, however, let me sum up the view very briefly in a nonquantitative criterion of emotional appropriateness, framed in terms of hypothetical belief warrant. The evaluative component is appropriate, we may say, as long as it rests on evidence that, if recognized, would yield prima facie warrant for the corresponding belief—and, if supplemented by further information, would yield substantial warrant for a propositional attitude with the same content.

My talk here of resting on evidence is meant to allude to the inferential requirements, themselves hypothetical, that were imposed on the causal derivation of emotion in my treatment of the suspicion case in Section (ii). The condition bringing in substantial warrant is an abbreviated attempt to allow for *both* nonevidential standards of significance and the evidential constraints that surfaced in my treatment of a "spillover" variant of the "hard sell" broker case in Section (i). Suspicion seemed to be *in*appropriate, remember, if based on just one disastrous experience with a broker; but in other cases of dealing with a broker, the appeal to general adaptiveness seemed to warrant suspicion on equally slight evidence. In the original case of intuitive suspicion, there was decisive *counter*evidence; and in the original "hard sell" case, the evidence was far from conclusive. I take it, however, that "substantial" warrant is still merely prima facie, in the following sense: Although it will not collapse as *flimsy* on internal examination, it may be undercut by further evidence just because its weight may depend on nonevidential considerations. But it is important that the nonevidential considerations pertain *to* the evidence—in a way assumed by the reference to "further information."

The information in question here is assumed to be *about* the evidence, that is—*true* of it, since "information" is taken to be necessarily veridical, though further information of the requisite sort may be available only hypothetically. It may include the further ingredients of belief warrant: reason for thinking that the evidence at hand represents enough of the total body of evidence to yield a sufficiently weighty generalization. But it also covers any reason for thinking that basing an emotion of the sort in question *on* the evidence at hand would be generally adaptive. In the latter case, what is warranted is not a belief but rather a propositional attitude with the same content—in short, the evaluative component of emotion. A case of "flimsy" warrant, then, will be one in which there is nothing about the evidence that would justify the evaluative component *either* evidentially or practically. But this does not mean that equally slight evidence could not yield a practical justification in another sort of case. I shall now apply this general view of appropriateness to the defense of some cases of rationally appropriate ambivalence.

5
Rationally Appropriate Ambivalence: Contrary Emotions

The word "ambivalence" was popularized in connection with psychoanalytic theories of motivation involving unconscious states that cannot bear scrutiny if only because they conflict with the agent's conscious states. But here I want to discuss some cases of conscious emotional conflict in defense of the rationality of ambivalence. For the word does not *imply* irrationality—particularly if rationality in the sense captured by the notion of appropriateness is in question, though ambivalence may also be seen as adaptive in some cases, even if we consider only the promotion of rational self-interest. The word "ambivalence" covers various sorts of two-directional motivating factors, including many I shall not be dealing with here. We sometimes use it just as an expression for any kind of indecision: "I'm ambivalent about so-and-so's worth as a writer," say. It may function, that is, as a substitute for "of two minds," without commitment as to whether or not the conflict is between states of mind of the same sort or active at the same time, though it *is* clear that both are taken as states of consciousness and as active at some time or other. I shall restrict attention here, though, to cases of conflict between two emotions, analyzed as comfort or discomfort directed towards evaluative propositions. These will be assumed to be occurrent emotions, even at times when their evaluative components are not actually present to consciousness. They need not therefore be "unconscious" in the sense that implies inaccessibility; but in any case, my treatment of unconscious emotions in Chapter 2 should allow for this possibility as well.

Further, I shall restrict attention to emotions whose "representational" rationality may be called into question, by analogy with contrary judgments, because their evaluative components conflict logically. Sometimes emotions simply give rise to contingent conflict—between desires, say, whose joint satisfaction is ruled out by the facts. The distinction may be illustrated by some variants of my central case of unconscious emotion in Chapter 2: jealousy, taken as fear of loss, combined with a fear of too much involvement. A motivational conflict might have persisted, in this case, even after jealousy had been made conscious—supposing that the love-object, or love-objects generally, would find it impossible, or impossibly hard, to maintain the acceptable mix of closeness and distance. We might well call this "ambivalence" and raise questions about the instrumental rationality (or for that matter, the fairness) of retaining both emotions. But the tension between them would not raise questions as to how they both could be *warranted*.

The beliefs corresponding to their evaluative components would be perfectly consistent, that is. They would be so, moreover, even if the (external) objects of fear—the two states evaluated as threatening—exhausted all the possibilities. In a variant of the case, for instance, the agent might have wanted to avoid *any* involvement, not just "too much," while at the same time wanting to avoid loss, taken as including any *un*involvement, even if brought about by her. Here we would have *logically* conflicting *desires*. But the two *fears*, or their evaluative components, would still involve no logical conflict themselves: both alternatives may indeed be threatening—for an agent already deeply attached to a particularly hurtful love-object, say. In any case, the connection between fear and the desire to escape is on my view merely contingent. Dread is always a possibility—fearful resignation to a hopelessly injurious relationship—if the agent cannot manage to block out one of her fears. What we want here, by contrast, is a case of contrary *emotions*—*hope* and fear, for instance, or the familiar "love/hate relationship"— with comfort and discomfort seen as directed towards contrary evaluations of the same object. For emotions that involve desire, but desire based on an evaluation of the object of desire, any motivational conflict of the sort just sketched should also take this form. For simplicity's sake, then, we may focus on emotions involving contrary evaluations.

In another variant of the jealousy case, we might suppose that the agent felt both comfortable and uncomfortable about anticipated closeness to the love-object. I shall return to a case of this sort; but first I want to examine a case of joy/sorrow ambivalence of the sort that briefly came into question in my treatment of identificatory love in Chapter 3. Since it arose in connection with pity, the case as set up earlier raised questions about the joint rationality of joy and identificatory sorrow. I shall modify it here by making the joy identificatory, in order to raise some harder questions about the rationality of the individual emotions as well as of the conflicting pair. For the ultimate aim of my discussion in this chapter is to allow for a more extended version of the view of emotional motivation that was outlined for some morally significant cases in Chapter 3. But this requires testing out my preceding account of appropriateness by applying it to some problematic cases. On my view, the joy/sorrow cases, along with other cases of ambivalence, involve no irrational conflict as long as the two emotions in them are warranted by different *reasons*. But in support of joy itself, in the case I focus on, I shall have to extend my account of appropriateness to cover identificatory emotions (i). I shall argue, then, that both emotions in the conflicting pair may be seen as warranted by "perceptual" reasons, or evidence, as supplemented by appeal to considerations of general adaptiveness, in accordance with the criterion of appropriateness set forth in Chapter 4.

My argument will include some detailed attention to questions about *self-regarding* emotions, both in cases where their rationality is usually taken for granted and in others where it is commonly denied—especially cases of *envy*, which I shall treat at length (ii). My discussion of these diverse cases will be meant in the first instance to show how my account of appropriateness can accommodate them. But secondly, I hope to exhibit some of the more interesting consequences of my account, with its reference to general adaptiveness. I shall show how the latter covers adaptiveness in a social sense, as well as rational adaptiveness, or value to the promotion of self-interest, and how it applies to emotions that are not instrumentally (or morally) valuable in the particular case at hand. I shall also attempt to pin down the notion of emotional contrareity, as basic to understanding cases of ambivalence. I shall then return to *love/ hate* ambivalence in order to construct a particularly hard case for the claim of rational appropriateness (iii). Besides answering some questions about the rationality of love and hatred considered individually, I shall defend their joint rationality even in a maladaptive case where both apparently rest on the *same* reasons.

(i) Identification and Warrant

Let us now turn to joy/sorrow ambivalence. Suppose that a good friend has just won some honor I had coveted myself, and I feel *both* glad and sad about his winning. I am comfortable, that is, at the thought that his winning is good, since it satisfies a desire of someone I identify with; and at the same time I am *un*comfortable at the thought that his winning is bad, since it frustrates a desire of my own. Thus analyzed in terms of my suggested pattern, my emotions can be seen to involve contrary evaluative attitudes with the same object: his winning. We need not suppose that I simultaneously experience a flush of gladness and a pang of sadness when I hear that he has won; on my account of occurrent emotions, this is not implied by the claim that I feel glad and sad "at the same time." I have "mixed feelings," and consciously so, though one feeling or the other may dominate consciousness at any given time. Or the two may yield a kind of "mingled" pleasure/pain; but they do not blend into some sort of intermediate feeling tone. This is what the case assumes, that is: The claim is not that this is the *only* possible reaction but just that it *is* possible and in fact fairly common.

Further, my mixed feelings here may be seen as directed towards the *same* object, even though the reasons to which they are tied might also be interpreted as qualifiers, picking out two distinct objects: that my friend's winning satisfied one of *his* desires and that it frustrated a desire of my own. The view of emotions I have defended does allow for multiple objects of the same feeling, where the agent would recognize them as such—and also in some cases of unconscious emotion where he would not. But my feelings here are still quite properly described as contrary emotions with "the same object" as long as at least one external object is evaluated positively and negatively by the internal objects of the two emotions. Once again, the claim is just that this is possible—and not uncommon. There might be a case where I am glad *only* that my friend's winning satisfied one of his desires; but on our assumptions, this is not it: I also am glad that he won. The fact that we can give two distinct reasons for my contrary feelings—whether or not we take them as yielding further objects, but as long as we let their apparent objects stand— gives us a way of defending both emotions as appropriate. In terms of my criterion of appropriateness in Chapter 4, each emotion is tied to a reason that, if supplemented by further information, would yield substantial warrant for its evaluative component. I shall argue that the criterion will fit both emotions as long as "substance" is assessed in practical terms but from different standpoints.

Where we have two reasons, that is, our appeal to practical considerations may justify contrary emotions; for it may be *generally* adaptive to act on each of them in cases not involving conflict. In the present case, in order to justify the two emotions, one reason requires supplementation by reference to the adaptiveness of identification with a friend while the other presupposes the adaptiveness of self-regarding emotion. We need to look at the case in more detail, though, in order to apply my criterion of appropriateness. The self-regarding evaluation seems initially to raise no questions, at least if we assume that its use of "bad" is nonmoral— though still "all-out," or at any rate qualified in the *same* way as the use of "good" in the contrary evaluation. If I evaluate my friend's winning as "bad-for-me," that is, I also evaluate it as in some sense "good-for-me" in the case as envisioned. Since the positive evaluation is taken to be identificatory, the case also supposes that it does not rest simply on a view of my friend's victory as ultimately promoting my own independent interests. I do not, for instance, think it likely that my friend will use the honor in some way beneficial to myself—or at any rate, that is not *why* I feel glad that he won. Rather, in the simplest sort of case, I evaluate his winning from *his* standpoint: I "feel as though" it were itself a benefit to me.

But how can this be rational, one might ask? Am I not simply picking up—via natural, but nonrational, psychological processes—an evaluation that is not really applicable to my own situation? My criterion of appropriateness in Chapter 4 should help us explain how this identificatory evaluation may be warranted, even though its corresponding *judgment* is indeed unwarranted. To apply the criterion, though—to make out my reason here as a prima facie evidence—we need to appeal to a rather generous notion of "significant perception." First of all, the standard of significance it relies on will not be dictated by the need for quick decision-making in my own interests, as it was in the case of fearful suspicion. Joy, on my view, is not an emotion that essentially involves a desire for action; and unlike emotions based on fear, it does not even typically give rise to a desire to act to falsify its evaluative component. It involves comfort at a positive evaluation; but it does typically give rise to a desire for *expressive* action—as well as for continued contemplation of its object—if only to heighten or sustain the comfort. There may be some cases resembling the present one where the agent's interests are served by the emotion just in so far as they require expressive action—to preserve a mutually supportive friendship, for instance. But in the first instance, I want to say, it is the *social* adaptiveness of mutuality, rather than its importance to rational self-interest, that prompts us to accept the identificatory evaluation as rational.

We might suppose, for example, that my friend's honor will in fact have only bad effects on our friendship—will widen the distance between us, say—in a way independent of my emotional response. The discomfort I derive from the honor now and in the future will outweigh any comfort I may experience at contemplating it with joy, even in combination with comfort at a view of myself as someone who identifies with friends. So it is false that his winning is good-for-me; and we may also grant that it is *evidently* false. In seeing things from his standpoint, though, I am not simply calculating the impact of his good on my own. Rather, I am ignoring the distinction between them, taking his good as if it *were* my own—though I am not deluded into thinking this is so. I realize that the two will soon part company—in fact, as well as in concept—but my joy on his behalf may be said to be warranted *by* my current conflation of them. For the moment, that is, our standpoints, or *perceived* goods, coincide. Or, in the looser sense of "identification," where it involves adopting the standpoint of a friend, I might instead be seen as ignoring the distinction between my own good and that of an imaginary third party, a friend related in the normal manner, without conflicting interests, to my actual friend in the case. I take it that an affectively registered awareness of the normal situation, as one of mutual support, is generally adaptive—sometimes even more so than seeing things directly from my friend's standpoint, though both figure in moral motivation, in the way sketched in Chapter 3. On my view, then, the fact that I do now identify with another person—even if indirectly, by way of a third party—yields prima facie reason for the judgment that our goods coincide; and the reason counts as "substantial" in light of its importance to social ends.

The nonevidential standard of significance that comes in here amounts to "adaptiveness" in a sense compatible with the recognition that my actual ends may *not* be served by identification in the particular case at hand. Perhaps in this instance my memory of identificatory joy will even make my friend's later distance harder for me to bear. But the general social value of identification with another person is still enough to warrant an evaluation from his standpoint, based on the perception of his good as my own. This use of "perception" may at first sight seem to conflict with my introduction of the term, in Chapter 4, for noneval-uative apprehension, interpreted as necessarily veridical. The "percep-tual" backing for identificatory emotion here is apparently spelled out in terms of a false evaluative judgment: that my friend's good is my own. Indeed, in Chapter 3 identificatory love was treated as a tendency to take on various fantasy-emotions. But in that case, one might ask how it can have the sort of *evidential* basis that seemed to be required for appropriateness in my last chapter. In reply, though, I would suggest that we make out identification as involving an act of perception (in the sense that extends to reflection) prior to the formation of the identifi-catory evaluation for which it then may be said to provide evidence. It yields adequate warrant for a temporally limited judgment that merely reports its results, that is: in the present case, that my perceived good now embraces my friend's. The act of identifying with another, then, brings together their *perceived* goods—their goods as presently perceived by the agent—as momentary ends of action.

This will not be enough to yield adequate warrant for a judgment that the two *goods* are identical—or even for a judgment that the agent will continue to conflate them. That degree of submergence in others' ends goes beyond anything envisioned here, in cases of ordinary iden-tification, without delusion or loss of self-regard. Rather, I want to say that the act of identification, taken as the perception of another's good as one's own, yields prima facie warrant for an evaluative judgment to that effect. But it is subject to gestalt shifts, of a sort that may overturn even a perceptually limited version of the judgment unless it is also limited to the present moment. By contrast, the "all-out" evaluation involved in identificatory love, as I interpret it, is *not* thus qualified: I "feel as though" someone else's good were *actually* my own or linked to my own in some lasting way as a result of identification. So adequate warrant for the corresponding judgment will depend on more than my current frame of mind. In the present case of "friendly rivalry," as I have set it up, the judgment would not be warranted, even "substantially," just by the evidence at hand, weighted in accordance with its importance *as* evidence of the likely benefit to myself of my friend's honor. Nor would the content of the judgment be warranted as a "snap" evaluation, with the evidence weighted in accordance with its importance to the immediate protection of my own practical ends. I take it that the present case leaves me ample time to express identificatory joy, if that would help to preserve a friendship I value. But I also assume that the importance of identificatory joy here is dictated more by my friend's interests or by the general interests of the social unit than by my own.

Even my own *general* interests—in community of feeling, say, as mainly shoring up individual self-esteem—need not in fact be served by the emotion; perhaps I am the sort of person who is not much benefited, on the whole, by others' similar responses. In the first instance, then, it is the *social* significance of the act of identifying with others—its signif-icance *for* others—that lends it substantial weight as evidence for an identificatory evaluation. The act amounts to a perception of someone else's ends as included among one's own; and it yields only prima facie evidence for a judgment corresponding to the evaluative component of emotion. Practical *commitment* even to one's own ends—and hence the adoption of an evaluative standpoint—must be taken as involving a jump beyond the simple perception of them as momentary ends of action. Their evaluation as genuine "goods," construed as ends that ought to regulate action, also depends on a judgment of significance. At the very least, it depends on a value accorded to consistent action over time and hence to continued pursuit of one's present ends—something that is not given in the recognition that action (or attention) is currently directed towards them.[1] Here it is extended to others' ends by a value placed on action on behalf of others.

(ii) Rationality and Self-Regard

At the beginning of Chapter 6 I shall supplement the preceding account by defending a distinction between appropriate and merely un-derstandable emotions that picks out identificatory cases from fantasy-emotions involving an element of delusion. But if my account is accepted, identificatory emotions may be counted as rationally appropriate, despite the fact that they do amount to fantasy-emotions, of a sort that may not be instrumentally rational for the agent—even in long-range terms, but in application to the particular case at hand. I have been dealing here with a case of joy on behalf of someone else, which would seem to be intrinsically pleasurable for the agent. But it is mixed with sorrow on one's own behalf and might well be overshadowed by it. Perhaps the joy or the fact that one has felt it even heightens future sorrow, as I suggested at one point; or perhaps it is mixed with further discomfort now if one feels it in the expectation that the friendship will fade with distance. In any case, there are other identificatory emotions that are intrinsically uncomfortable: sorrow, for instance, or embarrassment, at someone else's loss or *faux pas*. These may still be rational, though, in the sense of appropriate, as long as they are generally socially adaptive, even where they are not generally adaptive for the agent, as a reaction to prima facie evidence for belief. The claim that they are generally socially adaptive is meant as a claim about their usefulness in general terms to society as a whole. They are useful partly because of their connection to action—including expressive action, which signals to others both the agent's tendency to promote their interests and the simple fact that their triumphs and tribulations do "register" affectively on another being.

On the other hand, there would be nothing irrational, on my view, about *failing* to feel identificatory (or other appropriate) emotions if they do not serve the agent's interests in the particular case at hand. I shall also argue in Chapter 6 that representational rationality does not *mandate* feeling. For the moment, though, we may reapply our criterion of appropriateness to show that there is nothing irrational about feeling a *conflicting*, self-regarding emotion, one that is based on an evaluation of the situation from the agent's own standpoint. The fact that a desire of mine has been frustrated when my friend turns out to win the honor I had been hoping for provides a *non*identificatory reason for evaluating his winning as *bad*-for-me, that is. Granting that my sorrow fits the evaluation in degree, it is no less appropriate than my joy—perhaps just because its evaluative component is warranted as a belief or perhaps because it is generally useful in guarding against excessive submergence in someone else's ends. In either case, it seems that the explanation of the rationality of the conflict here depends on reference *both* to different reasons and to different standards of significance—the latter determining the weight assigned to the former. In terms of our criterion, each reason, identificatory or self-regarding, yields substantial warrant for the relevant evaluation if supplemented by further information of a different sort. The information may differ either in its evidential status or in the appeal it makes to considerations of practical adaptiveness.

This possible difference in the way the two reasons are supplemented will later allow for cases of contrary emotions apparently tied to the *same* reason. Here, however, where we do have different reasons, a variant case could also be defended by appeal to the same standard of significance. Most obviously, there might sometimes be self-interested grounds for adopting *each* of the two conflicting standpoints—and for emotional ambivalence in light of them but with control over its affective and behavioral manifestations. These latter include the degree to which and the occasions on which one dwells on each of the contrary evaluations, perhaps with affect, and perhaps with some tendency towards expression. Preserving a friendship without losing sight of my independent ends may require the capacity for spontaneous expression, but at well-chosen times, of both joy and sorrow, for instance. It may call for enthusiastic participation in my friend's celebrations, say, along with an occasional inner goad towards my own future achievement—a combination that might not arise from an intermediate response, the result of emotional blending. My contrary emotions, then, may both be useful in promoting my own ends—at least if they can be "tamped down" a bit more than usual or kept from full affective manifestation at the same time, with an important measure of *control* over what is felt when.

My discussion here has focused on a harder case, however, where joyful participation in my friend's celebrations and the like may be assumed to do no good at all for anyone actually affected by my actions in the particular case at hand. It will just place an unhelpful burden on my friend, let us suppose, since his honor brings with it responsibilities that genuinely require greater distance. Nor need my sorrow here serve even my own interests, in fact; but if appropriateness is in question, in the sense I have outlined, I still want to say that this conflicting feeling may be rational. Indeed, it may be rational in a way that depends on *social* adaptiveness—for another version of the case where appeal is made to extraevidential considerations of the same sort. These considerations of general adaptiveness, moreover, are to be distinguished both from instrumental considerations, individual *or* social, in the case at hand and from noninstrumental moral or quasi-moral values. My sorrow may be rationally appropriate, that is, in light of its general social adaptiveness, whether or not it is either controllable enough to be useful in my social situation or socially appropriate—a "suitable" feeling, let us say, for someone in that situation.

It seems "small-minded" of me, in this case, to dwell on my loss to a friend of one possible honor among many. Even granting this, however, I want to say something of my self-regarding emotion like what I said of its identificatory complement, where the latter is not adaptive, individually or socially, in the particular case at hand. The claim sounds odder when applied to one's own ends: that taking their perception as "significant" and the emotion based on it as appropriate depends, in part, on a *social* value placed on "registering" evaluations from one's own standpoint. This is not so implausible, however, if we assume that practical commitment to one's ends requires more than perception of them *as* one's current ends, or of action as currently directed towards them. By itself, such perception would not yield adequate evidential warrant for an evaluative judgment. One's ends must also be seen as *desirable* or as ends towards which action *ought* to be directed—in some, perhaps nonmoral, sense of "ought." Otherwise, in the present case, the fact that my friend's victory frustrates one of my desires would not imply an evaluation of it as "bad-for-me"—even ignoring possible conflicts among my current desires but supposing that I take the desire in question to be subject to change over time.

In short, the evaluative stance, even towards one's own perceived good, requires more than recognizing it as the object of current desire. In many cases, a desire can later be dropped. For that matter, even while it is still in force, it may be considered in the manner of a symptom of some disvalued addiction, to be mollified rather than satisfied. By contrast, holding in mind an evaluation, on the view suggested here, involves regulating future action accordingly—at the very least, permitting action to take its natural course as opposed to simply acknowledging it as the natural one as things stand. Practical *detachment* from one's own ends involves a kind of failure of self-identification; and it is to be avoided, except where it serves a particular purpose, as in a case of breaking an addiction. It is maladaptive in general—and socially, as well as individually; for the capacity for *moral agency* depends, in the first instance, on reliable pursuit of one's ends. It presupposes a general kind of motivational consistency: carrying out long-term plans and projects rather than simply making choices from a series of unrelated standpoints. Where the agent adopts *others'* ends, they must be unified by a sense of their bearing on his own. The alternative would involve either loss of a single perspective or submergence in the ends of someone else—real or imagined—and the threat that one's own ends might not be represented. In assessing the appropriateness of a self-regarding emotion, then, we accord a kind of *moral* significance to its vivid reflection of one's own standpoint—even where the emotion itself may be viewed as morally questionable. I now want to apply these remarks, not just to "unworthy" self-regarding emotions—feeling sorry for oneself, in the present case—but also to some that may seem to be morally vicious.

Unalloyed Envy. An extreme example—since it is sometimes thought to be ruled out as inappropriate in all cases—is one that we can extract from some variants of the present case: envy.[2] I shall discuss it first in unalloyed form, before it is tempered by ambivalence. It is sometimes taken to involve a desire to deprive another person of some "nontransferable" benefit: one whose loss by him would yield no equivalent benefit for oneself. With "equivalent" understood simply in terms of quantitative worth or importance to the agent, action on such a desire *would* seem to come out as *maladaptive*—irrational in "forward-looking" terms. But let us note, first, that the cases in question here might involve nontransferability only in some more limited, qualitative sense: The sort of benefit one envies another *for* may indeed be nontransferable, though one would gain another sort of benefit if he lost that one. In another version of the case of friendly rivalry, for instance, we might suppose that, besides feeling sorry for myself, I envy my friend his honor—even to the extent of preferring that neither of us has it to his having it and my not. Perhaps these are the only two realistic options, moreover: Any qualifications I have for the honor are those my friend possesses in greater degree, say, so that the honor would have gone to someone else, selected by different criteria, if not to him.

Must it be irrational, then, for me to prefer that my friend not have the honor—supposing that rationality limits me to the promotion of self-interest? Surely not; for there is another sort of benefit—the retention of our friendship, or our friendship-on-an-equal-footing—that I would have gained had my friend been passed over. Nor would it be irrational for me even to prefer that no one have the honor—to wish to be rid of what might be seen as an increase in social distance, something that diminishes my own perceived worth, just by supplying an example of superior achievement. This *comparative* view of things will be reasonable, moreover, as long as it appeals to a standard of merit according to which I know I am judged—whether or not I take the standard to be reasonable. Although the discussion of envy that follows will avoid economic examples, the financial notion of "what one is worth" should have obvious bearing on it, granting only that money is commonly regarded as a serious criterion of merit. In general, then, for envy to be rational, one need only benefit "by comparison" if the other party loses what he has.

But let us move on to a harder sort of case, with the aim of focusing initial attention on the appropriateness of envy, or its "backward-looking" rationality, as an emotion whose corresponding evaluative judgment may be warranted only prima facie. It might at least seem to be irrational for me to prefer that no one have the honor if its achievement by someone yields *benefits* for me overall—benefits that depend, in fact, on my losing out "by comparison" in the short run. Suppose that my friend's honor is some sort of teaching award whose bestowal on someone in my department will result in an increase in enrollments in my own courses and long-term benefits for me. Let us grant, too, that these would outweigh any present contentment I might experience at seeming to be as successful a teacher as anyone. Indeed, they might even be benefits of the same sort: The exposure to larger audiences eventually improves my teaching, say, spreads my reputation for success at it, and results in later honors exceeding my friend's. But the question of rationality must depend on what sort of "preference" is in question here. It is important that my envy need not involve an "all things considered" *judgment* that it would be better for me if no one got the honor. Nor need it involve an unambivalent *desire* that no one get the honor, a desire intense enough to issue in action where action is possible. This *would* seem to be irrational, on the assumption that the end that governs my preference—recognized worth as a teacher, say—is *dateless*. It would be another story if I really were after something—a history of attracting disciples among students, for instance—whose achievement depended on how soon I got the honor. But assuming that my end has been picked out correctly, an emotional preference, of the sort involved in envy as here conceived, need not be rationally inappropriate even in this case.

My negative evaluation of someone else's winning the honor will be appropriate, that is, as long as it is backed up by a *subset* of the reasons available to me—a subset that, if supplemented by further information, would yield substantial warrant for its evaluative component. This is to say that I may have adequate reason for "feeling as though" someone else's winning was a bad thing—worse, in fact, than no one's winning— even where the total body of evidence counts against the corresponding judgment. In reacting with envy here, I ignore the reasons for a positive overall evaluation of my friend's winning—reasons for thinking that the receipt of the honor by someone in the department will eventually be better for me than its receipt by no one. Instead, I focus on the *dis*value of the *immediate* situation: my lower rating, in comparison to another person, on a scale by which I take myself to be judged. But if it is appropriate, as it seemed to be in the preceding case, to react with envy to such comparisons where they do *not* benefit me overall, then it should be appropriate in this case as well. For the case exhibits the same connection to considerations of *general* adaptiveness—the "further information" referred to in the criterion of appropriateness—no matter how maladaptive the emotion may be in its situational context.

This assumes that the instrumental value of emotions in registering evaluative information affectively rests on their responsiveness to a partial view of the agent's perceptual situation. Here my envy serves to hold in mind an evaluative proposition that is not adequately warranted as a belief—and that may not even be a helpful object of attention in the particular case at hand. But it is of a sort that is useful in pursuit of self-interest and useful partly *because* it is resistant to qualification and counterevidence. For that matter, though it is about something rather trivial in this case, it may be *morally* valuable in general as a relatively immediate but sustained response to the perception of *inequality*. Even on *non*trivial issues, it may seem "small-minded" just to the extent that it is necessarily self-regarding: If felt on behalf of someone else, it simply would not be called "envy." But it is no less appropriate for all that—or no less so than *pride* in oneself, say, for qualities one may or may not admire in others. As with pride, envy allows for a special weight on matters affecting oneself; but this may let it serve a morally valuable purpose, whether or not it is morally valuable in itself. Like other self-regarding emotions, envy reinforces the agent's identification with his own standpoint and thereby promotes the motivational consistency presupposed by moral agency as well as by self-interest. But more specifically, envy provides an agent with a basis for an identificatory reaction to inequalities involving others, just insofar as it registers from his own standpoint the view of a similar situation from below.

As so far described, though, our case of envy need not involve a desire to *deprive* someone of a nontransferable benefit—a desire for *destructive* action, let us say, in order to *remove* an inequality. So far I have interpreted envy simply in terms of discomfort at a negative evaluation: the thought that the inequality is worse than no one's possessing the benefit. But this is not enough to link it essentially to desire, in the "motivating" sense that involves discomfort at an action requirement: the thought that I ought to do something to remove the inequality. At most, I have linked it to a preference for a different state of affairs, or a passive wish that things were otherwise. Of course, an object of envy may be something by now unchangeable: in this case, the honor already awarded to my friend. But one might object that genuine envy must still involve a desire for some sort of corrective action, erasing the comparative inequality by depriving the other party of some *other* benefit. Otherwise, the emotion would amount to no more than a comparative variant of *self-pity*, without the destructive element that calls the rational and moral value of envy into question.

I am skeptical of some of the philosophical demands imposed on the very notion of envy—including even "nontransferability," though I began my discussion by granting this. But I shall accept the demand for a destructive element at least to the extent of focusing my further discussion on a corresponding *subtype* of the emotion. I do think there may be another form of envy amounting to affectively agitated, or "smoldering," self-pity—destructive enough, in its way. However, I would agree that the really problematic subtype of the emotion involves a compound of envy and *anger*. This should be subdivided in turn, though, to reflect my distinction in Chapter 3 between personal and impersonal anger. The former may be said to yield personal envy involving *blame* and a desire for punitive action on the basis of a view of its object as responsible for an undeserved benefit—at a minimum, for not taking action himself to correct the inequality. The latter yields a compound of envy with *frustration* and remains impersonal in the sense of focusing only incidentally on a person, as part of the resented situation of comparison, with a more diffuse desire for destructive action aimed towards undermining the situation. Both emotions may be made less destructive by ambivalence, of course. But the main point for us to notice here is that, where we do not have warrant for a judgment of responsibility— responsibility for an undeserved benefit, of the sort that would yield blame, in this case—frustration-envy is available as an alternative response. The destructive element of frustration-envy may serve a positive purpose where it "energizes" the agent to compete for *attainable* benefits; but this alternative to punitive action need not involve depriving the other party of any *noncomparative* benefits. The possibility of this alternative form of destructive envy can be best established, I think, if we consider a less schematic version of the case of friendly rivalry. But first let us see why even its present version should not be taken to justify *personal* envy. In my argument up to this point, before compounding envy with anger, I have let the appropriateness of its evaluative component rest on *nonevidential* information, in accordance with the criterion of appropriateness offered in my last chapter. It might seem, then, that personal envy would be "substantially" warranted in at least some cases where the corresponding judgment is not. I may have prima facie evidence, in some cases, for a judgment of personal responsibility for an undeserved benefit—since my friend's competition did play a role, say, in gaining him a benefit I would *otherwise* deserve. But this will not be enough, as supplemented by reference to general adaptiveness, to warrant outwardly directed blame, taken as an emotion directed towards another person.[3] Such purposes as would be served by "feeling as though" my friend were *at fault* for his competition, that is, would be equally well served, in a case like this one, if I limited myself to impersonal anger. So the instrumental value of envy here, in a situation where no one is at fault, will not be irreplaceable in general terms. Although it may be easier—and hence understandable—for its destructive element to focus on a person, blame in the absence of responsibility would seem to be generally maladaptive.

Does the impersonal emotion really amount to destructive envy, though? Let us now look a case that should allow for some reference to experience in ruling out alternatives that lack the requisite destructive content, even as the case is made harder. X, a friend and colleague, chatters on, in an amiable enough fashion, about the enthusiasm and drive with which he approaches the task of freshman humanities teaching. Hearing this, I reflect on my own diffidence, with its negative effects on performance, and feel a pang of envy. As I experience this, it is clearly a negative feeling, aroused and outwardly directed, with X as the focus of attention. However, it does not amount to personal anger *at X*, involving a desire to deprive him of the general trait that I envy—uncritical enthusiasm, let us say—as a kind of punishment for outperforming me. In a different sort of case, let us note, where my envy had a different sort of object, the emotion *might* involve a punitive desire, even essentially—and for that matter, even appropriately. I might envy X, for instance, not just for his trait of uncritical enthusiasm or even for the teaching talent it promotes but also for his use of both to gain a student following. Perhaps I think he accomplishes this by misleading students about the difficulty of philosophy, so that my own labors go unappreciated. If so, I might hold X responsible for *some* object of envy, in this case—his student following—and I might have a desire to deprive him of it, even if it amounts to a nontransferable benefit. Because it sets a standard by which I may be judged, X's loss of his student following might transfer a kind of *comparative* benefit to me, according to my earlier argument. On these or similar assumptions, then, we might have a case of appropriate *personal* envy—reasonable enough in emotional terms, even though an attempt to act on it might not be.

These assumptions do not apply, though, to the case we are considering; so how can we say that my appropriate feeling there amounts to envy—as opposed, perhaps, to a compound of self-pity and admiration? My actual feeling in cases like this one seems to involve a pang of outwardly directed *resentment* with at least some degree of negative arousal—though it is usually limited in duration by the onset of an identificatory feeling since the real-life cases tend to involve ambivalence. At any rate, the destructive element of envy here seems to be directed towards the *situation*—including both X and myself—in which X has some traits judged higher than my own. I might want to undermine that situation of comparison, moreover, even if it ultimately benefits me, as in the schematic case sketched earlier. I might want to undermine it, in fact—let us now add, for a harder, "dog in the manger" version of the case—even if I do not really want the things I envy X *for*, apart from the comparative benefit of being rated higher. I need not *admire* X for possessing even the comparative benefit, in this version of the case. The comparative benefit, moreover, is not the only object of my envy: I also resent X's teaching performance itself and his possession of the personality trait that makes it possible.

On the level of judgment, then, my first choice here would be that X continue to possess the trait that ultimately benefits me. In so far as X's trait is an object of my envy, though, but not an object of desire, my first choice while I am in the grips of the emotion would be that *neither* of us possess the trait. This need not be irrational, on the view defended here, supposing that my envy does not involve blame or a punitive desire to deprive X of the trait. To the extent that my resentment focuses on X, I do not resent him for *doing* something but simply for *being there*— standing in my way, as it were, as an obstacle to my unqualified self-esteem. My desire to attack is directed towards a situation that includes him, the situation of comparison in which he gains some benefit over me—in this case, a benefit whose transfer I would not really want even if it *were* transferable. This means that on an emotional level I evaluate negatively the comparative state of affairs that I actually think is best for me: losing out to X in the short run. But as long as my response is adaptive, in general terms, I may be seen as responding appropriately here in reacting to relatively *immediate* states of affairs, considered in isolation, rather than withholding an emotional response until "all the facts are in." In my last chapter I defended an emotion based on fear as a "snap" reaction to a partial subset of the evidence. Here a similar treatment may be given to an emotion based on anger on the assumption that its reliability as a way of shoring up self-esteem depends on its responsiveness to a temporally limited body of information.

Note that these remarks are put forth in defense of the *emotion* envy, not of action based on it. The destructive element of my envy may be compared with what I might reasonably feel—but should not allow myself to act on, at least directly—after losing a point in a sports match. My appropriate reaction here does not amount merely to self-pity, even of the "smoldering" variety mentioned earlier; it also includes outwardly directed and aroused *frustration*—a form of anger, but without the view that I have been treated unjustly by another agent. If this feeling involves a desire to "lash out" somewhere, it need not focus on the other player. On the other hand, much like X, the other player *is* a convenient target, if only in thought: A few muttered curses, personal in content, would be reasonable enough as an expression of my emotion even though the emotion is itself impersonal. But any momentary urge I might have, say, to throw my racquet—whether or not at her—would be meant as a symbolic act of destruction, aimed at undermining the situation, rather than as a punitive measure, directed at an agent I take to be responsible for gaining an undeserved benefit. Moreover, my feeling here may be generally adaptive as long as its component of desire can "take on" a useful future object—with discomfort redirected towards a negative evaluation of a failure to improve my score, or something else that can still be affected by action. To say this, of course, is to grant that the rational expression of anger demands a fair measure of *control*. But assuming control, the emotion is generally adaptive in a way that self-pity is not—

supposing that both emotions reinforce the agent's identification with his own standpoint but that anger serves a further, "energizing" function, as outlined in Chapter 3.

    The preceding defense of envy considered in isolation made only passing reference to the various *conflicting* emotions that might serve to keep its component of desire in check—or alternatively, might complicate the case for its general adaptiveness. I say "conflicting" emotions rather than "contraries" since some emotions, such as fear of displeasing X, may oppose envy in motivational terms without exhibiting opposite content. But a genuinely contrary emotion might be used to set up a particularly hard case for the rationality of *ambivalent* envy, as we shall see. First, though, we need to work on picking out a contrary of envy; for the task is complicated by our analysis of the emotion as a subtype of anger and hence as essentially involving desire. It is easy enough to construct a contrary for envy taken as directed just towards X's possession of a certain benefit that I lack, analyzed as discomfort at a negative evaluation of the situation of comparison. We need only substitute comfort for discomfort and a positive for the negative evaluation in accordance with the simple notion of emotional contrariety that was used to limit our focus of attention as the present chapter began. But while that notion may of course be applied to cases essentially involving desire—assuming that the desire in question is based at least on an evaluation of some propositional (external) object of emotion—the notion leaves room for more than one contrary in such cases.

    In the case of my envy of the uncritical enthusiasm that makes X a better humanities teacher, what should we take as the contrary of the motivating desire based on my negative evaluation of the situation of comparison? On my view of frustration-envy, this desire amounts to discomfort at the thought that I ought to act to undermine the situation in some way—or, let us say, at a negative evaluation of my failure so far to act to undermine it. Constructing a contrary as we did earlier would seem to yield comfort at a positive evaluation of my inaction. Taken as based on a positive evaluation of the situation, this may be thought of as *one* contrary of envy, amounting to a kind of passive satisfaction at letting the situation stand. On the assumption, however, that I feel as though some action on my part is needed to *sustain* the situation, this would naturally give rise to a contrary *desire*, understood as discomfort at a negative evaluation of my failure to act in the way required. The result may be taken as an active contrary of envy, similar in structure to attachment-love, on my account in Chapter 3, as involving a desire for closeness based on comfort at a positive evaluation of the love-object. But as a contrary of an emotion based on *anger*, the desire in question here might best be interpreted as amounting to a variant of *gratitude*.

Personal gratitude of the usual sort is naturally taken as a contrary of *personal* anger since it involves a desire to benefit an object viewed as responsible for some benefit to oneself. With a propositional object, though—the situation of comparison—it might yield a contrary of *impersonal* anger and hence of the desire component of frustration-envy. Let us now see how we can extract this, along with a particularly problematic case of envy, from the hardest case in my preceding subsection: a "dog in the manger" case in which I actually benefit from the inequality that provokes my envy. We might now suppose that X's uncritical enthusiasm, besides being something I do not want myself, is something I benefit from *his* having—even in the short run and in a way that he is at least partly responsible for, though on our assumption he is not responsible simply for having the trait. X helps me, say, by reading my papers with the same enthusiasm; and on the whole I value my scholarly reputation above my reputation as a teacher. So my envy here is outweighed by gratitude to X for his *use* of the trait I envy. If we stretch the language a bit, moreover, I might be said to be *impersonally* grateful for the very situation in which X possesses that trait and I do not. Perhaps I think that the worth of my papers depends in the first instance on not waxing too enthusiastic about them myself. Here we seem to have impersonal envy and gratitude directed towards the same situation of comparison.

What I envy here, however, is X's possession of a trait that advances my own relatively *immediate* interests, a trait that I want only in the way that I want *everything*—or everything that anyone can have, whether or not one person can have all of it. In the sense allowed for by ambivalence, "wanting everything," where having everything is impossible, does not imply wanting the impossible. But there is at least a childish quality to the content of my "mixed feelings" here that throws them into question. My response resembles a child's insistence on keeping an out-of-favor toy, which interests the child only because it might be given away. It involves a kind of indiscriminate greed, first of all; but the objection to it is rational as well as moral: It would be *self-spiting*, not just *spiteful*, for me to act on its component of desire. To the extent that I do *not* act on it, though—or on the contrary desire provided by gratitude—I shall be uncomfortable. So my ambivalent envy may be maladaptive, individually as well as socially, in the particular case at hand. To establish rational appropriateness, though, we need only establish *general* adaptiveness—for the two emotions considered individually, not necessarily the ambivalent pair. Ambivalence may or may not undermine adaptiveness:

Although it rules out the full satisfaction of both desires, with proper control it may improve the agent's overall situation. Here my envy will be tempered with gratitude; and the alternation of the two emotions in thought may be helpful in ensuring that each is allowed to serve its purpose as a feeling without giving rise to action. On the other hand, ambivalence keeps us from explaining my envy here as based on a partial subset of reasons that can always be distinguished in *temporal* terms from those grounding my gratitude. The two emotions are assumed to be directed towards the same object; and my reasons for them, in cases like the present one, may have to be made out as equally short-term. Rather than simply making out cases of envy as involving "snap" evaluations, then, we may introduce a broader notion of "parti-resultant" evaluations for those resting on subsets of the evidence whose selection need not be justified by a need for quick action.

Some such notion, in fact, stood behind my earlier treatment of identificatory evaluations—on the assumption, as outlined in Chapter 3, that morally valuable action on behalf of another, of the sort that is prompted by identification, may be less likely to arise from evaluations from a neutral moral standpoint. One might suggest, indeed, that the combination of identification and ambivalence forces an agent not to lose sight of the fate of individuals, even where a wider view of things determines his choice of action. Emotions may thus function as a useful reminder of the moral importance of the individual standpoint—including, for self-regarding emotions, one's own. In the present case of envy, my emotion may be *generally* adaptive—and hence, on my view, rationally appropriate—as a counterweight to submergence in others' ends. The view of myself as dependent on others' action for the promotion of my own ends, as implied by gratitude, threatens a kind of submergence in X's ends; but envy balances this with a reminder of my independent standpoint. Envy may still be seen, then, as reinforcing my identification with "my own standpoint," despite the fact that the latter in this case embraces only a partial subset of my ends—and one not picked out by reference to time, as in my earlier case of "eventual" benefit.

We can mark off two subsets of my ends here, to reconcile envy with gratitude, by appealing to the distinction between my regard for the judgment of others, as grounds for "parti-resultant" envy, and my instrumental self-regard, as grounds for gratitude. This reference to different reasons, however, is not put forth as a way of effecting a *practical* reconciliation of envy and gratitude: It serves, at most, to support the claim that the conflict can sometimes be rationally appropriate. One of my reasons—regard for the judgment of others for its own sake—may seem to be instrumentally irrational in itself where it blocks the achievement of my ends. But this just means that the conflict is maladaptive in the particular case at hand. There may seem to be a conflict, too, between the reason supporting my envy in this particular case and the reason for thinking it generally adaptive: The former stresses dependence on others; the latter, *independence* of them. But this is not a *logical* conflict, we should note. Besides recognizing the distinction between dependence on others' *judgment* and on others' *ends*, we ought to acknowledge the different roles played by these two reasons in our assessment of the case. The former is one of my actual reasons, as the agent in the case, for feeling envy against my independent interests; the latter, one of "our" reasons, as theorists, for thinking that my emotion in the case is substantially warranted.

Let me end this section and move towards my next with an example indicating how contrary emotions *may* be reconcilable in practical terms, even where they both involve desire. Consider a possible variant of my envy in the present case, built on a kind of impersonal *hatred* rather than anger—a desire to *avoid* the situation of comparison rather than to undermine it. But I *can* avoid it, in the relevant sense, simply by not thinking about it, we may grant. My hatred here may be satisfied, that is, without overt action; and this sort of mental satisfaction need not defeat the point of the contrary emotion. The latter would seem to be a form of *love*, involving a desire for closeness, if only in thought, to the situation of comparison—perhaps because there are other respects in which I think it favors *me*. But an increase in mental distance, of the sort envisioned here, would not seem to make it any harder to achieve the corresponding form of closeness, as long as the two may be limited to different times. If we assume, then, that neither desire requires *constant* closeness or distance—as opposed to closeness or distance at the time when it is felt—they can each be satisfied well enough by alternation in thought. Whether or not the competing desires are themselves genuine contraries, they are based on contrary evaluations of the same object, so they still amount to components of contrary emotions. They conflict in the sense of competing for attention; but with some control, it should be possible to shift attention between the different reasons for them and thus to restrict their manifestations in thought to different times.

(iii) Masochistic Love/Hate

There may be cases, however, where love and hatred give rise to a practical conflict not resolvable by appeal to the possibility of satisfying conflicting desires at different times. Let us now consider a case of personal love/hate ambivalence, involving simultaneous attachment and aversion—a harder variant of the jealousy cases bypassed at the beginning of this chapter. The agent wants both to be close to X and to stay at a distance from him, let us suppose—and apparently not for reasons that allow for separate contemplation. For the very traits that excite her in X are deeply injurious to her self-esteem, and thus a source of hatred.[4] She does not love and hate X just in different respects—with X evaluated differently as a lover and as a companion, say. Rather, she cannot imagine X in *any* personal relation to herself, however close or distant, without discomfort at the thought that she ought to change it. X's off-and-on indifference, perhaps, keeps her on edge in a way that keeps up her interest. And let us suppose that this is the essential focus of her interest—combined, no doubt, with some other excitingly injurious traits that I shall sum up for simplicity's sake as "aloofness."

This case of love/hate ambivalence is of the sort commonly called "masochistic," whether or not it really involves a desire for pain for its own sake. It need not involve "representational" irrationality, however, but simply an unfortunate combination of emotional desires, which may not admit of instrumental rational control. I have artificially streamlined the case—leaving out traits that do not promise both harms and benefits—since I want to use it to test out my defense of contrary emotions as appropriate for different reasons. In this case, love and hatred apparently rest on the *same* reasons and apparently yield contrary desires that can only be maladaptive. For even in thought satisfying one of them amounts to frustrating the other. The agent cannot think of her reasons for loving X without simultaneously thinking of her reasons for hating him, it seems. Indeed, this may turn out to be true even if her reasons can be made out as distinguishable, though overlapping—as I hope eventually to show that they can. I shall argue, however, that both emotions may therefore be appropriate, on a conception of appropriateness that builds in reference to *general* adaptiveness, with the limitations I have outlined.

There is a prior question, however, concerning what it means in a case of this sort to assess attachment-love itself as appropriate or inappropriate.[5] That we do not ordinarily use these terms may be explained by appeal to the value placed on love in cases where it is *not* really warranted. We are naturally reluctant to point out misperceptions of the object that may serve a purpose for the agent—among others—and in any case are considered no one's business. But that does not mean that love is thought to be "blind" by its very nature to questions of warrant. The possibility of inappropriateness *is* occasionally considered; and we sometimes use related expressions—"unfounded" or "deluded," say—for loves that have *some* grounds, but grounds without a basis in "significant perception." *Groundless* love—a desire for closeness to the object without a positive evaluation of his relatively central traits—was marked off in Chapter 3 as a "deficient" case of the emotion. Where it is "un-founded" in *this* sense, the emotion may indeed sometimes be immune to any charge of inappropriateness. But such a case would have to assume that the emotion rests on no grounds whatever—even a positive eval-uation of the object's *non*central traits—to rule out any possibility of "representational" irrationality.

The fact that one does undergo emotional discomfort at the thought that one ought to move closer to a love-object may be criticized for its consequences, but not for its relation to some external body of evidence, where it does not rest on an evaluation of the love-object. On the other hand, it may be encouraged—for its energizing effects on the agent, perhaps—and it may be encouraged to *seek out* an evaluative basis, of a sort that would make it subject to rational criticism while perhaps also making it more useful. But if it is nothing but a groundless desire, its rational appropriateness does not come into question where it does not conflict with the agent's other desires. It might be shown to rest on some delusion about *itself*—about what it would take to *relieve* its component of discomfort—but that would seem to cast doubt on its genuineness rather than on its appropriateness as an instance of groundless *love*. "Deluded" love, by contrast, is unfounded in another sense: It does claim to be based on a positive evaluation of the love-object, of a sort that may be rationally undermined—at least in principle—but without necessarily undermining the emotion. A standard example would be love of someone for impressive qualities—kindness, courage, and other moral virtues, say—that any (other) fool could see that he lacks.

What about a case, though, where the love-object does possess the traits one loves him for but where these are so overshadowed by negative traits that others would consider them noncentral? The agent loves X for his kindness *to her*, say, and manages to block out his despicable treatment of others. This does seem to involve an element of delusion; and the agent's love of X may depend on it. But I do not think we should count her emotion here as inappropriate as long as it does not depend on a misapprehension of X-in-relation-to-others but at most on a failure of apprehension. To the extent that it is a willful failure, with potentially negative *moral* consequences, it may of course be criticizable in other ways. For that matter, if an "all things considered" judgment of X were in question, it would be criticizable as unwarranted. But that is not to say that the corresponding *evaluation* is unwarranted in the terms ap-plicable to emotion. For a case like this one begins to exhibit what I take to be the kernel of truth in the "love is blind" rejection of the possibility of inappropriate love, even in cases where its characteristic desire rests on a personal evaluation. My own view does allow for inappropriate cases, but its standard of appropriateness is extremely generous.

If it *is* just attachment-love that is at issue in the present case—and not personal *admiration* of X, say—then X's "central" traits will include any that are central to his character as manifested in relation to the agent. Love of X will count as appropriate in my terms as long as there is substantial warrant for a positive evaluation supporting the agent's desire for closeness to X. Relational traits—X's irreplaceable kindness to her and so forth—will be sufficient for the purpose, as supplemented by a general social value placed on *bonding*. Someone might try to talk her out of her love for X, of course, by getting her to see how he behaves in general. But his remarks should be interpreted as urging her to adopt a *contrary* desire—to dissociate herself, physically as well as mentally, from someone so vicious towards others—and to resolve the consequent maladaptive conflict in its favor. I take this, in short, to be a case where love and hatred may both be appropriate for different reasons, reasons whose significance is assessed in accordance with different conceptions of the general adaptiveness of the emotions based on them. As with our initial case of identificatory joy versus self-regarding sorrow, the two emotions may be distinguished *both* by their straightforward appeal to reasons *and* by their implicit appeal to standards of significance. Here we have two standards of significance, embodying two sorts of reference to general adaptiveness: to the value of forming bonds without too much overall assessment of a person and to the *dis*value of forming bonds that might very well discredit oneself and reward the undeserving.

I indicated briefly as I began this discussion that there are some cases where love will *not* be appropriate, since it does not rest on "substantial" evidence—rather than resting, as it does in the present case, on a substantial subset of the total body of evidence that is undercut by other subsets. The evidence in question here is assumed to be evidence for a positive evaluation of the object that is reasonably seen as central. As with personal anger, that is, love that is grounded in a personal evaluation must, if it is appropriate, involve warrant for a judgment of responsibility, in this case one that makes out the traits in question as positive traits *of* the object, important to an assessment of him in relation to the agent. But the insistence on centrality does not rule out all forms of *triviality*—*un*importance, in another sense—and all ways of rejecting the grounds for love as "insubstantial," even though not deluded.

One might suppose that the value we place on bonding is so high that evidence for *any* central-but-trivial positive evaluation of the love-object would yield substantial warrant for attachment-love. In fact, I think this is very nearly true. We would not dismiss an instance of the emotion as inappropriate if it were actually thought to permit bonding, even on the basis of the agent's peculiar tastes—for traits whose only value, say, consists in their ability to excite her interest. We would accept her love of X for his air of nonchalance, say—a trivial trait in itself, let us grant, but one that may be central to his nature—as long as the agent's evaluation of it did give rise to a desire for closeness. Our tolerance here may rest on a view that the emotion tends to *find* less trivial grounds as the agent achieves greater closeness; but if this general expectation is not borne out in the particular case at hand, that would not make us less tolerant.

We might dismiss as inappropriate, however, a love that is and can be based only on traits of trivial value *to* the agent *over time*. The traits excite her interest, say, but are trivial in themselves; and they block the satisfaction of her interest—along with its tendency to discover less trivial traits of the object—in a way that is nonaccidental. Here we seem to have a barrier to *general* adaptiveness—and hence to appropriateness, in our terms. The evidence for the agent's positive evaluation of the object, that is, would seem to be incapable of supplementation by further information indicating a tendency to yield comfort at close enough range to permit bonding. In fact, this might be thought to apply to the positive side of our case of masochistic love/hate, where the agent loves X just in response to his aloofness. By its very nature, that is, the trait would seem to block the sort of psychological closeness that love ultimately seeks. As a focus of attention, moreover, it would seem to resist supplementation by traits that do encourage psychological closeness. So a love that is based on it could never achieve its aim, one might say, without first abandoning its basis.

I think the "masochistic" case can survive this argument to inappropriate love. But assuming that the argument has *some* merit, our defense of the case must rest on distinguishing grounds for the agent's positive and negative evaluations of aloofness—and on recognizing different possible versions of the case. First let us put the argument into more general perspective. I make out "full-fledged" attachment-love, remember, as involving a certain configuration of internal objects: a positive evaluation of the love-object, a positive evaluation of closeness to the object, and a negative evaluation of failure to act in a way that is needed to end a distance. The negative evaluation, as an object of discomfort, is taken as yielding the desire that is characteristic of the emotion; and "comfort" at the two positive evaluations is taken as including arousal or excitation to the extent that this is pleasurable. But I need not claim that for the emotion to be felt all of love's internal objects must come into play as objects of comfort or discomfort at a given time. In particular, love can be love, on my view, in a case where the agent feels only discomfort. Perhaps we can also accept another sort of "deficient" case, however, where the agent *never* feels comfort at closeness—and never can, even in thought. This sort of love would seem to yield a higher standard of appropriateness, however—requiring nontrivial grounds for admiration, say—to justify the agent's discomfort; for it could not be defended as generally adaptive by reference to the social value of bonding.

On the other hand, love is typically seen as pleasurable for the agent, whatever the external barriers to satisfying its component of desire; so we will accept rather slim grounds for it in many cases where it is maladaptive in context. Thus, even if the agent's reason for loving X amounts to something trivial in itself—his nonchalance, say—it may still yield nontrivial benefits, in general terms, as an affective spur towards bonding, whether or not bonding is achievable in the case at hand. Only rarely, then, will appropriate love be expected to rest on grounds adequate for admiration: In the first instance, the emotion is encouraged simply for its pleasurable aspect for the agent. Hatred, by contrast, is *dis*couraged, partly for its *un*pleasant aspect for the *object*; so the standards for judging its appropriateness are typically higher. Its grounds must also be adequate to justify some discomfort for the agent; so the disvalue the grounds attribute to the object cannot consist merely in his tendency to give rise to that feeling—for another disanalogy with love. The traits the agent evaluates may still be relational and indeed may make reference to unpleasant feelings other than hatred. An agent may hate X appropriately, say, because of his cruelty towards her, taken as a tendency to hurt her feelings. But any such traits must be nontrivial, in a sense that rules out reference to an *idiosyncratic* response. The agent cannot *hate X* appropriately, for instance, just because of his air of nonchalance, even if she happens to respond to it with feelings of discomfort.

Now let us consider the case of "masochistic" conflict, where the agent loves *and* hates X because of his aloofness. How could this amount to an appropriate case of *both* emotions, viewed as genuine contraries? It is tempting to think of hatred, here, if it *is* appropriate in combination with love, as something less than full-fledged hatred of X: hatred of the situation of closeness to X, perhaps; or off-and-on anger towards X; or distaste for some of X's traits. But what we want is a case where full-fledged versions of both emotions are grounded in substantially warranted evaluations of traits that are not only central to X's personality, but also *nontrivial*, in terms of both value and disvalue, both viewed partly in relation to the agent. Love and hatred for the same traits would not seem to permit any gestalt shifts with regard to centrality. But what about the nontrivial value assigned to the traits in question? On the assumption that the traits grounding the agent's love make satisfaction of the desire for closeness impossible, both their value and their disvalue must be made out as nontrivial independently of her emotional response to them.

Alternatively, however, we might assume that the traits just make satisfaction of the desire unpleasant for the agent, to the extent that they give rise to hatred as well as love, and perhaps in greater degree, at close range. In that case, we may rely on "further information" about the affective benefits of the agent's love—and of her love considered in isolation but in light of the general value placed on bonding—even though those benefits are undercut by her hatred, in the particular case at hand. This second alternative involves rejecting an assumption of the preceding argument that the closeness love seeks must be ruled out by aloofness. It might be argued that some forms of love can be adequately satisfied by closeness in the sense of *favor*—in this case, say, by some sign of attention, probably rather slight, but with pleasurable effects augmented just because they are so hard to achieve. I insisted on a full-fledged case of both love and hatred, though; and this one might be thought to be deficient in a way I have not considered. Since the first alternative is at any rate the more demanding, I shall attempt to show how aloofness might be accorded nontrivial value and disvalue, *without* relying solely on its emotional effects on the agent.

We can sketch the requisite sort of gestalt shift, in this case, by bringing in the agent's reasons for attributing value or disvalue to X's aloofness. It *is* relevant that the trait glues her attention to him; but we need to take this as based on more than a masochistic streak in her nature. The trait also provokes a kind of admiration for X's impressive *unmanageability*, let us say—admiration of a general sort but not of the sort that is content to stay at a worshipful distance. For the excitement it generates depends on the agent's craving attention from X. She craves X's attention, say, partly *because of* the value she places on its independence of others' desires. But X's aloofness can also be seen as involving a kind of *cruelty*. She also wishes to be free of X, then, and appropriately so; for his off-and-on indifference is a source of serious harms to her, which he neither regrets nor tries to moderate—though he ought to do both in view of her history of attachment. We might say, then, that she evaluates X's aloofness differently, depending on whether she takes it as a generally admirable trait, one that makes his occasional attention count as a special *gift*, or rather as a denial of something that he *owes* her.

So love and hatred may sometimes both be appropriate—"for the same reasons," if that means "because of the same traits." But a full explanation of "the" reasons for two contrary emotions—what might be regarded as a *complete set* of reasons for each of them—must exhibit divergence at some point if both are to count as appropriate. This point of explanatory divergence is assumed to be *extrinsic* to the emotions in question, let us note. It is not enough that their initial reasons are built into different emotion components: those opposite evaluations of the same traits on which their components of desire are based, as in the present example. To show why the evaluations are both appropriate, the appeal to different reasons must reach further—sometimes even to different standards of significance. With the latter interpreted as reasons of another sort, we might now attempt to capture the very notion of emotional contrareity by appeal to different reasons. It seems that contrary emotions *are* just those whose defense as jointly appropriate, with the same external object, always requires reference to some difference in the reasons for them, beyond what is given in their internal objects.[6] Earlier I relied on a simpler characterization of contrary emotions, in terms of contrary propositions—with the latter understood, in the usual fashion, as propositions that cannot both be true—on the basis of my analysis of emotions in Part I. Granting, as I have throughout this essay, that positive or negative emotional affect is directed towards the corresponding sort of evaluation, contrary emotions may be taken as involving opposite affective components directed towards contrary evaluative propositions.

My treatment of the "masochistic" love/hate case might suggest, though, that contrary emotions involving necessarily unsatisfiable desires would require the more complex criterion. This rests on the assumption that some such cases may involve no element of comfort directed towards a positive evaluative basis for desire and hence no affective opposition. But any such cases will have to count as affectively deficient variants of the case I have discussed. For full-fledged cases of personal love we should have some comfort, if only in fantasy, directed towards a positive evaluation of the object. Indeed, as my earlier discussion of the contraries of impersonal envy should indicate, this also applies to deficient cases of the ordinary, evaluative sort—amounting, for love, to cases that rest on a noncentral evaluation of the object. At the very least, we would normally have some element of comfort at the thought of closeness to the object. However, where the desire for closeness is necessarily unsatisfiable, even in thought—just because closeness undercuts the reasons for one's positive evaluation of the object—a case of love may consist in pure *desire*, without any element of comfort.

Could the same be true of the contrary emotion, in some cases? Hatred would seem to involve at least an element of comfort at achieving an adequate distance from the object. But what if no distance *can* be adequate and still give rise to the comfort in question here? We might suppose, for instance, that the agent's negative evaluation of the object— as a basis for the desire for distance and thus for any comfort at achieving it—can be held in mind *only* at times when she is still "too close for comfort." Satisfaction of the desire would require not thinking of the object, that is—and hence would rule out comfort at a thought involving him. All we would seem to have, in such a case, is a conflict of desires. Both emotions would always and only be manifested in *discomfort*—at the thought that the agent ought to move closer to X and at the thought that she ought to move farther away. Unless we insist on unconscious objects of comfort, then—a move I would resist, without special evidence, for the reasons explained in Chapter 2—such cases would not seem to fit my simpler characterization of emotional contraries. One might be tempted to deny that such cases involve emotions; but according to my analysis, they involve particularly deficient cases of love and hatred, amounting to emotional *desires*.

To be sure, however, there may be cases superficially similar to this one but involving affect directed towards an unconscious evaluative component—one that is masked by another with greater apparent claim to appropriateness but without apparent affect. On a standard sort of view, the original affect, with its object, may be so painful that it is displaced onto a contrary evaluation or perhaps one that is linked to a contrary desire. I now am in a position to insert a brief word in defense of some of the more questionable psychoanalytic claims sometimes made about cases of this sort, where ambivalence is inappropriate since the reasons for it do not bear conscious scrutiny. We might suppose, for instance, that the agent's masochistic love for X is not really grounded in a value she places on unmanageability or the like. Rather, it seems to be a product of some earlier insecure attachment—to a rejecting parent, say, or some other object of infantile dependency in combination with fear. Perhaps a review of past love-objects indicates that her positive evaluation of aloofness vanishes in cases where closeness is somehow achieved.

Can we conclude, though, that her current love of X masks *occurrent* fear of an object she no longer has reason to fear—perhaps one that no longer exists—while retaining the assumption of basic rationality? In my main case of unconscious emotion, the jealousy case in Chapter 2, the agent was taken to be motivated by a *reasonable* fear, one that was rejected on something like moral grounds. But my treatment of long-term and fantasy-fears should allow for the unreasonable retention of a childhood fear, as in this case. To make out the agent as basically rational, we must just suppose that the original fear and its fusion with feelings of dependency were reasonable enough *as* childhood responses. For the tendency of emotions to persist beyond the occasions provoking them, sometimes by seeking out *new* objects, need not involve shedding their original objects. The latter, once masked, will no longer be subject to conscious scrutiny, as modified by the agent's rational development. So the agent's masochistic love/hate relationship may be inappropriate as well as maladaptive even on the assumption of basic rationality, where the real reasons for her two emotions fail to support both of them in present terms.

6
Justifying Emotion:
What One Ought to Feel

The case of masochistic love/hate based on unconscious fantasy, as discussed at the end of my last Chapter, should serve as a rather extreme illustration of the possibility of emotion that comes out as inappropriate, though understandable, on the generous notion of appropriateness I have defended. This is important because the notion has to have enough content to support an answer to both of the questions of emotional justification that were outlined in my introductory chapter. The first question concerned appropriateness itself; the second, the role of emotions as reasons for action, *assuming* appropriateness. In this chapter I want to address the second question and to draw some conclusions about what might be thought of as a second-level, or "forward-looking," justification of emotions, one that appeals to the role of appropriate emotions as spurs towards future action. If emotions can be shown to function as *reasons* for action—supplementing the reasons provided by dispassionate judgment, in the way sketched in Chapter 3—my argument in this essay may be taken as questioning the familiar dichotomy between emotion and reason. First, though, I need to demonstrate that the notion of appropriateness on which my argument depends can be made to support an intuitively acceptable treatment of cases.

I shall begin, then, by attempting to handle some questions about appropriate versus understandable emotions (i). For even as restricted to the evaluative component of emotion, my notion of appropriateness will apply to different—sometimes conflicting—responses, assessed according to different standards of "significant perception," as we have seen. The range of rationally acceptable responses also turned out to be wide when degrees of affect were considered—with reference only to their representational "fitness" to significant perception but on an interpretation that allowed for variable measures of fitness. Here I want to go on to argue that the *absence* of affect is also rationally acceptable—until one brings in instrumental value, or adaptiveness in the particular case at hand, as distinct from the general sort of adaptiveness that underlies appropriateness, on my view (ii). In an attempt to spell out what adaptiveness in the particular case amounts to, I shall offer a simple model of practical reasoning from emotion, showing how its component of affect may serve to reinforce the corresponding judgment. My argument here will lead me to take a closer look at the role of emotions in providing "pressure" towards action and to distinguish this motivational role from other ways in which they may function as reasons— most notably for *expressive* action (iii). Eventually, then, my complex argument in this chapter will focus on the question of the justification of action by emotion, a unifying theme of this essay as a whole. But it will approach that question by posing it in reverse and exhibiting the need for an answer in this form.

As my immediate aim in this chapter, that is, I shall argue that the claim that an emotion is appropriate, though it does give a first-level rational justification for feeling it, does not imply that one *ought* to feel it purely on rational grounds. This holds whether or not there is adequate warrant for the corresponding belief. Where an agent does have sufficient evidence for assenting to the evaluative component of emotion, he still may not have compelling reason for holding it in mind and for holding it in mind by making it the object of some degree of affect. But my argument applies with particular force to cases where belief is *not* adequately warranted; so its crucial final stage, concerning the motivational importance of appropriate emotions, will complete my rebuttal of the common view of emotions as at best mere concomitants of belief. On this view, emotions may be seen as understandable in light of our animal history but of no independent rational value in developed human motivation—as excused rather than justified, in short. The view seems most plausible if one focuses on extreme cases of emotional arousal— agitated states like terror—of a sort that are rarely very helpful in civilized practical life. Terror may sometimes make one run faster; but that is not always the best response in cases where fear is appropriate. Even where it is, moreover, the cool acknowledgment of present danger has less chance of producing a confused and counterproductive response. To pave the way for an alternative view, I have insisted that we recognize the wider range of affective states that can reasonably count as "occurrent" emotions—and as adequately warranted in many cases where belief is not.

Although my argument here will both depend on and strengthen the contrast between emotion and belief, we should note that its immediate point, about what one ought to feel, is not directly *about* that contrast. If the point is expressed as a claim that second-level emotional justification demands "more specific" reference to adaptiveness, the intended contrast is to first-level justification, or appropriateness, with its underlying reference to *general* adaptiveness. My argument will not presuppose a view about the adoption of beliefs on similar instrumental grounds. But it will assume that strictly *logical* requirements impose constraints on the representational function of beliefs that do not apply to emotions. Feelings as such need not be consistent with each other; nor does the notion have any clear meaning for the compound of affect and evaluation, except in a sense I have allowed for by assuming that positive or negative affect is directed towards an evaluation whose value corresponds. There is no set of premises, in short, that forces one for consistency's sake to draw an emotional conclusion; but affect brings with it important constraints on action, as we shall see.

(i) Appropriate Versus Understandable Emotions

At this point, let us turn back to the contrast between emotion and belief that was drawn in terms of first-level justification, or warrant. There are dangers in my weaker notion of appropriate emotion; and I want to confront them in some detail before proceeding further. Whatever the limitations on appropriateness as a justificatory category, we must keep it from applying to any and every understandable evaluative thought. It was stretched to cover quite a number of questionable cases in my last chapter, often on the assumption that their affective elements were controlled or minimal. But disproportionate affect is not the only, or even the central, issue here. I now want to show that we can distinguish appropriate from merely understandable emotions—rationally acceptable only in the sense of excusable—in a way that cuts across differences in warranted affective strength. My defense of the distinction will bring together a number of the cases introduced in my discussion up to this point, with complexities illustrating the variability tolerated by the notion of "fitness to significant perception."

At the end of Chapter 4 I attempted to pin down that notion somewhat with a nonquantitative criterion of appropriateness—but only, at that point, on the basis of some cases of fearful suspicion, which now need to be reviewed in light of my discussion of rational ambivalence. My criterion required that the perceptual evidence for an appropriate emotion would yield substantial warrant for the evaluative component if it were supplemented by further information, including appeal to considerations of general adaptiveness. But the latter were assumed to apply to the evidence at hand. The "snap" evaluation of a broker as untrustworthy just because of one bad experience with a broker was *not* thought to be warranted in the situation requiring protection of the agent's financial interests, even supposing that further evidence would in fact bear it out. So I did recognize at least one case of inappropriate suspicion, moderate in affective strength, that might be thought to be understandable in light of the agent's history. Prima facie evidence of the tendency to deceive was lent substantial *psychological* weight by his past experience. But the resultant emotion was treated as a "spillover" case—involving the association of an evaluation to perceptual cues of insubstantial *rational* weight—on the model of the Fido case in Chapter 2. However, somewhat weightier evidence was thought to warrant suspicion in other cases, including cases where the agent was in no position to assess the weight of the evidence and even where he knew of evidence that undercut it. The same reference to general adaptiveness did seem sufficient here to license a jump in emotional terms beyond adequately warranted belief. In one case, indeed—the case of the "hard sell" broker—it was thought to yield substantial warrant for an evaluation that further evidence would decisively disconfirm.

At some stages in the (possible) gathering of evidence, then, the practical value also assigned to a contrary emotion, hopeful *trust*, might have been taken to warrant *ambivalence*. But this would not seem to hold for a similar case where disconfirming evidence was already at hand. So here the suspicion cases seem to part company from my cases of rational ambivalence in Chapter 5. Where the weight assigned to a particular subset of the total body of evidence was determined by a need for quick decision-making in self-interest, it was held to depend on limitations in the amount of evidence available to the agent. By contrast, the perception of another's end as my own was thought to be sufficient to warrant joy on his behalf, even *in the face of* decisive evidence that my ends would in fact be frustrated by his achievement. Its weight—and the full weight of the evidence for the contrary emotion, sorrow—rested on appeal to a general social value placed on registering different standpoints of evaluation. But this introduction of multiple standards for assessing the evidence in favor of emotion complicates the notion of substantial warrant—and with it the distinction between appropriate and merely understandable emotions.

In the "hard sell" broker case, we might suppose that further acquaintance over an extended period makes it clear that the broker is perfectly trustworthy, reliable even when he does adopt an overeager approach. Yet later, when he does, the agent's feelings of suspicion recur, prompted by association to other situations but directed (at least momentarily) towards the situation at hand. This amounts to another spillover case, based on a habit of linking the emotion to a partial subset of the evidence. A particular subset still stands out against the overall background because of its significance in situations of limited information—as this one no longer is. The persistence of suspicion is understandable here not because of some peculiar feature of the agent's history or psychological make-up but because of its appropriateness in a more common sort of situation in which it is generally adaptive. The agent's perceptual cues still yield prima facie evidence of untrustworthiness—as they did even in the idiosyncratic spillover case—but the weight of that evidence is now insubstantial relative to the total body of *available* evidence. A "parti-resultant" evaluation is not warranted, in short, where forming one *on* the evidence at hand would not be generally adaptive.

By contrast, in the cases of ambivalence compatible with full information, we were dealing with "parti-resultant" evaluations whose limited evidential basis was not determined by the amount of evidence available at a given time. Different subsets of the total body of evidence thus continued to stand out as significant relative to different standpoints of evaluation, both at least arguably worth adopting at the *same* time. The weight of the evidence for emotion did not depend solely on its importance to the agent's protection of his immediate interests—or on any *single* standard of assessment—so it did not depend on the current availability of counterevidence. There is a fine line, however, between appropriateness and understandable spillover, in such cases; for they were defended by reference to general utilitarian considerations that might be pushed too far, especially in justifying a personal evaluation. I now want to see how my account may be made to handle cases of personal *hatred*, where we would naturally impose a particularly high standard on evidence for appropriateness.

"Parti-Resultant" Hatred. First let us pause for some further review and expansion of related cases. My notion of "deficient" anger, as introduced in Chapter 3, allowed for an impersonal variety of envy that was defended as appropriate in Chapter 5, where my account was briefly extended to impersonal hatred. This involved hatred of the *situation*— of the situation of comparison with a friend, for instance, balanced by simultaneous identification with him and justified by its reinforcement of the agent's standpoint of self-regard. *How much* the latter should be taken to justify is a matter of judgment, though. We need to rely on rough impressions to determine just what qualifying factors an agent can be expected to incorporate into his emotional evaluations—and just how important it is that he hold in mind some such evaluation, even at the cost of leaving out qualifications. I accepted as appropriate, for instance, a case of frustration-envy in the face of a warranted belief that the friend's achievement would ultimately result in a situation of comparison favoring oneself. In view of some of the functions of emotional evaluations, it seems reasonable enough to focus attention on the current situation, reacting to it without considering its more remote effects.

On the other hand, I did not accept as appropriate cases of personal envy where the agent's negative feelings focus on the friendly rival himself. One might also "feel as though" the friend were *at fault* for the situation of comparison, that is, even in the knowledge that he is not. We may count such cases as understandable spillovers, on a view of impersonal anger as another self-regarding option in them—though one that is often harder for the agent, since it requires a higher measure of control. Because of its very "deficiency," in my terms, we can see why it might sometimes come to focus on a person as a more satisfying target of the urge to attack. But under normal circumstances, presumably, an agent can be expected to avoid this and still achieve the reinforcement of self-regard that makes envy generally adaptive. The distinction between appropriate and merely understandable emotions thus can turn on *how* "unmalleable" a given emotion is—the degree to which it resists qualification, in contrast to belief. In cases of personal hatred based on envy, what is in question is the ability of the agent to restrict the emotion to a broader evaluative focus, with the situation as its (external) object. But in other cases, the alternative to personal hatred is a variant of the emotion with a narrower focus—on some of the object's traits, say, as opposed to the object himself.

To decide whether hatred is appropriate, in such cases, we must make some contextual assumptions—for instance, about the surrounding relationship between agent and object that is potentially a factor in determining the significance of some pieces of perceptual evidence. To illustrate some possible variations, let us now alter our previous assumptions about love/hate ambivalence, in Chapter 5, and suppose we are dealing with a case of long-standing attachment-love, so far relatively unalloyed. A reason normally thought sufficient to justify hatred—of one's former broker, for instance—might not be thought to do so in the context of historical attachment. This is not just to say that the feeling involved in personal love makes personal hatred—for some injury to one's financial interests, say—less *likely*. Indeed, it may sometimes be *more* likely, at least if short-term hatred is accepted as a possibility. Anger may quite readily spill over onto one's view of a person's relatively central traits, where the latter are already objects of attention since the person in question is a love-object.

However, while the feelings associated with love make momentary hatred understandable in such cases, the surrounding history of attachment may make it inappropriate. To the extent that hatred, like love, may be based on an historical evaluation of its object—if only because it may be based on something he has done—it involves at least an implicit claim of historical significance. Long, largely positive interaction may make the current evidence for a negative evaluation insignificant relative to the overall background of available evidence, even though a "snap" reaction is not in question here. But some grounds for anger—a single but serious betrayal, say—may be thought important enough in themselves to stand out against the background, justifying at least short-term hatred, even where there are weightier grounds for love. So there may be some cases of appropriate love/hate ambivalence that are neither "masochistic" nor instrumentally irrational—supposing that hatred sometimes is needed to balance a tendency towards submergence in another agent's ends.

Hatred might be thought to be so "all-out" an emotion, though, that it always ought to reflect the *total* body of evidence.[1] I think we have to allow, however, for at least some cases of appropriate hatred in response to just a few pieces of information. The point will be most easily seen for cases that do not involve a background of available evidence weighted towards the contrary emotion; but it can be applied to such cases as well. It seems clear, for instance, that hatred would be justified, in "backward-looking" rational terms, if felt towards someone solely because of his vicious racism. It may be *morally* preferable to limit oneself to some less condemnatory emotion—especially if there is reason to think that the object of hatred is not bad in every way or without qualification. But this is not the same as what is at issue in considering the appropriateness of the emotion, on the view that can be drawn from my discussion of other "morally significant" emotions in Chapters 3 and 5.

There are some emotions whose very concepts are refined to build in normative constraints, as we saw in Chapter 3; and their rational appropriateness may depend on the general *social* value of their reflection of a certain evaluative standpoint. But particularly in deficient or tamped-down form or in combination with their contraries, they may be appropriate even in cases where their moral worth might be disputed. Personal hatred, like anger and envy, is an unpleasant emotion for its object, among others, even where its affective component is not all that intense or enduring—though more so, of course, where it is. Like the corresponding sort of love, moreover, personal hatred properly rests on a relatively central evaluation of its object. The result is a high standard of evidence for full-fledged instances of the emotion; but it is not an impossible standard. Surely racism is a trait of enough significance to justify a personal focus for hatred, where it does amount to a central trait of the object, so that he is at least causally responsible for it. It might be possible for the agent to limit himself to hatred of the trait, say, while declining to evaluate the person who exhibits it—or declining to avoid him, acting only mentally, perhaps, on the desire for distance that is essential to hatred. But the general adaptiveness, and hence the appropriateness, of the emotion here depends on its role in discouraging the trait in question; and it would be undercut if accomplished without distancing oneself, if only symbolically, from its bearer. In cases where there are strong reasons for qualifying the negative evaluation of the racist, a kind of external qualification, through ambivalence, would provide a more manageable alternative to hatred focused only on the hateful traits in question.

The preceding discussion suggests that at least some forms of love/ hate ambivalence may be rationally appropriate, whatever the moral status of hatred considered in itself. They may be morally valuable, for that matter—most clearly in cases where hatred is based on identification with a third party, as in the case of offense that was introduced in Chapter 3. Hatred on behalf of the target of the insult may be socially adaptive in general terms as a spur towards social exclusion of the racist. But we now need to consider some more basic questions raised by the inclusion of *identificatory* emotions as appropriate—as rationally warranted even by a subset of the total body of evidence. The "evidence" here was made out, in Chapter 5, in terms of an act of perception: taking the ends of another as one's own. We need to recognize constraints, however, on the imaginative generation of appropriate emotions, if we are to accept some cases of fantasy-emotion as appropriate without accepting all.

In my treatment of cases of identification with others in real life, the agent was assumed to receive at least some distant *external* perceptual input—from sense-experience or perhaps just from third-party accounts of others' experiences. As extended by an imaginative perceptual act, this was taken as yielding substantial warrant for an identificatory evaluation when supplemented by further information about the general value of the resulting emotion. But a similar treatment would seem to apply to emotions with *fictional* objects, if we count fictional representations as pieces of perceptual evidence—slight in themselves, but supplemented here, perhaps, by information about the general adaptiveness of the *experience* of identification. The value of the experience may be moral as well as nonmoral: The usual appeal to catharsis and the like may be reinforced by appeal to the development of the capacity for identification in real life, particularly as extended to a circle beyond one's friends. Thus, for instance, hatred of Simon Legree might be seen as appropriate, just in so far as it has a kind of textual justification that would not apply to emotions based on misreadings.

A more complex conclusion, though, is suggested by our treatment of emotions based on fantasy alone—on purely imaginary constructions of the agent, rather than perceptual input from fictional representations. Common psychiatric parlance in reference to amusement—with "inappropriate laughter" for laughter not prompted by the external situation—might suggest that we should rule out all of these, at least on the assumption that they are maladaptive in the particular case at hand. But amusement at one's own thoughts, if one's thoughts are genuinely funny, would seem to be *rationally* appropriate even where one fails to communicate them to others—and where they exhibit a detachment from social surroundings that may be maladaptive. Perhaps a persistent habit of unexplained amusement is here assumed to involve amusement with no intelligible object; or perhaps a different (social) norm of appropriateness has come into play. Otherwise, we would have to rule out, as rationally *in*appropriate, identificatory emotions experienced by the creator of fictional objects before he actually puts them into publicly perceptible form. But this would sit oddly with an acceptance of such emotions as appropriate once the job of creation is complete.

Suppose I make up my own private horror film scenario, dwelling on some rather unlikely fates that might befall me—particularly fiendish forms of execution, say—with no intention of writing them up for others and in fact no benefit to myself. In this case, let us grant, the pleasure of objectless feelings is outweighed by their transformation into object-directed discomfort, and I derive no later or higher-order comfort from the recognition that my scenario *is* just a fantasy. But an emotional response of some sort or other may still be adequately warranted simply by the material, it seems, without reference to its adaptive value. Much depends on the nature of the emotion in question—on its strength, of course, but more fundamentally, on its internal object, and hence on what sort of emotion it amounts to. Supposing that it does amount to one of the varieties of fear, there is still a question whether it involves fear *for myself*—for myself in real life, that is, as distinct from some imaginary character in my fantasy. In reaction to my own imagined horrors, if I felt the usual sort of self-involved fear—discomfort at the thought that some such injury is likely to befall *me*—my reaction would seem to be inappropriate. What matters here is the detailed content of my emotion, not just whether it involves discomfort at a fear-evaluation. For my fear might be appropriate if it amounted instead to fearful *revulsion*, directed towards the very thought of such horrors—or the thought of their applying to an acknowledged fantasy persona.

We might add, then, to the list of things covered by "perception," in my extended sense here, "imagination *recognized as such*." And we might insist that the recognition of the imaginary status of an external object of emotion be preserved within a full statement of its appropriate content. This requirement will not pose a problem for some self-induced fantasy-emotions, such as amusement at an envisioned possibility. But it will rule out any that are directed towards something seen as real—if only the agent himself, as a secondary external object of some emotions—

in a way that extends to responses to fictional representations. The acceptance of real-life identificatory emotions as appropriate, *without* a similar limitation, will depend on the further information concerning practical adaptiveness that is available to supplement their basis in external perception. In such cases, the agent is assumed to have evidence adequate to establish the existence of another subject of experience, whose ends are then taken to bear on his own by a kind of self-warranting act of imagination, in the way sketched in Chapter 5. By contrast, in fictional and self-induced fantasy cases, the agent's adoption of a new set of ends would not have the same tendency to give rise to socially adaptive action, where the ends lack an independent bearer. Such instrumental value as these fantasy-emotions have would seem to be largely a matter of the agent's *experience*—and to be sufficiently well served, in general terms, by an emotion that recognizes their imaginary status.

My way of distinguishing cases here may have some odd results; but I think they can be swallowed with a bit of further explanation in terms of general adaptiveness. Consider, for instance, my cluster of cases of fantasy-*pride*, in Chapter 3. If genuine pride must be self-involved, the cases will come out as inappropriate, except where they involve identification with an actual person. In the first-person case, where imagining impossible gymnastic feats gives rise to a feeling of pride on my part, my feeling was made out as having an indefinite internal object rather than one that attributes to me some specific praiseworthy feats. But the self I see here as praiseworthy for something-or-other presumably may be quite specific—and not an acknowledged fantasy construction. In that case, however, my pride would seem to be inappropriate even if it is adaptive in the particular case at hand—and even if it happens to apply to me on other grounds, by analogy to the falling rock case in Chapter 4. The emotion would also be inappropriate in the more familiar case where I vividly imagine some future achievement as if it were already a *fait accompli*. But a different assessment would seem to apply to the case where my emotion is based on absorption in the accomplishments of an Olympics gymnast. For pride, however, what is generally adaptive is an emotion based on identification in the looser sense—just because it must remain rather indefinite and avoid attributing the accomplishments in question specifically to me. And in fact, an act of identification in this sense may be seen as serving effectively to place me within the circle of friends or supporters on whom another's achievements reflect praise.

In any case, even where we take an emotion to be *in*appropriate, that is not necessarily to say that one ought not to feel it. This point may need to be stressed as we make the transition to my next section; for in discussing emotional justification people often tend to interpret a claim that some emotion is inappropriate as a flat charge of irrationality. As here interpreted, however, the claim means merely that the emotion is not warranted *by* significant perception and hence is not justified in "backward-looking" terms. It may still be justified in "forward-looking" terms, as *instrumentally* rational—if only because, where it amounts to a state of comfort, it serves as an end of action, including the action of contemplating fictional representations or engaging in fantasy. Just as fear felt at a horror film may sometimes yield greater pleasure on the whole where it goes beyond what is strictly warranted, so an agent may have reason in a particular case to fool himself emotionally with respect to pride.

In the rest of this chapter, assuming appropriateness, I shall fill out the view sketched initially in Chapter 1 of the role of emotions in practical reasoning, particularly as spurs towards future action where they amount to states of discomfort. For the moment, though, my earlier example of pride-based confidence, the feeling that one is up to any task, should make clear some of the limitations of appropriateness as a justificatory category. The example indicates that the practical justification of emotions involving comfort neither implies nor is implied by their *representational* rationality. For instance, we might suppose that, in preparing myself to perform some difficult task, I would do best to generate some inappropriate pride. My pride may be based on fantasy, or on the "feeling as though" some future achievement is already realized. In any case, it amounts to a relaxed attitude that is assumed to be adaptive under the circumstances, allowing for actions that turn out to justify pride in retrospect. Without some such instrumental justification, moreover, in cases where it *is* appropriate, there would be no compelling reason to think that I *must* undergo the emotion. A belief that I am praiseworthy—in those respects in which I have reason to think that I am—would do just as well for representational purposes, it seems.

This presupposes a view of emotions as subject to some, even if limited, forms of control: there are long-range strategies for generating emotional states, and often one can avoid spillovers and disproportionate affect. In another sort of case, however, one might suppose that a strategy helpful in generating enough confidence to handle some crucial past situations gives rise to a tendency to "rest on one's laurels," with pride undercutting the necessary motivation to work. Later occurrences of pride might then count as "merely understandable"—as emotions one strictly ought *not* to feel from *both* the representational and the instrumental standpoints, but emotions that are nevertheless excusable in light of the agent's history. Other cases might be cited involving disproportionate affect rather than a spillover to other cases and with explanations in terms of social norms or physiological constitution rather than the agent's history. I shall now stop with this case, however, and turn to the more complex question of second-level emotional justification: what one ought *to* feel—if anything.

(ii) Rationally Required Feelings

The standards of appropriateness are rather generous, even if not all-inclusive, as we have seen; and their generosity leaves room for a range of acceptable responses, including even contrary emotions, in many cases. But we do often speak of emotions as if they were required—in a rational sense, or so it seems, as well as in various moral or quasi-moral senses.[2] Nor are such claims limited to emotions like pride that clearly function as ends of action, and might therefore be seen as required by self-interest. When we say, for instance, that one ought to feel grief at the loss of a love-object or anger at an insult or guilt about some past misdeed, we may seem to be saying that failure to feel the emotion in question would in some way be unreasonable under the circumstances. Such emotions are uncomfortable for the agent; and our claim is not a claim of moral requirement, presumably. But I now want to argue that the claim should then be interpreted as a claim of instrumental rationality, appealing to the special role played by emotions in practical reasoning.

My main example here will be anger at an insult; but in my next section I shall also attempt to handle some cases that do not essentially involve discomfort at an action requirement. The range of possibilities for analyzing emotions is wide, as we have seen; but it would be best to focus initially on one fairly common and clear-cut sort of example, re-fining the account of emotions as spurs to action that I sketched in Chapters 1 and 3. My argument in this section will center on anger, then, and will occur in two stages: First, I shall consider *representational* rationality, arguing that it does *not* require feeling as a supplement to belief; next, I shall turn to *instrumental* rationality, arguing that it some-times does. Let us begin, then, by asking whether, *apart* from its possible practical importance, and considered solely from a rational standpoint, the feeling of anger has any real point. It might seem just foolish to undergo discomfort if one can avoid it.[3] If one *can* get by with the cool recognition that one ought to punish X for some injury or offense, why not simply record the evaluation without affect? From the standpoint of representational rationality, the obvious answer is just that one ought to see things as they are—and that belief is not always sufficient or suffi-ciently reliable.

But why not? It seems to be capable at least in principle of recording any qualitative distinctions available to emotion, including some that emotion is less likely to record, on my account. It does introduce different quantitative measures, as we saw in Chapter 4; and these might be thought of as capturing something about the situation—the importance of the object, perhaps—that is not represented by belief strength. But belief plus degrees of attention would seem to do the job—*if* the job really needs doing; for it is not so obvious that one is required to represent *everything*. There may also, of course, be cases where appropriate anger shortcuts adequate *warrant* for belief— analogous to the suspicion cases in Chapters 1 and 4 but here involving a "visceral" response to an insult not yet "digested," say. However, my claim is just that a feeling of anger is unnecessary here as well, unless we appeal beyond the strictly representational functions of emotion. As an object of attention, the content of an *unwarranted* belief corresponding to anger—that one ought to punish X for the wrong he has done—would seem to do just as well as a way of summing up the situation, if that is all that is in question. The agent may be more likely to dismiss it than the content of an appropriate emotion; but there would seem to be a point in holding it in mind only on the assumption that an immediate response to anger is required in this case.[4] If it is not, then perhaps one ought ideally to limit oneself to a suitably qualified evaluative judgment: that there are some signs that one ought to punish X, for instance. Nor would this vaguely worded judgment be so difficult to come up with in advance of the sophisticated cognitive processes involved in assessing belief warrant.

Some apparent counterexamples to my view here turn out to be cases where a "snap" emotional evaluation is required, in addition to warranted judgment, for the cultivation of general *habits* of adaptive response. Perhaps it would be useful to feel angry at X, say, because one ought to develop a pattern of response that is helpful in other cases, though it is not otherwise helpful in this one. But if so, anger would be adaptive "in the particular case at hand," in the sense I have in mind here. It would be adaptive, that is, on this particular occurrence—since it serves as a way of cultivating the habit in question—even if it is not of much use in this particular interaction with X. The "ought" derived from considerations of habit formation would thus be practical, prescribing an emotion for its usefulness to *later* action. Although the reference to action may not be spelled out explicitly, it is a "specific" reference, of the sort that does not come into my notion of appropriateness.

In answer to some other possible objections, we should note that the difficulty of *limiting* oneself to a qualified judgment would be relevant *only* to a practical "ought." An ideal "ought"—applied in the first instance to states of affairs, rather than actions (what ought to be the case rather than what one ought to do)—is all that may be in question here for "ought-to-think," taken as a representational requirement of belief.[5] But this would not seem to imply "can"—meaning "can by the exercise of choice." Nor would it imply that an alternative state of affairs is unacceptable. Thus, our denial that one ought to feel angry on the grounds that one ought ideally to hold a qualified judgment instead should not be taken as meaning that the *absence* of feeling is required. The claim is just that anger is *not* required—until we move beyond representational considerations. It is worth stressing, too, that what is denied by this claim is just that the feeling is *required* for its representational role, not that it plays one. We might grant, in fact, in the case just sketched, that anger serves to depict something about the situation that belief cannot capture—to "portray" in affect the sort of violent punishment that the object of anger deserves, say. But whatever one would lose by feeling nothing, the absence of feeling cannot be equated with a failure to draw some logically obvious conclusion.

This is to say that an affectless response to a clear-cut body of evidence would not really be analogous to a standard case of failure to *believe* what one ought—where an agent withholds assent out of self-deception, most notably. Someone might refuse to recognize an insult out of doting fondness for its author, say, despite beliefs recording all the evidence on the matter, along with the relevant values. He might refuse, that is, to acknowledge that X has wronged him, though he would make that judgment of anyone else in X's position who came out with the same remark. But if his other beliefs did commit him to that judgment, denying it would be logically *inconsistent*. Even in a case where the agent felt the corresponding emotion, but as long as he withheld assent from its evaluative component, his belief system would contain a logical gap. Given the judgments he made or would make about others or in general, along with his awareness of the facts of the situation involving X, his failure to judge X's behavior as insulting would amount to a violation of representational rationality. For emotions, by contrast, there seems to be no parallel requirement to *react* similarly in affective terms to similar cases. Apart from practical purposes, rationality does not require a consistent outlay of *attention*; so an agent is not "committed to" an emotional response to his beliefs, even supposing that he exhibits one in similar cases.

This argument presupposes, of course, that the agent does hold some relevant beliefs. A rational requirement to assent to *any* evaluations—or for that matter, to have a *system* of beliefs, as defined in terms of logical coherency—might indeed rest on considerations of instrumental rationality. But this is an issue that we may leave open for present purposes. On the other hand, there are some issues concerning different sorts of requirement to feel that deserve at least a detour at this point, since they might be confused with the requirement of representational rationality that my argument here has denied. Some practical "oughts" appeal to ideals of emotional sensitivity or to the role of emotions as ends of action. Although my primary concerns lie elsewhere, claims about what one ought to feel for its own sake or for the sake of others or for the sake of one's own emotional satisfaction are important; and it is important that we distinguish them from the claims I mean to be considering.

Emotional Ideals and Ends. At this point I shall limit myself to a few illustrations based on variants of the case where an insult merits anger. Without reference to the importance of anger from a purely rational standpoint, the claim that I ought to feel angry might be justified in a number of different ways *either* in registering evaluative information or in reinforcing the reasons for adaptive action. One might say, for instance, that I ought to feel angry because anger is required to maintain a certain kind of *dignity* under the circumstances. Any lesser response— hurt feelings, for instance, as well as simple indifference—would amount to letting myself be "walked all over" and would be obtuse or insensitive in a way that may be said to resemble a failure of perception. Similarly for a failure to feel angry in response to an insult to someone else— feeling sorry for him instead or simply judging that I ought to avenge the insult but without registering the evaluation affectively or perhaps even focusing much attention on it. A lesser response might not be thought to be sufficiently satisfying to the other party—just in view of his interest in community of feeling, of the sort that came into my treatment of identificatory love in Chapter 3.

It should be evident, though, that these claims bring in more than considerations of representational rationality. The moral or quasi-moral values to which they make appeal are values of a sort that may come into the notion of appropriateness, as "further information" affecting the weight placed on a given body of evidence, in the way indicated for social adaptiveness in Chapter 5. But as such they can yield only a judgment of rational acceptability—as one option among others—until we bring in reference to adaptiveness in the particular case at hand. Here, where feeling and absence of feeling are the options, it is clear that both cannot be taken; but in order to decide in favor of one of them— undergoing the feeling—we must assume that it is actually needed to promote the value in question on this occasion. In the case of anger for oneself, to maintain one's dignity, for instance, an extrarational assessment of the feeling in itself or of oneself as undergoing it in certain situations seems to be brought in, in accordance with a personal ideal of emotional sensitivity. The feeling is assessed positively, that is, as satisfying the ideal, rather than for its representational or other relation to some distinct state of affairs. To yield an ought-judgment, though, the ideal must be viewed as something that requires anger on this occasion: I ought to feel angry at X, perhaps, because I have let his insults go by unanswered too often in the past.

To the extent that it genuinely makes no reference, even implicitly, to the value of *expressing* anger to X, the ought-judgment here is not a judgment of instrumental rationality, strictly speaking. The feeling may be seen not as a means to something further, presumably some sort of action to ward off future insults, but as an essential *part* of something— the preservation of dignity—that is valued for its own sake. In the case of identificatory anger, the appeal is to a social ideal of shared feeling; and this might also be taken to yield a moral or quasi-moral ought-judgment, if it also makes no reference to the instrumental value of action on others' behalf. In Chapter 3 I indicated that some of our obligations to others require *feeling* something on their behalf, as something that is valued for its own sake. Since we can often generate emotions by performing voluntary actions, such as dwelling on certain evaluations, this should give us a noninstrumental basis for an argument to a practical "ought-to-feel." The latter will be an "ought" of the sort that does imply "can," remember—meaning "can by the exercise of choice," though not necessarily "can at a moment's notice" or "can with a guarantee of success."

A similar argument would apply to "oughts" like the one just considered, with its appeal to dignity as an individual, taken as a moral or quasi-moral ideal. Further, in both sorts of cases the positive assessment of anger may sometimes be rational rather than moral, but without being reducible to a judgment of representational *or* instrumental rationality. Dignity, or shared feeling, may be seen as valuable just insofar as it is satisfying to the agent, say—to take the simplest sort of case. Here the emotion may be viewed simply as an *end* of action—as prescribed by an ideal of *rationality,* then, but prescribed for its own sake, not as a means to something further. Its description as "satisfying" may amount to an assessment of the emotion in itself, that is. One may "take comfort," for instance, in the fact that one feels things strongly or in concert with others even where the object-directed feelings in question are themselves unpleasant. At any rate, for present purposes, the point is just that more than representational rationality stands behind our ought-judgments in such cases—but also more than instrumental rationality, since the emotion itself is taken as an end or as part of an end of action.

The role of emotions as rational ends of action is a role *in* instrumental *reasoning,* though, since actions may be chosen as means to emotional satisfaction. Indeed, along with the moral value placed on them, their role as ends, particularly in cases of pleasurable feeling, provides an important supplement to the narrower issues I now wish to focus on, with emotions viewed as *spurs to* action. The combination of roles allows for a kind of "double-action" motivational account, as illustrated by the case of anger. It is a commonplace that anger "feeds on itself"—that we naturally want to dwell on it, despite the fact that it involves discomfort. My appeal to a positive assessment of the emotion in itself or of ourselves as undergoing it in certain situations is part of what explains this fact and with it the special motivational force of anger. We should note, too, that even an intrinsically uncomfortable emotion may sometimes involve or give rise to an element of comfort *apart* from any assessment of it. In particular, on my account in Chapter 3, anger involves comfort at a positive evaluation of revenge. A positive emotion, by the same token, may sometimes involve or give rise to discomfort at an action requirement: As Chapter 3 also indicated, with regard to attachment-love, discomfort may even be an essential component in its analysis. So the argument I shall go on to give—for practical reasoning from the need to escape emotional discomfort, as illustrated by a relatively simple case of anger—will have multiple application to motivating states that an agent acts *both* to escape and to sustain.

Even as extended by my comments on emotional ideals and ends, the "escape from discomfort" view of emotional motivation, as initially sketched for action from anger in Chapter 3, is not designed to yield an account of *all* reasons for action. In my next section I shall consider some other possibilities for explaining even emotional motivation. But in any case, I do not deny the possibility of action purely to attain some coolly valued end since I do not claim that all action is emotional. In fact, since "motivation" is understood in a way that requires something more than goal-directed behavior—some sort of quasi-causal "push from behind," with prior conditions seen as *making* the agent act—I do not claim that all action is motivated.[6] What I do maintain is that action is commonly made more likely by a kind of subliminal "reasoning" from emotion, as a supplement to judgment. If my view at first sounds paradoxical, that is because it cuts against the standard dichotomy between emotion and reason, just insofar as it brings together motivation and justification. I take this to be a welcome result of my ensuing argument, however. To put its point provocatively, then: By contrast to our reasoning *to* emotion from perception, practical reasoning *from* emotion does sometimes yield a judgment of "ought-to-feel." Or it would if reconstructed in terms of judgments about the agent's need to escape emotional discomfort.

   This is obviously a complex view, particularly when spelled out in the standard vocabulary applied to practical reasoning. It would be simpler just to sum things up in the terms of my earlier treatment of action from anger, with the affective component of emotion made out as adding "motivational force" to a judgment-based desire for action, in the simplest sort of case. But although something like this will still stand behind my view here, I now want to take the view further by showing how the extra "force" provided by emotion augments the agent's *reasons* for action, as well as its psychological triggering mechanisms. It will be crucial to my defense of "ought-to-feel" that emotions put the agent in a position to perform a certain piece of practical reasoning. At this point, however, some general words of clarification might help to avert natural misunderstandings of the argument I shall attribute to him. Most importantly, my claim that the need to escape discomfort provides a reason for action from emotion should not be taken as a claim that action from emotion follows a process of deliberation about emotional discomfort and alternative means of escape. But nor is it just a claim that *there is* a reason to justify action—as distinct from one that actually functions motivationally as *the agent's* reason—given by the need to escape discomfort. Rather, it is meant as a claim that discomfort provides a *rational* "push from behind" in the generation of action from emotion, even if it is not on the tip of consciousness prior to action—and even if, in some cases, it is not easily accessible to consciousness after-the-fact.
   The piece of practical reasoning I shall go on to sketch may be thought of as "subliminal," in the sense I defended for the case of subliminal reasoning to *emotion* in Chapters 1 and 4. In "reconstructing" it, I shall not take myself to be describing a set of unconscious inferences but rather to be filling in gaps in what in fact is in many cases a leap from emotion to action, warranted even where its grounds are not recognized. The result will not be so different from the application of standard accounts of practical reasoning to the many little purposive actions performed more or less automatically in everyday life. In crossing the road, for instance, I begin by shifting my weight onto one foot. If asked the reason for my action or even for the extended action of walking, I may not have much to say besides "to get to the other side." Even if I did have some further ends "in mind," I need not have *borne* them in mind as I walked or before I began to walk, deliberating about alternative ways of achieving them. But these are plausibly taken as my reasons for walking—and indeed for taking that first step—however comical it would be to make out a logically adequate statement of them as describing my prior reasoning *process*, conscious or not. Similarly for at least some cases where I might be hard put, even after-the-fact, to provide any reason at all—for shifting my weight out of restlessness, say.

It might be objected that emotional behavior typically *starts out* as a more or less automatic response, preceding any developed capacity for reasoning, rather than a response based on reasoning that later becomes unnecessary, as in the present example. This does mean that a syllogistic representation of "emotional reasoning" may be particularly artificial—more so, at any rate, than a similar attempt to capture the reasoning that gets me across the road (as opposed to my shifting out of restlessness). But although emotional behavior is not *initially* purposive and may never be fully brought within rational control, action from emotion in adult life—along with the very nature of emotions, as I argued in Chapter 3—has been modified in light of information about its consequences. In its developed state, then, action from emotion does not merely have relief of discomfort as an incidental result, on my view. Rather, it has been *seen* to have that result, at least subliminally; and it has taken the particular form that it has at least partly *because of* that perception, with one of its functions coming to serve as an end.

If I rebuke X out of anger at his insult, on this account, I am not merely lashing out at X. I am exercising a choice among optional responses, weighted for their usefulness in discharging my anger as well as in getting back at X—compatibly with my other aims and the other exigencies of my situation. Even if the response is more or less automatic, it is something I *allow* to happen—and something I can *make* happen on other occasions. It seems to be at least semi-voluntary, then, and is naturally thought of as an action. It rests on a reason or reasons that may be represented in terms of judgments about emotional discomfort and alternative ways of relieving it, even if it would be absurd to suppose that the agent acted only after running through a syllogism.[7] In the present case, we may ascribe to me what might be called a "self-centered" judgment of the following form:

I am uncomfortable at the thought that I ought to get back at X.

This is meant to capture my awareness of my anger—but with anger analyzed along the lines proposed here. The judgment may be thought of as subliminal, even if I do know that I am angry, since I may fail to pay much explicit attention to the affective component of my emotion: *discomfort at* an action requirement, of the sort that yields a motivating desire. My attention may be focused entirely on X—on evaluations of his past misdeeds and his possible future payment for them rather than on my current state of feeling. Still, we may take my response to be *based on* a self-evaluation—not solely on the "object-centered" judgment corresponding to the evaluative component of anger:

I ought to get back at X.

I need not actually *hold* this second judgment, as we have seen, in all cases where I "feel as though" it were true; but even supposing that I do hold it, it may not be enough to explain my choice among possible alternative responses to anger.

For not every response to anger is reasonably seen as a way of getting back at its object. Instead of rebuking *X*, or in combination with a rebuke, I might do a number of things for which my anger counts as a motivating reason, though I know that they will not achieve revenge. I might mutter a few inaudible curses; or entertain fantasies of wringing *X*'s neck; or kick Fido; or make an angry face; or simply attempt to work off anger by removing myself from *X*'s presence and engaging in vigorous exercise. This is nothing like a full list of possible responses, of course. But it should serve to illustrate the range of options available to someone acting out of a state of anger that falls short of a blind rage—as it usually does, let us grant, once the infantile "lashing out" response has been shaped into its adult form. By that time, besides recognizing revenge of some sort as the "proper aim" of anger, the agent has come to see this *and alternative* manifestations of the emotion as *outlets* for its component of negative feeling.

The agent sees the manifestations of anger, moreover, as outlets yielding a degree of satisfaction that is typically greater as they resemble the proper aim. Even those, like my facial expression, that were initially reflex reactions have been brought under some control, to the extent that they now can be *used to* discharge anger on the basis of some degree of choice with or without a process of deliberation. They have come to have a purpose, that is—a purpose not fully explainable in terms of a desire to achieve the emotion's aim, though their relation to that desire explains why they are satisfying. Most can be viewed as symbolic realizations of the aim of anger—not just as ways of alleviating essentially objectless anger *symptoms*. Although they obviously do not achieve the aim, they are seen as serving to relieve the agent's discomfort at his failure (so far) to achieve it—something not given in the object-centered judgment.

To show how anger provides a reason for its outlets, then, we need to bring in the self-centered judgment. Its reference to discomfort is what justifies the various alternative actions manifesting anger; and it also *reinforces* the justification for *direct* action on the emotion. For an action that would get back at *X* may function as *both* aim and outlet of my anger—presumably the most satisfying outlet, if relief of discomfort is all that is in question, just because the others are indirect. In combination with a complex set of background judgments about the relative effectiveness, wisdom, and permissibility of various ways of getting back at *X*, the object-centered judgment might be sufficient to yield a specific action requirement. All alternatives to rebuking X might be evaluated negatively, that is, just insofar as they fail to achieve adequate and acceptable revenge. But it is important that another argument to the same conclusion is possible, since a rebuke is also seen by the agent as the most effective way of discharging discomfort. An ought-judgment prescribing a rebuke may thus be derived from the self-centered judgment, along with a complex set of background judgments about alternative ways of relieving discomfort, plus a general ought-judgment prescribing its relief.

This argument from the self-centered judgment may be needed to explain an agent's decision to rebuke X in certain cases where the argument from the object-centered judgment would not go through—where X would not be affected by a rebuke, say, though it is still the most satisfying outlet for anger. But even where both arguments would yield the same conclusion, the argument from the self-centered judgment may be needed to get the agent to *act on* the argument from the object-centered judgment. By itself, that is, the recognition that an action requirement has not yet been fulfilled is something that may or may not weigh heavily on an agent's mind, prompting him to take action. It involves a kind of cognitive/practical dissonance, of course; but this "inert" variety of weakness of will seems to be not merely possible but also rather easy to live with—at least on many familiar occasions and for many "basically" rational agents. Like any belief, an action requirement need not always be held in mind; but action-oriented discomfort absorbs attention *now* and exerts a kind of pressure towards *immediate* action.

Affectless Desire and Inertia. Reinforcing an action requirement with discomfort, in the way just illustrated, will still have a point, on my view, even where the action requirement coincides with a *desire*—but in what has been called "the philosopher's sense," extending to affectless preferences. I may not be much moved by the fact that I "want," in this sense, to get back at X—as I do, let us grant, when I hold the object-centered judgment corresponding to anger but without discomfort at my failure to act on it yet. Someone might object, though, that a basically rational agent who did have this desire and who had no stronger conflicting desires necessarily *would* act on it. If so, the argument from the self-centered judgment would seem to be superfluous as a way of reinforcing the argument from the object-centered judgment. It would seem to be replaceable by an argument from the desire to act in accordance with the object-centered judgment or by a version of the original argument that brings in a general desire to act as one ought. But the objection is questionable, if it has any content—if it rests only on a claim about action on desire (as opposed to ought-judgment) and does not trade on our natural interpretation of "desire," or of "strong desire," as involving uncomfortable affect. Where a desire for revenge is at issue, this interpretation is hard to avoid; so let me switch, for a moment, to a case that also may serve to illustrate the breadth of the philosopher's notion.

Consider my desire (while writing this book's first draft) for a home computer. I do want one—would like to have one, even think that I ought to get one, in view of some of my other desires—but am not especially *eager* to get one, or not yet. Having avoided acquainting myself closely with the array of choices and their relative advantages, I am not in even a mild state of discomfort at putting off the purchase. Nor am I uncomfortable at the prospect of doing without a home computer forever, though I do evaluate it negatively. The prospect of shopping for one, on the other hand, is something I regard as *both* an onerous task and a probable source of pleasure—in a way that about cancels out, it seems, yielding a kind of *inertia*. I have no real urge to do the shopping as long as I keep the prospect at a comfortable temporal distance. If I did allow myself to dwell on it in immediate terms, though, I would develop a *motivating* desire, we may suppose. Contemplating the possibilities, with an eagerness both pleasurable and involving some element of discomfort until satisfied, I would cease to regard the task as onerous once I let it absorb my imagination. However, my current desire for my own home computer is clearly not like this at all. It is more than an idle wish—I have the money set aside and expect to do the shopping at some point—but it is nothing like a pressing emotional urge.

What if I never got around to acting on this desire? Assuming no change in my external circumstances, would it necessarily be irrational for me to leave it in its initial state, with an end in mind but easily postponed into the ever-receding future? I do not see why we should say so, supposing that postponement is still regarded as an option. It would seem to be a reasonable option, in that case, since the end I have in mind is required by nothing *besides* affectless desire. Of course, I cannot postpone action forever and still satisfy the desire. But it is important that the view of rational action in question here makes no independent appeal to an ought-judgment, even one that prescribes maintaining the desire. It is quite consistent with rationality simply to *drop* an optional desire—along with any further desires that might seem to yield an ought-judgment—if a now-or-never choice is ever forced on me.[8] This also applies to a desire whose object is temporally specified as an action in the immediate future. If I want a home computer now, I am rationally committed *either* to getting one now or to dropping my desire in the time it would take me to get one; but I am not committed to getting one now—*simpliciter*—unless we suppose that I must maintain the desire.

That I have the desire now is not sufficient reason for requiring me to take action on it without either some emotional pressure that keeps me from just dropping it or an ought-judgment that rules out this other option.

At least as applied to one particular affectless desire, then, my motivational inertia in response to a now-or-never choice would not be irrational in itself. It would be a different story, of course, if I generally dropped desires requiring action or dropped all of my current desires now or attempted just to drop one that did exert emotional pressure. But all that is in question here is the view that an agent *must* act on any desire he has insofar as he is rational. Nor would it do to appeal to a stronger, conflicting desire—a desire to avoid having to act on the one I drop—to reconcile this conception of rationality with the philosopher's sense of "desire." This familiar move is questionable unless it is question-*begging*; for unless intensity of desire is available to explain emotional strength—as it is when we move *away* from the philosopher's sense—there seems to be no noncircular rational "push" towards action on the stronger desire. It is not clear that an agent's behavior must always bear out his preference rankings, say, if the latter are taken as an independent measure of strength. But if "stronger desire" is interpreted simply as "desire considered more important," the claim that a basically rational agent must act on his strongest desire would simply amount to a veiled rejection of the possibility of weakness of will. We may grant, then, that the addition of desire to my reconstruction of emotional reasoning in terms of ought-judgments would not eliminate the role it assigns to the need to escape emotional discomfort.

Let us now return to the case of anger at X, noting how the affective component of the emotion may add a kind of motivational force to desire and belief—in the first instance just insofar as it serves to hold the evaluative component in mind. To the extent that I am uncomfortable about not yet acting on it, the thought that I ought to get back at X is not something I can simply drop or ignore, in the way that I could drop or ignore an affectless desire or belief, to avoid having to act. This point will apply to more cases than we ordinarily classify as emotions; but I take this to indicate that the motivational influence of emotional pressure is not limited to motivation *by* particular emotions. It is a pervasive explanation, even if not the only explanation, of action; for negative affect directed towards an action requirement is what actually forces work of an agent. The threat of continuing discomfort, in short, supplies a self-interested *and pressing* reason for action from the agent's standpoint; and it gives us the basis for at least a limited sort of argument to "ought-to-feel."

Since anger puts the agent in an escape-situation, the cost of withholding a response to it mounts over time; so the emotion reinforces any independent reasons—self-interested or not, but ignored *without* affective cost—for thinking that he ought to take some action in revenge. Even on our assumption that the agent does hold the object-centered judgment, then, the piece of practical reasoning I have sketched may depend for its motivational force on the argument from the self-centered judgment. Appeal to the need to escape emotional discomfort may be necessary to get the agent to perform an action of the sort that the object-centered judgment makes out as required. But then we would seem to be able to construct an argument to "ought-to-feel" from the judgment prescribing a specific action, essentially by reversing the agent's argument from the self-centered judgment, to derive an ought-judgment of its starting point. It would follow from the action requirement, that is, that the agent ought to be in a position to *apply* the argument from the self-centered judgment—and thus, on standard assumptions, that he ought to undergo the emotion it attributes to him.

This argument to rationally required feeling assumes that the emotion in question is already justified in "backward-looking" terms, as implied by the notion of "second-level" justification. The argument thus presupposes warrant for the object-centered judgment—or rather, for a corresponding evaluation, since this is no longer attributed to the agent as a judgment, on the argument's reversal of our artificially "judgmentalist" reconstruction of his practical reasoning.[9] The argument also assumes the truth of the specific action requirement drawn from the object-centered judgment and the strict necessity of a certain emotion to its fulfillment. There will be important cases, though, where only something weaker can be granted—a recommendation of action, most notably; but also, where this recommendation is important enough, a recommendation of advance steps that would tend to *ensure* its fulfillment. In such cases, the emotion would be "adaptive," in my terms, even if it is not strictly required. Its adaptiveness may depend on a kind of practical illusion, moreover, in which the agent appropriately "feels as though" action is required.

An extension of our argument to fit such cases can appeal, we should note, to one sort of practical illusion that seems to be allowed for by the argument as it stands. For some false judgments about the agent's own state of discomfort will be needed to capture certain cases of action from anger that came up briefly in Chapter 3. Although the self-centered judgment, as limited to the present, is assumed to be self-warranting, its implications for action will depend on reference to the future, with discomfort viewed as *continuing* unless and until the agent acts to relieve it. A possibility of error on this score must be located in the agent's complex set of background judgments about alternative ways of relieving discomfort. Our argument relies on these background assumptions to capture the *pressing* nature of action-oriented discomfort as a state that does seem to require action and indeed favors more or less immediate and direct forms of action for its relief. This phenomenological "slant" may sometimes be illusory; but it is just this illusion, if so, that would seem to be mandated by our argument.

Although our argument was stated, then, in terms of the need for affective strengthening of judgment, we can see how it might be extended to evaluative strengthening, of the sort that came into my earlier cases of the special motivational role of emotions. In the case of identificatory anger discussed in Chapter 3, we attributed to the agent a view of action as required of him in particular in a case where it was merely recommended, or made out as the responsibility of a group to which he belonged. Here, we might say, the emotion's special motivational role traded on a phenomenological slant towards the *agent*. In the case of fearful suspicion in Chapters 1 and 4, on the other hand, we attributed to the agent a view of injury as likely, *simpliciter*, in a case where (for all he knew) it merely seemed likely relative to "some signs." This removal of qualifications amounted to a form of evaluative strengthening that was justified in general "forward-looking" terms by the need for quick decision-making in self-interest, since the evaluation here gave rise to an action requirement in context. In the present case of nonidentificatory anger, we may appeal to a kind of illusory time-pressure combining elements of both of our earlier cases. For the emotion's slant towards immediate and direct discharge may be practically adaptive even in cases where it distorts the agent's view of his options for acting on the object-centered evaluation.

There may be variants of the present case, for instance, where revenge would be sweeter if achieved later; but some illusion on this score might still be helpful just in so far as it keeps an agent from waiting for an impossibly ideal time for action. It may not be strictly true, say, that I ought to rebuke X for his current insult. A response to the next one would do just as well, perhaps, in curing him of the general tendency; and my later rebuke might be better planned, given the time-lag. But it might equally just be postponed indefinitely into the future without some pressure from present anger at least to formulate plans immediately. In short, the pattern of second-level justification I have sketched here should extend to emotions yielding actions not themselves required—with the dates, agents, and other specifics attributed to them—except as a way of ensuring the fulfillment of a more general action requirement. This means that our extended argument will have to allow for a gap between the agent's evaluations and our own; but it will still turn on the motivational role of emotions as pressuring the agent towards action.

(iii) Emotional Pressure and Escape from Discomfort

The argument I have offered for rationally required feeling as a supplement to evaluative belief rests on a view of emotional pressure as slanted towards action that would satisfy an ought-judgment requiring fulfillment of the emotion's proper aim. But the argument's reconstruction of the agent's practical reasoning extends more widely, as we have seen, to cases where what is given independently of emotion is a weaker ought-judgment, which I make out as strengthened by emotional evaluation. The reconstruction also allows for some indirect ways of acting on an emotion that are designed to achieve partial relief of the agent's discomfort at failing to fulfill the action requirement. We should now note that these may be used to pose some problems for my view of emotional motivation, with its basis in the need to escape discomfort. They amount to ways of *expressing* the emotion, whether or not it involves a "proper aim"—or even an aim that is limited to a particular situation, as in a case where essentially passive *sorrow* gives rise in context to a desire to change the surrounding circumstances. For I make out a motivating desire in terms of discomfort directed towards an unfulfilled action requirement, of a sort that apparently does not apply to the full range of emotions capable of expression.

Emotional expression should here be taken as limited to action that bears some intentional connection to the emotion's *content*. My view of emotional motivation, remember, depends on a general account of emotions in terms of affect directed towards evaluative "internal" objects, as distinct from affective emotion *symptoms* seen as merely accompanying evaluative states. The view would not apply, then, to action just to lessen the symptoms of anger, without connection to its internal object—engaging in vigorous physical activity, say, just in order to "work off" the emotion without even deflected or symbolic aggression towards X. Such action may of course be a help in discharging discomfort. It may also be one's wisest option in light of conflicting requirements in some cases—sometimes even fully satisfying in cases where the emotion simply fades with time. But it is not the natural response and is normally unsatisfying as the sole response to anger. Nor is it happily described as action "from" anger, unlike even the least direct ways of acting on the emotion's aim—kicking Fido, for instance, also without any conscious aggression towards X.

On the other hand, expressive outlets initially unconnected to an emotion's aim, such as the facial contortions typical of anger, may *come* to fulfill it as both the aim and the outlets of emotion are shaped by social learning. Gritting one's teeth in frustration, say, may become a way of making a face *at X* and achieving a kind of revenge. Even as so far stated, then, my view can accommodate some cases of expressive behavior. In other cases behavior expressing anger would seem to count as action "from" the emotion even though it does *not* involve action on its aim; but a simple extension of my view could accommodate these too. We might appeal to the experience of "containing" an emotion, seen as allowing for an element of *anticipatory* discomfort, action-oriented even for emotions that are themselves passive. Discomfort at the thought that one ought to *express* one's sorrow, say, might be seen as arising in context from its element of discomfort at a negative evaluation of the situation, on the view of emotional affect as capable of "taking on" further objects· that I outlined for cases of fear in Chapter 2. However, this account may seem questionable in application to emotions not involving *felt* discomfort—especially comfortable emotions, such as *joy*, that often seem to "press" for expression, though they come out as essentially passive, on my view. For that matter, it interprets the desire for expression as something general—something important in practical terms (to social communication, say), but something whose motivational force may seem to be connected only incidentally to a particular emotion. Yet just because the scope of expressive behavior extends to all emotions, at least potentially, it might be taken as the paradigm case of emotional pressure.

On a closer look, however, cases of expressive action seem to admit of division into those that can be brought under some extended version of the "escape from discomfort" view and those that do not really involve emotional pressure. We should note, on the one hand, that responses to comfortable emotions may be made out as occurring under anticipatory pressure as long as the agent is threatened with more or less immediate discomfort at containment. If I "jump for joy," say, I may be seen as motivated by discomfort at the thought that I ought to express my joy in some such exuberant fashion, whether or not I am aware of present discomfort. It is enough that I am aware from past experience of the discomfort involved in containing the feeling, or its more extreme manifestations. On the other hand, the same action may occur *without* pressure; for joy behavior may sometimes amount to a deliberate attempt to *dramatize* the uncontainable quality of the emotion—a sense of its affective component as overflowing boundaries, as the word "exuberant" suggests.

Where I do act under pressure, my discomfort may sometimes be "masked" by comfort or experienced in light of a heightened state of comfort to which it yields. But at any rate, I may act in such cases before I am actually *in* a state of discomfort. I may not have the purpose of avoiding it—"escaping" it in a broader sense—explicitly in mind; but an explanation in terms of a need to escape discomfort should fit this case at least as well as certain "automatic" variants of my central case of anger. Sometimes an agent might react to an insult, that is, before he has time to feel the desire that I take to be essential to anger. He may act in order to *head off* discomfort, so far feeling only comfort at the thought of revenge. We have no distinct name for the constituent of anger that prompts action here. Perhaps this should not be thought of as a case of action "from" anger, strictly speaking. But it is surely a case of action motivated by a *part* of anger—comfortable in itself but deriving its motivational force from the pressure of *impending* discomfort as the agent anticipates the full onset of the emotion. The explanation is simpler, if anything, in application to joy, where the emotion has only one constituent assigned to it "essentially" and thus may be viewed as complete before action.

Whether all expressive action is like this is of course another question. Sometimes a response to joy, such as smiling, is so automatic that one might be tempted to count it not as an action at all but rather as a reflex reaction—on the model, say, of *beaming*—even supposing that it is susceptible to indirect or negative forms of voluntary control. In at least some cases, though, including cases of the same behavior, it is clearly reasonable to suppose that the agent acts deliberately *to express* joy—without any element of discomfort, perhaps, but in that case without any real pressure. The aim might be to communicate feelings of joy to others for the sake of social reinforcement or simply to "portray" joy dramatically to oneself—or to no one in particular—in order to sustain or heighten its pleasurable aspect. If no other motive is involved here—one is not "pressed" to communicate by feelings of insecurity, say—the action in question would not seem to count as an action under pressure. Emotion may still be said to provide a reason for it beyond that given by the corresponding judgment; but what emotional pressure adds is a reason whose satisfaction cannot be postponed without a *mounting cost* in continuing discomfort.

By itself, a positive *goal* does not exert pressure in this sense, though it might sometimes be said to provide a "pressing reason" for action—most obviously, where it is assumed to be temporally limited: expressing joy while someone is around to share it, say, or before the feeling passes.[10] There is a cost, of course, in the sense of something missed, if one postpones action beyond the time when it would be effective. But this is not a "mounting cost" in the sense of an accumulating penalty: a bad state of the agent that adds up over time. It is the latter sort of cost that seems to be imposed by more or less immediate emotional discomfort on an agent who fails to express his joy. With a bit of explanatory inventiveness, moreover, we may allow for it in an account of expressive behavior as action motivated by emotional pressure. Thus, smiling from joy is sometimes checked in adult life. The difficulty of containing oneself in such cases might be explained, say, by reference to a sense of *incompleteness* felt, by comparison with past experience, in foregoing an expression of joy. But then, where the behavior is *not* checked, one might appeal to this uneasy feeling as something the agent acts to avoid—assuming that he does act under pressure.

Being satisfied *without* an explanation would seem to involve treating the behavior as a reflex reaction. This is surely implausible even for smiling, which did originate as a reflex reaction, but to something other than joy. It seems especially odd, though, in application to more complex behavior—inviting someone out to lunch, say—whose very performance rests on learning, even if it is sometimes automatic in the sense of "unreflective" in adult life. At any rate, my account of emotional motivation is meant to apply only to cases of *action* from emotion—and not necessarily to all such cases. I might smile, for instance, just to indicate to someone that I am happy with something he has done. Here my smiling amounts to an action and one that has emotion as its expressive subject matter. But it is not motivated in the sense of "driven" or "impelled"— a sense that suggests *causation*, though my account is designed to leave open the question whether emotion causally *necessitates* action where it does involve pressure. Perhaps all action is caused, that is; but the fact of emotional pressure does not give us reason for assigning some special, nonrational role to emotions in this regard. On my account, it allows for a choice among optional ways of discharging discomfort—and thus for an element of freedom, but in a situation that also sets up some limitations on freedom by making alternatives difficult for the agent in the way just indicated. We do commonly speak of emotion as *making* an agent act, operating as a kind of "push from behind" in the explanation of behavior. My claim here is just that action that does not fall under some version of the "escape from discomfort" view does not arise from emotion in this sense, whether or not a reference to emotion is needed to explain it in other terms.

We ought to allow for cases of *indirect* causal or quasi-causal influence, though: ways in which emotion may affect the likely *form* of behavior and through it one's choice of action, say. On a standard picture, sorrow *inhibits* action—is expressed in hushed tones, a slowed gait, and so forth— whereas joy has the opposite, arousing or energizing, effect. Both may be said to cause certain changes in behavior, then—sometimes even to cause behavior itself—without reference to a need to escape discomfort.

However, they should not be said to *motivate action*, in my sense, though they do have an important influence on what one can do effectively and thus on what one decides to do. The inhibiting effect of sorrow, for instance, may explain why I walk slowly; but we need to appeal to something else to explain why I *walk*. Given that other sources do supply an initial reason for action, though, sorrow may determine how one responds to it. If a slowed gait is likely to make me poor company on a walk, say, sorrow gives me a reason for declining an invitation to take one. But here the emotion is not itself seen as *making* an agent act. Rather, it influences his choice of what to do by affecting the likely form of his behavior.

Still, it might be objected, passive sorrow does sometimes seem to trigger an action directly—if only the mental action of dwelling on its object, as when one declines an invitation in order to be alone with one's sorrow. I shall deal with this sort of case in extreme form in a moment. The point of the present objection might stand out more sharply, however, for positive actions of the sort that result from the "expansiveness" of joy: issuing an invitation oneself, most obviously.[11] Emotion may indeed seem to "push" the agent here—at least towards a particular *range* of behavior, leaving room, once again, for a choice among options. But first of all, we can appeal back to the need for emotional expression as a way of explaining such cases. For it is unclear how emotion can manage to motivate action, in the sense I have indicated, unless it is part of a state of affairs with which the agent is uncomfortable—or with which he would soon *become* uncomfortable if it endured unchanged over time. This amounts to an extension of the "escape from discomfort" view; but by locating the agent's discomfort in the more or less immediate—and hypothetical—future, we now detach it from the particular emotion in question, even in its situational context. The agent who acts out of joy, on this account, does not act in response to the feeling of joy *per se*. Rather, he acts in light of the expectation of another feeling he would have if his joy were not expressed. But his action does express the evaluative content of the emotion.

Secondly, though, we should note that there are other ways in which joy may indirectly influence the agent's choice of action. It may affect his behavior's likely form and thereby its likely rewards for himself and others—making him more animated in conversation, say—so that he ought to take account of it in deciding what to do, as in the case of sorrow just discussed but with a positive action as its upshot here. In some cases, too, an emotion may influence action by way of its effect on mental state. My estimate of my likely worth as a luncheon companion, for instance, may itself be directly influenced by joy or sorrow—not as a result of reflection on the emotion, that is, but as part of the emotion's characteristic arousal or inhibition. Besides affecting optimism or pessimism, an essentially passive emotion may affect one's interests—and hence, perhaps, one's openness even to the thought of social interaction (or of food). Emotion influences an agent's very perception of his possibilities, one might say; so it may have a *more* than formal effect on what he does, apart from any general need for expression.

For joy, these indirect effects can sometimes give the appearance of emotional pressure just because the state is one of arousal; but they do not involve the kind of affective *coercion* that I take as definitive of the notion. One might even be tempted to hold that the felt quality of an emotion like joy in some cases simply involves a sense of *urgency* without any element of discomfort. Joy may seem to provide a "push" towards action, just insofar as it distorts the agent's temporal assessment of his options. Perhaps it simply yields a thought that action must be taken in a hurry. This might seem to give us a new, discomfort-free candidate for emotional motivation; but I would balk at applying the term, if only because the "push" here does not really seem to be emotional. An affectless action requirement might be said to be *caused* by emotion, in such cases; but it would not seem to yield emotional *pressure*, in the full sense I have in mind here, unless it at least provides its own backing in emotional discomfort. Unless a failure to satisfy it gives rise to discomfort itself, that is—a kind of restless tension, say—it would not seem to incur the sort of mounting cost that I take as definitive of action under pressure.

Grief and "Subjection" to Emotion. Let me now pause to look at an extreme case of emotional passivity. I want to see how my view of emotional motivation applies to *grief*, an uncomfortable emotion that seems to be *necessarily* passive—to lack an aim, in the sense of an object of some motivating desire it gives rise to, even in context, unless one includes expressive action itself.[12] As an extreme form of self-sustaining sorrow, grief apparently poses a problem for the view of emotional motivation as explained by a need to escape discomfort. It poses a special problem because its object, as standardly conceived, is not just a state of misfortune but particularly one that is immune to any efforts at improvement. I would analyze the emotion as discomfort directed towards an evaluation of some state of affairs as an *irrevocable loss*. The emotion then comes out as passive—with odd results for cases of *anguished* grief, where its affective quality is surely active enough (in the sense of "aroused") and where it often gives rise to extremely demonstrative behavior. What it means to call the emotion itself passive, though, is something about its evaluative content. Its analysis rules out action to improve its object; so it cannot give rise to a desire for action—at least assuming a basically rational agent—except by reference to a general need for emotional expression.

However, the need for expression, as applied to grief, is itself problematic. It seems to yield a desire to make the situation *worse*—in the first instance, to dwell on the object of the emotion, "wallowing" in grief in a way that *increases* discomfort. On the standard conception of the emotion an agent in the grips of it is "subject" to it in two overlapping senses. First, his control over both the emotion and its behavioral manifestations is at best severely limited. Grief typically "comes over" one, sometimes seeming to compel action against one's better judgment. It therefore provides a fairly clear case for the traditional view of emotions as responsible for weakness of will and other forms of irrationality. My approach to emotional motivation pushes the opposite line, stressing our modicum of control over emotions in an attempt to show how they also work *against* weakness of will as motivational supplements to judgment. The approach depends on interpreting emotions as rational motives for action just insofar as they amount to states of object-directed affect: comfort or discomfort *about* some evaluative proposition. But it need not be taken as conflicting with the traditional view, or at any rate with its treatment of the cases it chooses to emphasize. In adopting this approach, I do not deny that emotions resist practical control—just as they resist qualification, a kind of evidential control, on the account of emotional appropriateness that I argued for in Chapter 4. Rather, my claim is that the ways in which emotions resist control are themselves sometimes useful in rational terms, particularly in getting the agent to act to achieve their aims, viewed as something independently valuable.

Here is where grief poses a special problem, though, as a kind of experiential "dead end." A second sense in which an agent may be said to be "subject" to the emotion makes it out primarily as something *bad* that happens to him—and that tends to perpetuate itself, without an ameliorative aim. It amounts to a state of discomfort directed towards an evaluation of the situation as hopeless, and the natural behavioral responses to it often seem to make the situation worse. Yet these clearly include *actions*, even if actions performed under pressure. They are not limited, first of all, to reflex *re*actions, though of course the emotion may involve these too: bursting into tears, most obviously where the agent lacks behavioral control. Nor, secondly, do expressions of grief just amount to formal properties of actions performed for independent reasons: "moping" around the house, say, where that connotes behavioral inhibition—a particular way of doing what one does. We can also think of some clear-cut actions (though they often amount to negative actions) that are themselves done *from* grief: declining invitations to go out, for instance. But how can such actions be made out as rational in light of the emotion? Along with the tendency to dwell on the loss, they seem to be designed to make a hopeless situation worse by subjecting the agent to further sources of discomfort.

To some extent, this problem is shared with other forms of sorrow. As I noted briefly in my discussion of identificatory cases in Chapter 3, sorrow often seems to have a tendency to sustain itself as a passive state of discomfort by prompting the agent to dwell on his misfortune. But the emotion does sometimes give rise to a desire for action in contexts where action would improve the situation; and its self-sustaining quality might be made out as sometimes contributing to this ameliorative aim. Dwelling on the object of sorrow, that is, might be seen as designed to improve it by changing the agent's attitude towards it, perhaps at the cost of an increase in more or less immediate discomfort but in the expectation of greater overall good.[13] It is important, however, that more than emotional improvement is in question here, even if it ultimately depends on a change in emotional state. Thus, for instance, one might attempt to make the best of a bad situation by focusing attention on its details—learning enough about it, say, to turn it into an opportunity for *intellectual* improvement. Dwelling on misfortune in such cases may be seen as a strategy for overcoming it—for "mastering" it in thought.

This form of explanation may seem to be only a small part of the story, though, even for ordinary sorrow. It says nothing about the sense in which one is *expressing* the emotion (as I think we would say intuitively) by dwelling on its object. For grief, however, the explanation may seem not even to apply to action *from* the emotion—as opposed, perhaps, to action *on* it. If grief necessarily lacks an ameliorative aim, one might question how it can itself function as a reason for action, even granting that its element of unpleasant affect makes it capable of improvement by the strategy just indicated. Dwelling on its object, for instance, may serve to elicit an intense experience of it, of a sort that is needed to prevent later discomfort—given that the agent is subject to the emotion in some form or other. In what follows I shall refer to this as the self-interested explanation of grief behavior. In fact, I think some version of it does apply to cases of action expressing grief, and I shall later assign it a secondary role in explaining them. But it seems to be unable to make them out as motivated by the *content* of the emotion—as opposed to a desire to alleviate its element of discomfort.

For other cases, on my account, the desire to alleviate emotional discomfort can be seen as *reinforcing* a desire based on the content of the emotion. Or in the "judgmentalist" terms of my earlier reconstruction of practical reasoning from anger, a "self-centered" judgment about the agent's discomfort may serve to reinforce an "object-centered" judgment corresponding to the emotion's evaluative component. The need to alleviate emotional discomfort can thus be taken as explaining the *pressure* exerted by the affective component towards achieving the emotion's aim since its full satisfaction depends on that of the aim. It also provides an explanation of indirect forms of action on emotion, such as making an angry face, as expressive "outlets" yielding symbolic satisfaction of the aim. But grief can have *only* outlets, it seems: Its content provides no link between a desire that operates *on* the emotion and one that arises *from* it since it essentially involves a view of the object as hopeless.

We seem to have a problem, then, for the view of grief behavior as action motivated by grief. I think we can handle it, however, by inquiring into the reasons why an agent sometimes ought to "subject" *himself* to the emotion, on our intuitive account. For grief is one of the prime examples of an emotion one ought to feel in typical cases where it is appropriate. Despite the fact that it resists control, it may often be brought on voluntarily, sometimes by the very act of dwelling on its object. Yet just because of the "punishing" features of action from grief, an *instrumental* rational requirement to undergo the emotion—on the grounds that it would be useful to the agent's pursuit of his ends—seems to be ruled out. Is the discomfort of grief, as compounded by grief behavior, instead prescribed simply for the sake of an accurate *representation*—of the negatively valued situation that constitutes the emotion's object? If only rationality is in question here, it is unclear why accuracy should be *required*, at the cost of subjection to discomfort. However, representational considerations may indeed play a role in an alternative sort of justification of emotion appealing to a moral or quasi-moral requirement.

If we bear in mind my earlier comments on extrarational assessments of emotion in the subsection on emotional ideals, we might appeal to an obligation to "portray" the sense of loss in the medium of emotion either for the sake of one's own ideal self-image or as a way of honoring the dead. Thus, berating himself for emotional "numbness" at the death of a close friend, an agent is not satisfied with the *belief* that he has lost something irreplaceable. Feeling is something he requires of himself, perhaps just as someone who cares about others—to fulfill an ideal of emotional sensitivity, that is. Or feeling may be seen here as something owed *to* others, in the way that came into my discussion of identificatory love in Chapter 3. To say that grief is *socially* obligatory in the second case, moreover, should not be taken just as a claim about conventional behavior at funerals and the like—hence my term "quasi-moral"—though of course such claims are often made as well. On an altruistic explanation like this one (which I shall adopt here, for contrast with the self-interested explanation), the emotion may be thought of as satisfying an interest of the person now deceased—no less plausibly than action to satisfy interests expressed in a will.

On some such account, at any rate, the very discomfort of grief may be seen as serving to dramatize the agent's sense of loss—in a way that also begins to make sense of grief *behavior*. By inflicting further discomfort on himself, the agent depicts the very hopelessness of his situation in affect, one might say. His self-subjection to grief is thus explained as serving some purpose—as a spur towards expressive action. It is not explained, though, as a spur towards action useful in achieving some proper or contextual aim of his emotion. We may think of grief behavior as arising instead from the passive content of the emotion, as the aim of an associated desire with the same moral or quasi-moral source: the desire for expression, here focused specifically on grief. But this desire calls for interpretation in terms of escape from discomfort. For an explanation of grief behavior along the lines I have sketched so far would be not sufficient to capture the sense in which it amounts to action under pressure—to "motivated" action as opposed to action coolly chosen for its expressive value.

Action "motivated" by grief, that is, would seem to have the emotion as both its reason and a kind of *goad* towards its performance: a "pressuring" reason, in short, or one that actually pushes the agent to act and indeed to act soon. On my account of emotional motivation in other cases, this is what is supplied by discomfort—but more or less immediate discomfort of a sort that imposes a cost on postponing action. It may be unclear, though, how this can come into our altruistic explanation of grief behavior—or what else that explanation supplies instead, besides a reason for deliberate action—action with the *goal* of expressing grief. The self-interested explanation I rejected earlier, as extended from cases of action on the ameliorative aim of sorrow, might not seem to help us here, even granting the extension, if it appeals to a desire to prevent *long-term* discomfort: the side-effects of suppressed grief, most obviously. Action to improve one's affective state in the long run cannot be *driven by* discomfort one avoids much later. However, there are ways of bringing in a temporally limited version of the self-interested explanation once the self-sustaining quality of grief has been explained in other terms.

For positive cases, such as joy, where action to sustain emotion is unproblematic, a purely expressive aim can serve as the object of a motivating desire if emotional containment is itself seen as threatening the agent with more or less immediate discomfort. As with joy, of course, grief can exhibit other forms of pressure—or pressure in another *sense*, covering affective quality (a "bursting" feeling), or pure time-pressure, as well as the sort of affective *coercion* that is suggested by my talk of "exerting" pressure. But the emotion's quasi-causal influence, as a goad towards action, seems to turn on the sense of pressure I have stressed. In the case of grief, then, we might say that the object of obligation, on the altruistic explanation, is a felt *need* to express a sense of loss. The pressure exerted by grief may thus be explained by reference to some worse state of discomfort the agent would undergo *in* "bottling up" the emotion—not just as a long-term side-effect of doing so. Action to escape this worse state, moreover, would seem to be compatible with action to subject oneself to *further* discomfort, as required by the obligation to undergo grief, on my account. For that matter, all we really need to say here is that the grief-stricken agent "feels as though" he would experience worse discomfort at containment. His thought may be illusory—an overreaction to discomfort currently felt—and still add genuine motivational force to the desire for expression.

So the need to escape emotional discomfort seems to play a role, after all, in explaining grief motivation. It would not be sufficient on its own to explain the agent's choice of action: but it seems to explain the *haste* with which the choice is made. The self-interested and the altruistic explanations of grief behavior may be seen as coinciding, in fact, in their insistence on the haste that the first supplies. The very pressure exerted by grief on the self-interested explanation favors a choice of the first expressive action that comes to mind; but on the altruistic explanation this may be part of what is required of an agent in the grips of the emotion. It may be important to the expressive value of grief, that is, that the agent not deliberate on the purposes of his action. Part of real grief, or adequate grief, perhaps, is a blindness to the ends of grief behavior. It must not be measured out or fitted *to* a purpose, even one that is altruistic; rather, its expressive end demands that it be *torn from* the agent, much as was the object of his grief. But acting this out deliberately would of course defeat the purpose; hence the need for a secondary mechanism prompting action in response to more or less immediate discomfort.

In a case of "numbness," then, someone might reflect on his failure to fulfill his obligations to the dead by reminding himself reproachfully of his relationship to the object of loss: "But he was my closest friend!" Or the reminder might be meant less as a reproach than simply as a goad to attention—to memories that might elicit the emotion. But ordinarily, no such deliberative maneuvers will be necessary to elicit grief; and none would be desirable in view of what is required of the agent in feeling it. Similarly for the agent's reasoning *from* the emotion to action. As with anger, a choice must be made among alternative modes of expression; but on this matter, too, extended thought would not be suited to the purpose. It might seem that any thought *for himself* would be ruled out here, as well; but my general view of emotions allows for multiple objects of affect, with some objects "masking" others that remain unconscious.[14] Conjoining our two explanations should let us accommodate subliminal reference to self-interest, then, as what *motivates* the agent's altruistic focus in cases of action from grief.

It should be sufficiently clear, by now, that I do not take the "escape from discomfort" view of emotional motivation to yield an all-embracing account even of action explained by reference to emotion. There may be cases of fully deliberate expression of emotion—for the sake of social reinforcement, perhaps, or perhaps for art's sake. But where action is explained by reference to emotional *pressure*, the view implies that we act with limited freedom. Only in rare cases are we totally out of control— so sad that we cannot help dwelling on the object of sorrow, say, or so angry that we must lash out in revenge. But there are limitations on our freedom just insofar as action is required of us in order to escape a state that is seen as hard for an agent to put up with. According to a view I have defended elsewhere, an action is unfree where alternatives to it would be too hard to expect of the agent, even if he is not strictly incapable of them.[15] But full unfreedom, even in this sense, does not seem to be characteristic of emotion, or even of pressuring emotion, if we let the category extend beyond states of extreme agitation—and especially if we consider the full range of actions it explains.

In my state of anger at X, for instance, I *can* control the urge to lash out—at a mounting cost in continuing discomfort but a cost made more bearable by my other options for discharge, including mental action. The cost would be higher for avoiding even symbolic or deflected forms of revenge; and no doubt it would sometimes be high enough for full unfreedom. Even if not, though, the failure to take direct action on anger—to fulfill its proper aim—normally involves some degree of discomfort. The discomfort is hard to put up with partly because the agent sees it as coming upon him soon and continuing without a let-up, so that it interferes with further deliberation. But a barrier to further deliberation can sometimes serve our ends. Thus, insofar as we value emotion as a supplement to dispassionate judgment and desire, it seems that we sometimes value an element of unfreedom. In the way that setting up social obligations may be used as a strategy for reinforcing the reasons for action in self-interest by limiting our *permissible* options, so the cultivation of pressuring emotions promotes our ends by limiting our *reasonable* options to action. This is what stood behind my earlier argument to "ought-to-feel," and my claim that a pressing emotion forces work of us.

Cultivating identificatory emotion, on this view, forces us to work on behalf of others. It adds a self-interested and pressuring reason to the recognition of our social obligations, as if reversing the strategy in the analogy just cited. The practical value of an identificatory emotion will not always depend on the truth of the corresponding judgment, moreover, but rather on that of a recommendation corresponding to a desire its evaluative component gives rise to in context. If I feel sorrow on behalf of someone else, say, in a case where the feeling is adaptive, it need not be true that something bad has happened *to me*—or not without a circular reference to my own affective response to this identificatory evaluation. What makes the feeling adaptive is the fact that it comes to focus on a requirement to mitigate the other's suffering— perhaps just by expressive action, sometimes by action designed to improve his circumstances, but at any rate, by *my* action. A parallel *non*-identificatory emotion—discomfort at the thought that something bad has happened *to him*—might not have quite the same force for action, as we saw in Chapter 3.

Hence my detailed discussion of the appropriateness of identificatory emotion in Chapter 5. An emotion based on taking another's standpoint in imagination, compatibly with self-regarding emotion, is often important for the satisfaction of others' interests in our action. Because of the possibility of ambivalence and its general adaptiveness in social terms, the emotion will be able to accommodate interests at odds with our own—but without undermining the perception of our own—in the particular case at hand. My earlier discussion thus exhibited the "parti-resultant" nature of emotional evaluations—their appropriate basis in a partial subset of the evidence—as the source of a kind of evaluative strengthening of judgment by emotion. My treatment of emotional pressure in this chapter fills out this view of emotion's special motivational force with an account of its affective strengthening of judgment. Emotion makes a requirement of action harder to resist, in short, by making it an object of discomfort. This means that binding oneself to others via shared feeling will impose limitations on one's freedom; but they are limitations that may be adaptive as spurs to *moral* action.

If my argument here is correct, then, emotions play an important role in both prudential and moral reasoning. They are valued for their practical adaptiveness in a way that depends on interpreting them as states of limited freedom. But by arguing this, I have in effect reversed a standard picture of the clash between emotion and reason. Emotions, viewed as reasons for action, are here seen as justified in part for their very resistance to rational control. My defense of this claim was based on an analysis of emotions and their representational justification, in earlier chapters, that distinguished them from beliefs by the resistance of their evaluative contents to logical and evidential control. But according to my argument in this chapter, by removing them from the full control of the will, the lesser *practical* "malleability" of emotions effectively sets up a check on weakness of will. By subjecting himself to emotional pressure, an agent erects a barrier to the will's moment-to-moment flexibility. Our claim that he "ought to feel" in such cases means that he ought to commit himself by means of emotional pressure to following through on some of his long-term desires.

In light of this brief summary of the results of my overall argument, we may now see some of its broader implications for emotion-versus-reason. My title was put in the plural since my results here were drawn bit by bit from the exploration of diverse cases. Moreover, my title merely conjoined the two categories, with nothing to suggest opposition, as in the standard picture. For on the view I have defended, emotions *are* reasons. They can indeed function as irrational forces—because of their tendency towards "spillover," for instance, but also because in extreme cases they subject an agent to motives beyond his control. In the cases I have stressed here to balance the standard picture, however, emotions also add motivational force to rational judgment and desire. My argument thus can be said to yield a general justification of emotion; for its account of what one ought to feel in particular cases yields an answer to the question why one ought to feel *anything*.

Passion, on this view, may be seen as working in the service of reason. It is neither slave nor slavemaster, as on the Humean account, but rather plays something more like the role that Plato assigned to the seat of emotion in the tripartite soul, properly executing reason's commands despite a rebellious tendency.[16] Here, however, its rebellious tendency is made out as a side-effect of something valuable. For my own view depends on not relegating passion to a separate status or sphere, with reason's commands interpreted as deliverances from on high, but treating it instead, one might say, as a somewhat independent member of the reason family. The link to judgment via evaluation is crucial to this alternative since it gives us a new way of cutting into the conventional emotion/reason contrast. Instead of treating emotion as opposed to reason, judgmentalism, the view I have argued against, may be seen as attempting to do away with the contrast by analyzing emotions as modifications of judgment, assumed to be reason's basic instrument. But this is accomplished at the cost of ascribing to emotions no role in practical reasoning *besides* that of judgment. The alternative view I have defended here analyzes emotions as sharing a common content with evaluative judgments and thus a rational (justificatory) role in the generation of action. Their role is a special one, however, since emotional evaluations motivate by way of *affect* rather than assent. It is also a widespread role, let us note; for my view of the nature of emotions extends affect beyond extreme cases, granting even to "calm passions" motivational force as supplements to detached judgment and desire.

NOTES

1 Reasons to Feel: Sketch of an Argument

[1] See Errol Bedford, "Emotions," *Proceedings of the Aristotelian Society*, 57 (1956-1957), 281–304; O. H. Green, "Emotions and Belief," in N. Rescher (ed.), *Studies in the Philosophy of Mind, American Philosophical Quarterly*, Monograph No. 6 (Oxford: Basil Blackwell, 1972), pp. 24–40; Jerome Neu, *Emotion, Thought and Therapy* (Berkeley: University of California, 1977); and Robert C. Solomon, *The Passions: The Myth and Nature of Human Emotion* (Garden City, N.Y.: Anchor, 1978). With the qualifications explained in ch.2, n. 2, I would also include William Lyons, *Emotion* (Cambridge: Cambridge University, 1980); cf. also the accounts of pride cited in ch. 3, n. 2.

These contemporary views are put forth as alternatives to views derived from René Descartes, *The Passions of the Soul*, in E. S. Haldane and G. R. T. Ross (trans.), *The Philosophical Works of Descartes*, vol. 1 (Cambridge: Cambridge University, 1970), pp. 331–427. But the general line goes back at least to the Stoics; for a detailed historical survey, see H. M. Gardiner, Ruth Clark Metcalf, and John G. Beebe-Center, *Feeling and Emotion: A History of Theories* (Westport, Conn.: Greenwood, 1937). To minimize difficulties for readers unfamiliar with the literature on this subject, I shall limit the main argument in my text to a simplified account of alternative views. In general, though my own view has much in common with others, (especially Aristotle's and Hume's) I shall relegate any textual mapping to footnotes; see ch. 2, n. 7 and ch. 3, n. 8.

2 Emotions Without Essences:
Varieties of Fear

[1] See my "Emotions as Evaluations," *Pacific Philosophical Quarterly*, 62 (April 1981), 158–169; and "Emotions, Reasons, and 'Self-Involvement'," *Philosophical Studies*, 38 (August 1980), 161–168. For similar views, see George Pitcher, "Emotions," *Mind*, 74 (July 1965), 326–346, and Kevin Donaghy, "Emotion Without Judgment," in F. D. Miller, Jr., and T. W. Attig (eds.), *Understanding Human Emotion, Bowling Green Studies in Applied Philosophy*, vol. 1 (Bowling Green, Ohio: Bowling Green State University, 1979), pp. 36–42.

In "A Case of Mixed Feelings: Ambivalence and the Logic of Emotion," in A. O. Rorty (ed.), *Explaining Emotions* (Berkeley: University of California, 1980), pp. 223–250, I presented a preliminary argument against the *identification* of emotions with judgments. I would now modify a number of my points and aims there; see ch. 4, nn. 1, 3, 8, and ch. 5, n. 6. Here I merely sketch my later argument against the view that emotions *entail* their corresponding judgments—an argument I do still accept but need to defend against objections—as a way into a more general discussion of cases of "occurrent" emotion. My hope is that, to the extent that judgmentalism can be defeated by argument, some of the various cases in Part I will tell against it. But my primary aim here is to defend my alternative analysis as a reasonable framework for addressing the justificatory questions to be dealt with in Part II.

² Except for its emphasis on current mental involvement, my account here resembles Lyons' attempt, in *Emotion, op. cit.*, to explain apparently nonjudgmental emotions as reflex reactions to "embedded" evaluations from past experience (see pp. 86–87). I would stress Lyons' brief suggestion on p. 88 that the evaluation must in some sense be "active" in the current situation, even if it is not then conscious. Unfortunately, however, the case he uses to illustrate this suggestion on p. 89 does seem to involve unconscious *belief* (cf. pp. 76–77).

In general, it is unclear to me to what extent Lyons departs from judgmentalism. Although he does not refer to evaluations as beliefs, the distinction seems to be terminological: He restricts the noun "belief" to factual judgments; but he seems quite ready to use belief *verbs* in connection with evaluations (see, e.g., pp. 34–35, pp. 58–59, p. 86, and p. 89). Moreover, while he denies that evaluations are "cognitive," on the grounds that they appeal to an agent's "personal" rating scale, he does seem to allow that they are extended to others, on the model of universalizable evaluative judgments (cf. pp. 59–60 and pp. 78–80). In any case, I include even my own account among "cognitivist" views to the extent that, like Lyons' theory, it bases emotional on cognitive distinctions.

Lyons takes emotions to be picked out as the particular emotions they are by reference to their evaluative components, but to be picked out *as emotions* by the fact that their evaluative components cause "abnormal physiological changes." I shall go on to present some cases that might be used to question his "causal-evaluative" theory—on the assumption that feelings *result from* physiological changes, where the latter do yield emotions. For a more general defense of physiological bases (whether or not "abnormal changes") as necessary but not sufficient for emotions, see Georges Rey, "Functionalism and the Emotions," in A. O. Rorty (ed.), *Explaining Emotions, op. cit.*, pp. 163–195. See also ch. 2, n. 7.

³ See esp. David Sachs, "On Freud's Doctrine of Emotions," in R. Wollheim (ed.), *Freud: A Collection of Critical Essays* (Garden City, N. Y.: Anchor, 1974), pp. 132–146, and Harvey Mullane, "Unconscious Emotion," *Theoria*, 31 (1965), 181–190. The view I adopt here seems to fit the less "strict" account in Sigmund Freud, "The Unconscious," in J. Strachey (trans.), *The Standard Edition of the Works of Sigmund Freud*, vol. 14 (London: Hogarth, 1953). It is meant to provide an alternative to Mullane's purely dispositional account (see "Unconscious Emotion," *op. cit.*, e.g., pp. 184–185), but without presupposing Freud's detailed conception of unconscious "contents."

⁴ My treatment of the jealousy case as involving a confusion of two varieties of *fear* depends on my broad understanding of "discomfort"; cf. ch. 2, n. 7. A nice account of the range of object-directed feeling that may come into play here—and a nice expression for it, "being bothered"—is provided in Daniel M. Farrell, "Jealousy," *Philosophical Review*, 89 (October 1980), 527–559, esp. pp. 538–539 (cf. p. 543). See also Annette Baier, "Master Passions," in A. O. Rorty (ed.), *Explaining Emotions, op. cit.*, pp. 403–423, for some suggestions that come up in discussing qualifications on the self-content characteristic of *pride*: "unrest," "unease," and the like.

Farrell has remarked in correspondence that jealousy provides some good cases of emotion without judgment: cases where the very thought that the love-object *could* favor someone else is enough to provoke the feeling. We have to interpret this carefully, though; for if we treat jealousy as a variety of fear, a belief in the possibility of loss of favor might seem to ground the emotion in such cases. See Robert M. Gordon, "Fear," *Philosophical Review*, 89 (October 1980), 560–578, for an account of "uncertainty" emotions as including fear—though not all varieties if my later treatment of horror and dread is correct. In any case, the object of fear has to be seen as a *real* possibility—as something that might very well come to pass—and not just as barely conceivable. Farrell's suggestion would seem to apply most readily to jealousy as a deluded form of fantasy-fear, in cases analogous to those I go on to discuss.

⁵ For some highlights of the debate over objects and causes, see esp. Ludwig Wittgenstein, *Philosophical Investigations*, G. E. M. Anscombe (trans.) (New York: Macmillan, 1953), sec. 476, p. 135, and *Zettel*, G. E. M. Anscombe (trans.) (Oxford: Basil Blackwell, 1967), sec. 488, pp. 86–87; G. E. M. Anscombe, *Intention* (Ithaca, N. Y.: Cornell University, 1963), sec. 10, p. 16; Anthony Kenny, *Action, Emotion and Will* (New York: Humanities, 1963), pp. 12–14 and pp. 60–62; D. F. Pears, "Causes and Objects of Some Feelings and Psychological Reactions," in S. Hampshire (ed.), *Philosophy of Mind*, (New York: Harper & Row, 1966), pp. 143–169; Irving Thalberg, "Emotion and Thought," in *ibid.*, pp. 201–225; and J. R. S. Wilson, *Emotion and Object* (Cambridge: Cambridge University, 1972). I shall not join this fray, in what follows, though I shall feel free to rely on an intuitive notion of object-directedness in the expectation that anything I have to say can be translated into the technical talk of a given theoretical conception. On my account, the application of the intuitive notion to emotions is derivative from its application to the two components of emotion; but I shall avoid commitment to a particular view of the latter. For the less philosophically familiar notion of an object of the affective component, my hunch is that an analysis could be based on causal hypotheticals about objects of *attention*. These would have to be extremely complex, however. They might tell us, for instance, that the agent's attention to the feeling in question would result in a thought corresponding to the evaluative component of emotion, if we rule out mental barriers of the sort indicated in my treatment of unconscious emotions.

⁶ See Kendall L. Walton, "Fearing Fictions," *Journal of Philosophy*, 75 (January 1978), 5–27, for an account of this and similar reactions as involving a kind of play-acting on the part of the viewer. Walton denies that real *fear* can be involved here—with no judgment that one is in danger and hence no desire to flee the theater—even where full fear symptoms are experienced. On my view, however, we may still have an evaluation sufficient for occurrent fear. Even if the emotion is generated by play-acting—and its *object* is known to be unreal—it may still be a genuine instance of emotion. I shall have more to say about fantasy-emotions—in particular, about the moral significance and appropriateness of those that involve emotional identification—in Chapters 3, 5, and 6.

⁷ See Aristotle, *Rhetorica*, in R. McKeon (ed.), *The Basic Works of Aristotle* (New York: Random House, 1941), pp. 1325–1451, Book II; René Descartes, *The Passions of the Soul*, *op. cit.*, Part Second; Benedict de Spinoza, *The Ethics*, in R. H. M. Elwes (trans.), *Benedict de Spinoza: On the Improvement of the Understanding; The Ethics; Correspondence*, (New York: Dover, 1955), pp. 45–271, Part III; and David Hume, *A Treatise of Human Nature* (Oxford: Clarendon, 1888), Book II. All talk at least partly in terms of pleasure and pain, though some include desire as an independent factor and some (especially Aristotle and Spinoza) distinguish among emotions on the basis of their evaluative content.

Moreover, even those philosophers who identify emotions with particular sensations (especially Descartes and Hume) bring in evaluation and desire, along with physiological changes, when they describe either the causal generation of emotions or what they are sensations *of*. In Thomas Hobbes, *Leviathan* (Baltimore, Md.: Penguin, 1968), Part I, Ch. 6, pleasure and displeasure are apparently taken as sensations of the bodily motions constituting "Endeavour," or appetite and aversion, with evaluations defined in terms of these motivational states (see pp. 119–120). I reverse the definition, in effect, taking motivating desire as derivative from a certain *sort* of evaluation, as an object of discomfort, with the latter seen as essentially a state that an agent would want to get out of.

For an argument that such affective states do not *reduce to* desire—but in what I have called "the philosopher's sense"—see Michael Stocker, "Psychic Feelings," *Australasian Journal of Philosophy*, 61 (March 1983), 5–26, esp. pp. 10–18; cf. ch. 3, n. 8. I doubt, too, whether they can be explained entirely in physiological terms across different stages of animal and human development. Although I assume that they do have a physiological basis of some sort, I would be surprised if it turned out to be a simple one—or one that did not involve cortical activity, as a product of both evolution and a kind of social "shaping" to be indicated in my next chapter. In any case, they do not amount to perceptions *of* "bodily" occurrences, on the view I adopt here; cf. esp. William James, *The Principles of Psychology*, vol. 2 (New York: Dover, 1950), esp. p. 449. Nor do they always involve bodily *feelings* (as distinct from generalized mental tension, say); cf. Moreland Perkins, "Emotion and Feeling," *Philosophical Review*, 75 (April 1966), 139–160.

I take physiological changes to *yield* emotions, moreover, only where they do yield comfort or discomfort *about* some evaluative proposition. My mouth may water as I go past my favorite food in the supermarket, presumably as a result of an "embedded" evaluation of it—see ch. 2, n. 2—but I do not *crave* it in emotional terms unless I am discomfited, on some level or other by the thought that I must get it. If my treatment of cases of mixed affect is correct, though, I need not see myself as uncomfortable on the whole or even be aware of the element of discomfort in my overall state of feeling; cf. Lyons, *Emotion, op. cit.*, p. 58.

It is also worth noting that unmixed occurrent states of comfort, such as simple joy and pride, taken as states one would want to stay in, may or may not involve "bodily upsets," in the sense of changes from the bodily norm, if we allow for long-term occurrent emotions without full-blown emotion symptoms. Cf. Lyons, pp. 60–61; and William P. Alston, "Emotion and Feeling," in P. Edwards (ed.), *Encyclopedia of Philosophy*, vol. 2 (New York: Macmillan, 1967), pp. 479–493, esp. p. 486, for a similar view of occurrent emotions as involving a "disturbed state of the organism."

3   Some Morally Significant Emotions:
Rewards and Punishments

[1]   See Lawrence Blum, "Compassion," in A. O. Rorty (ed.), *Explaining Emotions, op. cit.*, pp. 507–517, esp. pp. 514–516, and *Friendship, Altruism and Morality* (London: Routledge & Kegan Paul, l980), esp. pp. 144–151; cf. also William Neblett, *The Role of Feeling in Morals* (Washington, D.C.: University Press of America, 1981), esp. pp. 9–11.

[2]   See Donald Davidson, "Hume's Cognitive Theory of Pride," *Journal of Philosophy*, 73 (November 4, 1976), 744–757; Philippa Foot, "Moral Beliefs," *Proceedings of the Aristotelian Society*, 59 (1958–1959), 83–104; and Gabriele Taylor, "Pride," in A. O. Rorty (ed.), *Explaining Emotions, op. cit.*, pp. 385–402. Cf. David Hume, *A Treatise of Human Nature, op. cit.*, Book II, Sec. II, esp. p. 277. In what follows, my use of the term "praiseworthy" to capture the positive self-evaluation characteristic of pride follows Davidson but fits some cases better than others; "important," "powerful," and the like might be substituted where the more general term seems questionable.

[3]   This case first emerged in conversation with Jerrold Levinson about his claim that feelings in response to music are objectless and therefore *cannot* be emotions; see, e.g., "Music and Negative Emotions," *Pacific Philosophical Quarterly*, 633 (1982), 327–346, esp. pp. 331–332. As I understand it, Levinson's argument would seem to rule out other

indefinite fantasy-emotions besides the responses to programmatic music that raise the question most forcefully. For a view more like my own, particularly on the explanation of fantasy-*fear*, see John Morreall, "Enjoying Negative Emotions in Fiction," *Philosophy of Literature*, 19 (April 1985), 95–103.

⁴ My rather cautious claim here, though it rules out suspension of judgment (at least for beliefs that may be borne in mind), owes much to criticism of an earlier version by Timothy Williamson. The "must" in it is normative; for the claim amounts to a consequence of the Principle of Logical Charity—a constitutive rule of "basic" rationality, applied to the question whether an assumption or other predicative thought should count as a belief. Note that this is not itself a justificatory question, though issues of "backward-looking" justification come up in attempting to settle it. In any case, the justificatory questions need not be regarded as completely settled at this point to support so cautious a claim.

In particular, one need not maintain that a belief could never be justified by "forward-looking" considerations—in this case, by its usefulness to the agent in generating confidence—either in the absence of adequate evidence or against the preponderance of evidence currently available. What the claim rules out as inconsistent with basic rationality is a belief not backed up by a minimal kind of corresponding faith in the total (hypothetically available) body of evidence: faith that the belief in question could survive a full inquiry. This does accord backward-looking considerations a kind of primacy for belief that they do not have for emotion, on my view; and the point will be extended when I do turn to justificatory questions. But as far as I can see, it is perfectly compatible with reasonable arguments for faith of the usual sort: the choice to adopt a belief that is not yet, or could never be, *established* by the evidence. See esp. William James, "The Will to Believe," in *The Will to Believe; Human Immortality* (New York: Dover, 1956), pp. 1–31, e.g., p. 11, for the limitation of the most familiar argument to matters that "cannot . . . be established on intellectual grounds."

In the case of confidence that I have set up here, it is important that the agent already recognizes decisive evidence *against* at least an unqualified belief corresponding to the emotion's evaluative component—and that holding the latter in mind requires actively ignoring such counterevidence. The case should not be confused with one in which the agent simply fails to consider the question whether confidence is justified. Nor is it put forth as the only possible case of confidence exceeding its grounds. Perhaps a more thoroughgoing form of self-deception, involving a deluded *judgment* about the grounds for confidence, is sometimes both possible and preferable in forward-looking terms. But the present case, with its split between judgment and emotion, does seem to represent an alternative to this and one that may be easier for some agents to manage.

It also lets us appeal to a notion of logical coherency as definitive of the system of beliefs; and this means that my argument here amounts to more than a bare appeal to intuition. It provides us with general support, that is, for the view that a change in beliefs, whenever confidence is called for, would have to involve a change at multiple levels in the system, including the level of beliefs about the grounds for one's beliefs. This makes it less plausible to suppose that the requisite belief change occurs so readily, given that the agent has to work to avoid confronting the counterevidence.

I should acknowledge, of course, that my argument does involve an appeal to intuition on the particular case described, just insofar as it requires imagining a change in confidence without a change in one's beliefs about the grounds for it. Since some readers may find such cases hard to imagine, I have briefly inserted the alternative example of *optimism*, which may be recognized as unfounded without quite the same problems for self-esteem. However, a nicely concrete example—a more sophisticated version of popular "self-help" affirmations—can be extracted from a handout found in a doctor's office on the use of biofeedback to control migraines. The technique described involves repeating a sentence on the model of "my whole body feels quiet, comfortable and relaxed"—something that would be roundly rejected, if questions of evidence were even considered, by a patient still in the grips of a migraine.

The efficacy of the verbal behavior recommended here might depend on its eventually *generating* a belief; so perhaps it is just as well that biofeedback instructions tend to blur over philosophical distinctions on such questions. In any case, the fact that this seems to be standard in psychological discussions generally is among my reasons for minimizing explicit reference to them in this essay. For we also need to say that the affirmation here initially falls short of belief, insofar as it is taken as *inducing* relaxation. When the agent begins to repeat the affirmation, he still presumably trusts the evidence of his senses about a current state of pain. The affirmation is supposed to effect a *change* in that evidence— to the extent that the agent holds it in mind as an "assumption," in my terms.

⁵ This rough account is suggested by the alternative to judgmentalism sketched in Amelie Oksenberg Rorty, "Explaining Emotions," *Journal of Philosophy*, 75 (March 1978), 139–161; cf. Ronald De Sousa, "The Rationality of Emotions," *Dialogue*, 18 (1979), 41– 63. If my argument here is correct, it seems that this "attention/salience" view does not really represent a *nonpropositional* alternative to evaluative theories since it requires implicit reference to evaluative *predicates*.

⁶ The general point is nicely illustrated by Stanley Schachter and Jerome E. Singer, "Cognitive, Social, and Physiological Determinants of Emotional State," *Psychological Review*, 69 (September 1962), 379–399. Difficulties in replicating their experiment undermine its detailed use in defense of cognitive theories of emotion; but perhaps this may be explained by the fact that it relied heavily on social cues, under conditions inducing various sorts of *conformity*. Since the subjects were students and participation in the experiment was a way of achieving extra points on the final, reluctance to admit to anger at the experimenter was taken as explaining some apparently disconfirming results; see p. 391. But a tendency to identify with the "stooge" posing as a fellow subject and setting up the "cognitive" situation might equally be brought in to account for some results that did confirm the experimenters' "cognitivist" hypothesis.

⁷ See John B. Watson, *Behaviorism* (Chicago: University of Chicago, 1930), p. 154, for bodily rage responses apparently elicited shortly after birth. Some more recent psychologists use facial expressions to pick out certain emotions, including anger, as *innate*, even though they do not seem to occur until some months after birth; see, e.g., Carroll E. Izard, *Human Emotions* (New York: Plenum, 1977). The innateness hypothesis is traced to cross-cultural studies in Charles Darwin, *The Expression of the Emotions in Man and Animals* (Chicago: University of Chicago, 1965). Photographs in support of it, however, do not exhibit the distinctions at issue here, most notably that between blame and simple frustration. For an apparent rejection of the latter as potentially *justified* anger in adults, see Gabriele Taylor, "Justifying the Emotions," *Mind*, 84 (1975), 390–402, esp. pp. 394–395.

Wittgenstein suggests that their lack of clear temporal distinctions, of a sort that presuppose language use, makes dogs and other animals incapable of experiencing emotions like hope and remorse; see *Philosophical Investigations, op. cit.*, Part II, sec. i, p. 174, and *Zettel, op. cit.*, secs. 518–519, p. 91. I think we can allow for shorter-range versions, though, sometimes with indefinitely specified objects—the hope that some food will be shared fairly soon; or a kind of remorse (indistinct from social shame) at a freshly discovered lapse from continence. In any case, if my argument here succeeds, a similar point would seem to apply to emotions, like anger, that Wittgenstein does attribute to animals. It applies to human infants as well, on the assumption that they lack the appropriate concept of responsibility.

[8] See Aristotle, *Rhetorica, op. cit.*, Book II, sec. 2, 1378a31–1378b5, pp. 1380–1381. Cf. Abraham I. Melden, "The Conceptual Dimensions of Emotions," in T. Mischel (ed.), *Human Action: Conceptual and Empirical Issues* (New York: Academic, 1969), pp. 199–221, esp. pp. 203–204, for an account that drops the insistence on pain or discomfort as an element of anger. I shall take issue with this in my ensuing discussion, while granting that not all cases of anger involve discomfort on the whole—as opposed to that element of discomfort that the desire to attack brings in.

Along with Aristotle, I take some, but only some, emotions to involve a desire for action—what I call a "motivating" desire, since it involves discomfort at an unfulfilled action requirement. My overall view is not quite "conative," then, though it is designed to yield an account of those emotions that do yield motivating desires in context whether or not they are *essentially* directed towards action, as anger seems to be. With comfort taken as a state one would want to stay in and discomfort as a state one would want to get out of, all emotions *would* seem to yield desires in "the philosopher's sense." The latter is nicely illustrated, for instance, by Anthony Kenny's definition of "Volition" in *Action, Emotion and Will* (New York: Humanities, 1963), pp. 214–215.

For a view of emotions as essentially *passive wishes*—and hence quite sharply distinguished from "motives," even those ascribed by emotion *terms*—see R. S. Peters, "Emotions and the Category of Passivity," *Proceedings of the Aristotelian Society*, suppl. 62 (1961–1962), 117–134. Cf. also "Motivation, Emotion, and the Conceptual Schemes of Common Sense," in T. Mischel (ed.), *Human Action: Conceptual and Empirical Issues* (New York: Academic, 1969), pp. 135–165, esp. pp. 159–162. In the later paper, Peters gives a restatement of his view to accommodate the element of "intuitive appraisal" stressed by Magda B. Arnold, a psychologist, as part of a more action-oriented account in *Emotion and Personality*, vol. 1 (New York: Columbia University, 1960), esp. pp. 172 and 177. Cf. also Arnold's "Human Emotion and Action," in T. Mischel (ed.), *Human Action: Conceptual and Empirical Issues, op. cit.*, pp. 167–197.

Alston, in "Emotion and Feeling," *op. cit.*, pp. 480–481, would apparently count both of these views—along with my own and any other *evaluative* accounts—as "motivational," having ruled out the possibility of identifying emotions with action tendencies, as on Arnold's view. He argues this by showing that not all emotions are associated with particular actions—essentially Peters' point, with grief as an especially forceful example; cf. ch. 6, n. 13. We may grant this, however, while allowing for a stronger tie between *some* emotions and action via motivating desire, of a sort that adds something to standard evaluative accounts, but without an all-embracing causal theory of motivation; cf. ch. 6, n. 6.

[9] The case (which I have modified to distinguish it from simple *deluded* love) appears in Robert Kraut, "Objects of Affection," in K. D. Irani and G. E. Myers (eds.), *Emotion: Philosophical Studies* (New York, N. Y.: Haven, 1983), pp. 42–56; see pp. 51–53. My discussion of it stems from an earlier, unpublished paper, in which Kraut had not yet allowed for variable standards of knowledge; cf. p. 53. In any case, on Kraut's nonevaluative view of love, it apparently would require only *knowing who* the object is—not necessarily knowledge of the sort that would yield an adequate evaluation of the object.

For a contrasting account of love, closer to my own but with judgmentalist underpinnings, see Gabriele Taylor, "Love," *Proceedings of the Aristotelian Society*, 77 (1975–1976), 147–164, esp. pp. 151–153; cf. pp. 154–157. Taylor brings in some cases from literature that exhibit the central features of Lisa's case on p. 160; but she apparently treats them as "defective" only in the sense of *unjustified*.

In more extreme contrast to Kraut's view, Lyons suggests that the word "love" has only a *dispositional* use; see *Emotion, op. cit*, p. 55. But feelings of tenderness at the thought of the irreplaceable value of some object would seem to count as *one* occurrent state of love, and the one that is most commonly called "love," even though it is not the only manifestation of the emotion, on my view. I would grant, however, that the term is not limited to emotions but is sometimes applied to a relationship without much affective content. A relationship is not enough for occurrent love, of course, any more than pride as a trait of temperament is enough for occurrent pride.

A similar point might be made, though, for feelings of tenderness alone, in response to what seems to be Kraut's view of love. I wish I had saved a *Doonesbury* cartoon passed on to me by Stephen Stich, in which the familiar football huddle somehow has launched into an argument about which states amount to emotions. After some protests at the suggestion of "insouciance," "horniness" comes up and is roundly rejected. Presumably, it is taken as a "pure" feeling—"pure" in the sense I have brought in earlier, not even amounting to a desire for "I know not whom," though as with coffee-induced edginess, it might very readily "take on" an object, whether indefinite or simply available. I would say the same of "horniness of the heart," despite the difference in localization—and even where it is a reaction to some *particular* object, as on Kraut's view.

[10] This assumption must be taken to rule out quite a lot: most notably, insults that could apply to me on some other basis (sex, say, or my individual traits) and insults that in context would have indirect negative effects on my interests (by interfering with social interaction, for instance). But the resulting case, though artificial, is not impossible; in fact, it is based on a real-life case, in which X had more or less been rendered harmless by age. I have described the case in somewhat more detail here than I did in "Identificatory Love," *Philosophical Studies, op. cit.*, in order to answer some questions about whether imagination is really needed to generate an identificatory evaluation. (See also ch. 3, n. 11.)

It might be thought that a fantasy-evaluation is unnecessary to make sense of emotional identification just because it could be replaced by the agent's judgment that he is vulnerable to the same *sorts* of harms as the other party, along with the affective response he *would* have if actually subjected to such harms. However, I take it that the affect here must be more than an incidental accompaniment of the judgment—if that judgment or some related evaluation is to provide it with intentional content, of the sort I have defended as essential to emotion, as opposed to objectless sensation. But if so, an adequate response to a case of the sort I sketch here would still seem to require some element of fantasy.

Sadness about my *actual* vulnerability to insults in general, that is, or to an insult that was leveled at me in the past, would yield a kind of *self*-pity rather than an identificatory emotion. But if my discomfort were directed towards a thought of myself as undergoing some particular but *hypothetical* insult, then my emotion would seem to involve imagination, after all. Similarly, for that matter, if my emotion rested on hypothetical assumptions about the effects of the actual insult—e.g., of everyone's doing likewise. However, I shall later suggest another way of making the evaluation here rest on something less specific—and hence, I think, more plausible—than the view of myself as undergoing the *same* misfortunes as the other party. Although it will allow for the retention of my own standpoint, it will still admit of interpretation as a kind of fantasy-evaluation; cf. the distinction between "central" and "acentral" imagination introduced by Richard Wollheim in *The Thread of Life* (Cambridge, Mass.: Harvard University, 1984), esp. pp. 72–76.

[11] I have added a few words to my earlier version of this argument in order to allow for Karen Hanson's objection that "*any* representative of mankind *in my position* . . . [might be said to] have some responsibility for action." It is important to this case that, insofar as I am angry, I see myself as *fully* responsible for punishing X, in the sense of being picked out for individual action by a requirement to punish him.

This is not to say that the action I should perform must be *specified* fully or must amount to the fullest *sort* of punishment. Rather, the intended contrast here is to *shared* responsibility, with no definite parceling out of subtasks among the individuals in the group that bears it—whether mankind at large or those representatives of it who are present on this occasion. The case assumes that *full* responsibility actually devolves only on some such group rather than on any individual in it. It might be compared, say, to a case where some group bears responsibility for collecting from its members a certain amount of money for famine relief but no individual is himself responsible for contributing a particular amount—at least until the group decides on a procedure for allocating responsibility.

In the present case, of course, there is no such procedure—or even, let us assume, any particular "natural" way of dividing the labor. No one is picked out by talent or the like as the best group member to avenge the insult; and adequate vengeance does not require action on the part of all group members. It might be said that everyone in the group bears "some responsibility for action," meaning that each partakes in the general group responsibility. But the agent still may bear no individual responsibility, even for seeing to it that the *group* punishes X—though he must "feel as though" he is responsible for some such action, insofar as he reacts to the insult with anger.

However, once I bring in the looser notion of identification, it will be clear that this fantasy-evaluation need not involve simple self-projection into the position of the target but rather a more direct assumption of responsibility for him. This means that my account of motivation by identificatory emotion assumes more than simple self-interest. It also makes it clear that the notion of responsibility that comes into play here cannot be one that rests on a past action of the agent, or anything else attributable to him as cause, as in my earlier treatments of pride, anger, and attachment-love. I have discussed this notion in more detail in my article "Unfreedom and Responsibility," in F. Schoeman (ed.), *New Directions for Responsibility* (Cambridge: Cambridge University Press, 1987), pp. 63–80. For present purposes the analogy to responsibility for famine relief might help as a brief illustration, since it involves taking responsibility for corrective action whether or not one is held responsible for the problem.

[12] Both lines of objection were suggested to me by Harvey Green's comments on an earlier version of this Section at the University of North Carolina at Greensboro Symposium in Philosophy, in March 1985. But the bulk of the second—that portion assigned to its own subsection—was not actually spelled out by Green. For an earlier discussion of some of the questions it raises, see my "A Case of Mixed Feelings: Ambivalence and the Logic of Emotion," *op. cit.*; cf. ch. 5.

4 Perceptual Warrant: Suspicion Revisited

[1] See De Sousa, "The Rationality of Emotions," *op. cit.*, p. 132; cf. p. 133. De Sousa avoids the *word* "truth" in his ensuing discussion for reasons he indicates here; but he still seems ready to mix other notions of "success" with notions of warrant in his treatment of the "intrinsic" rationality of emotions. Cf. my "A Case of Mixed Feelings: Ambivalence and the Logic of Emotion," *op. cit*, esp. pp. 235–236.

[2] A conversation with William Harper enabled me to see this—and alerted me to some exceptions to the tendency of "reliability" accounts of knowledge to detach the notion from that of justified belief. I owe thanks, too, to Andrew Woodfield for an earlier discussion of current accounts—and for the spatial perception example that comes up later in this chapter. The particular reliability account that I consider here is based on some suggestions I found in Robert Kraut, "Visceral Fear" (Unpublished paper, 1982)—but with modifications to accommodate the suspicion case.

My concern here is not with knowledge, I should say, except to the extent that it does involve warranted belief. It is worth noting, however, that on some accounts of the sort considered here—with reliability taken as *sufficient* for knowledge—our original suspicion case would seem to come out as a case of purely "emotional" knowledge, without even *un*warranted belief.

³ Note that a qualified judgment, as here conceived, though it may report a prima facie reason, is not itself a prima facie *judgment*. I take it that a prima facie judgment is one that is based on a subset of the total body of evidence but whose content is not limited to reflect the limitations on the evidence. Thus, in the present case, "X is untrustworthy" would be prima facie, considered against the same background of evidence as that which justifies the qualified judgment given here. We may say that the qualified judgment, by contrast, is justified *as* an "all things considered" judgment (as distinct from one that is "all-out," or *un*qualified), since its qualifications let it stand against the background of the total body of evidence. Although this usage does not fit some contemporary interpretations of "prima facie," I take it to be in line with the original application of the term to unqualified judgments of duty, or right action. (See ch. 4, n. 5.) My comments on "qualified" judgments and emotions, in what follows, should be taken as superceding my discussion in "A Case of Mixed Feelings: Ambivalence and the Logic of Emotion," *op. cit.*, pp. 233–234.

⁴ It is important that this distinction—between a judgment itself and the act of forming it—does not have a short-term parallel for emotions just because emotions exhibit some features of both belief and action. Assent to a proposition may be treated either as an action or as the result of one; so it preserves the ambiguity illustrated here. Although assent may result from a long-term action of *cultivating* belief, in cases where more is required than treating a subset of the total body of evidence as if it were complete, it also may involve just *adopting* a belief, presumably a short-term action, as in the present case. An inappropriate but adaptive emotion tendency—towards anger, say, where there are grounds only for sadness—admits of cultivation, of course, as a long-term parallel to the present case. But the emotion cannot simply be adopted at will, in some way analogous to a decision to stop considering counterevidence; for it involves holding a proposition in mind *by* feeling comfortable or uncomfortable about it—something not subject to direct voluntary control.

There is no act of *feeling* that carries over to emotions the distinctions applicable to assent, in short. So we cannot detach our assessment of emotions as belieflike states from a forward-looking assessment, in the terms usually applied to action, simply by assigning the two assessments to different items, one of which amounts to "the emotion itself." The fact that we *can* make a similar distinction for belief, as illustrated here, allows us to claim that nonevidential considerations do not apply "properly" to belief without denying that they may sometimes be used to justify an act of belief formation. In any case, it should be noted that my own claim here is framed in a way designed to avoid these complexities: Nonevidential considerations are said not to apply properly to belief *warrant*, which is understood as limited to backward-looking justification.

⁵ My second example of this interpretation, using "insofar as" to introduce the qualifier, is modeled on Davidson, "Hume's Cognitive Theory of Pride," *op. cit.* Where a qualified judgment of this sort is held "all things considered"—in light of the total body of evidence, that is; (see ch. 4, n. 3)—I take it that it cannot be merely "prima facie," though Davidson apples this term to his examples. I should note, however, that on my view there are some cases of dilemmatic ought judgments where both notions might apply; see my "Sophie's Choices: More on Exclusive Requirement" (Unpublished paper: American Philosophical Association, 1986).

⁶ This point is in response to Adam Morton's suggestion, in conversation, of a coherence theory including both emotions and beliefs, as illustrated by examples like the one I go on to cite. It might indeed be possible to translate my rough-and-ready talk of "fitting the facts," here, into talk of coherency. We would then have to be careful, though,

about which sorts of practical considerations properly apply to beliefs as opposed to emotions and acts—including acts of cultivating belief (cf. ch. 4, n. 4).

What about those very general *preferences*, such as simplicity, that guide our choice with regard to systems of belief? I would question whether these should be interpreted in terms of emotions rather than evaluative beliefs—assuming that they do involve evaluations. What makes them seem "emotional" is apparently just the fact that they are not seen as warranted in the terms applied to beliefs—or not until coherency considerations are brought in. In any case, they might be more fruitfully understood in terms of *acts of choice*—and as justified in practical terms at least partly by their effects, including their intellectual effects, in determining the structure of the agent's belief system.

Of course, one might say the same of the choice, say, of a God-centered way of approaching intellectual inquiry (as Morton suggested). This sort of preference, along with simplicity, would seem to *yield* an evaluation, which might be said to be justified by its effects. However, we ought to distinguish between justification for the corresponding belief and justification for the act of forming it. In case there seems to be no distinction here, consider the "hard sell" broker case, where my belief that the broker is untrustworthy is *not* justified, since it is the result of "jumping to a conclusion." I may still be justified *in* jumping to a conclusion—in my act of assenting to the belief without adequate evidence (cf. ch. 4, n. 4)—given my perceptions and needs.

In short, an intellectual error may be justified in practical terms without its ceasing to be an intellectual error. The point applies, as far as I can see, to the acceptance of a groundless belief, whether in the interests of theory-building or of psychological security. Emotional warrant seems to combine the two notions just distinguished—justification for belief and for belief formation—since emotions may be seen as combining some aspects of belief and action. But this is a reason, I take it, for exercising some discrimination in according them a role as sources of warrant.

[7] Jerome A. Shaffer, in "An Assessment of Emotion," in K. D. Irani and G. E. Myers (eds.), *Emotion: Philosophical Studies, op. cit.*, pp. 202–220, seems to assume that a "general" justification of emotions must justify most cases of emotion. But a general justification of eating, say, does not require that most acts of eating are in fact beneficial. Indeed, one might argue that eating would be justified "in general" even if people were prone to eat unwisely. A general justification of drink, say, might be extracted from a view I heard in England, that one bottle of scotch per day was good for the constitution. That more than one bottle was not recommended—and, perhaps, that drinkers of one would be likely to keep going—might of course affect one's practical advice; but as far as I can see, it would not undermine the justification, at least if scotch made an *irreplaceable* contribution to health. Shaffer's conclusion, I should say, is that we would be better off with no emotions. I shall attempt to rebut this, in effect, in my final chapter.

[8] See "A Case of Mixed Feelings: Ambivalence and the Logic of Emotion," *op. cit.*, for an argument from the possibility of rational ambivalence to a rough distinction between emotional appropriateness and the corresponding property of belief. In the present work I have attempted to deal with the more basic issue first and to provide a general account of emotional appropriateness; but some may find the issue of ambivalence to be first in order of intuitive persuasiveness. As presented here, though, the argument involves a stronger case against judgmentalism; cf. ch. 2, n. 1.

5 Rationally Appropriate Ambivalence: Contrary Emotions

[1] This may be seen as a partial application of my argument in "Conditional Oughts and Hypothetical Imperatives," *Journal of Philosophy*, 72 (May 22, 1975), 259–276, esp.

272–273. With ought judgments taken as prescribing ends of action, they might be used to represent what I here call "practical commitment" to ends, as opposed to the simple perception of them *as* momentary ends.

Note that, according to my earlier argument, if continued perception of one's present ends were *unavoidable*—if one were unable to drop the ends, that is—they would come out as practically mandated, even without a judgment of value. In the present discussion, however, I assume that they are "optional" ends—even morally, since there is no requirement that one maintain one's ends or their conflation with those of another on any particular occasion. To cover this sort of case, then, ought judgments of the usual sort will have to be supplemented by what my earlier argument called a "first-person ought"; cf. *ibid.*, p. 275, n. 32. This amounts to a prescription issued by and limited to the agent, embodying a choice among equally acceptable ways of acting on some general personal or social value. My argument in this essay should indicate how the choice may be prompted by emotion.

² The variant cases I go on to discuss are drawn largely from discussions in ethics— and largely from conversation, so I shall not attempt to attribute them to particular authors. For a rejection of envy in the literature on emotions, see Taylor, "Love," *op. cit.*, pp. 149– 150, esp. p. 150; and "Justifying the Emotions," *op. cit.*, pp. 401–402. Although Taylor seems to mix together questions of moral and rational justification, here and elsewhere, her discussion of envy suggests that it may be seen as involving a kind of intellectual incoherency. I shall not attack her particular argument since it rests on an analysis of the emotion that differs from my own. But the variant of envy that comes closest to fitting it is the compound with that I shall refer to as "personal envy," in what follows.

³ I give a different treatment to *guilt*, interpreted as *self*-anger, in "Moral Dilemmas and Guilt," *Philosophical Studies*, 43 (April 1983), 117–125. The self/other distinction makes an important difference if we grant that frustration-anger is necessarily outwardly directed. I would make out self-anger as playing a special moral or quasi-moral role in a kind of ritual cleansing of an agent of the taint of involvement in evil, even in some cases where the blame for evil properly belongs to other agents—or to none. A similar point holds for other interpretations of guilt—as I hope to show in a fuller treatment of the subject now in progress.

⁴ This example was suggested to me by Roger Wertheimer in some comments, in correspondence on "A Case of Mixed Feelings: Ambivalence and the Logic of Emotion," *op. cit*, esp. pp. 236–237. Wertheimer's own example concerned *anger* with someone, resting on grounds *overlapping* with those for one's love of her; but I want a case of *hatred*, as a genuine *contrary* of love, where the reasons for the two emotions actually seem to be the same. Indeed, in what follows, I hope to make the case as hard as possible for the claim that both emotions are appropriate, as well as for the claim that they are so for different reasons.

⁵ For contrasting treatments of this topic, see, e.g., Mary Warnock and A. C. Ewing, "Symposium: The Justification of Emotions," *Proceedings of the Aristotelian Society*, suppl. 31 (1957), 43–74, and Taylor, "Love," *op. cit.* Below I hope to defend the appropriateness of love in my "masochistic" case, while allowing for the possibility of inappropriate love. I shall treat hatred only briefly here, by contrast with love, postponing some further questions to my next chapter; see ch. 6, n. 1.

⁶ This amounts to a modified version of the account of emotional contrariety suggested in "A Case of Mixed Feelings: Ambivalence and the Logic of Emotion," *op. cit.*, p. 236. Providing a definition of the notion is not essential to my overall aims here, as it was there, in answer to doubts about its status as a "logical" notion. In any case, my analysis of emotions in Part I provides me with an alternative criterion as well as a way of recasting my earlier suggestion in a more defensible form.

It is important that this modified version refers to what is *required* by the defense of two emotions as jointly *appropriate*. There may of course be noncontrary emotions that do in fact rest on completely different reasons—and could not be appropriately exhibited for the *same* reasons—just because they are emotions of completely different sorts. But presumably their difference can be established simply by examining their internal objects, without reference to any *extrinsic* reasons. It should also be clear that the reasons for genuinely contrary emotions may overlap; cf. ch. 5, n. 4.

6 *Justifying Emotion: What One Ought to Feel*

[1]   A similar point was made by Richard Sorabji—but apparently on the question of *what counts* as hatred and framed in terms of the emotion's *strength*—in discussion of my case of appropriate suspicion in Chapter 4. I *would* allow for affectively weaker, or "tamped-down," varieties of hatred, as I did for fear and other emotions that a dictionary might make out as necessarily strong. But in any case, the example I discuss here might be defended without stretching the term "hatred"—or substituting something weaker, such as "personal distaste."

[2]   For a version of this view, but entwined with issues of moral requirement, see Taylor, "Justifying the Emotions," *op. cit.*; cf. Aristotle, *Nicomachean Ethics,* Martin Ostwald (trans.) (Indianapolis: Bobbs-Merrill, 1962), e.g. Book IV, ch. 5, p. 101. I owe thanks to Daniel Farrell for pressing some of the questions and cases of *rational* requirement that I take up in this section.

[3]   For a similar treatment of *shame*, see Arnold Isenberg, "Natural Pride and Natural Shame," in A. O. Rorty (ed.), *Explaining Emotions, op. cit.*. esp. p. 367. Isenberg apparently equates the "reasonableness" of an emotion with its utility, however; cf. p. 374. "Natural" shame seems to come out as "merely understandable," then, since he has no separate category of appropriateness.

[4]   Similar comments might be applied to less mundane cases of "emotional insight" where time pressure is not at issue. Thus, it might be thought that a certain visceral fear-reaction to death captures something that belief could not record quite so memorably. But an agent still may raise the question why he needs to be burdened with this insight—until one brings in its probable force for action.

In general, affect may indeed be required to hold evaluations in mind; and this might be viewed as a "representational" *function* of emotions. But the *requirement* to feel them still is not strictly representational, if it rests, as I expect, on reference to some practical purposes served by attention to their evaluative components.

[5]   My distinction here between ideal and practical "oughts" is meant to correspond to "ought-to-be" versus "ought-to-do"; see my "Conditional Oughts and Hypothetical Imperatives," *op. cit.*, p. 261. I have tried to leave open the question whether the practical category applies to "ought-to-think"; for despite the verb, what would seem to be in question here is not itself an action, though it may be the result of one (see ch. 4, n. 4). But in any case, an ideal "ought" would seem to be sufficient for a representational requirement. My later argument for an instrumental "ought-to-feel" will be limited to a practical "ought," in accordance with my argument in the article just cited (cf. ch. 5, n. 1 and ch. 6, n. 8).

[6]   This way of explaining the notion of motivation comes from R. S. Peters, *The Concept of Motivation,* (New York: Humanities, 1980); see esp. pp. 37–51. Although I adopt Peters' general understanding of the term, which seems to cohere with a dictionary definition, I do not assume, as he does, that it requires an all-embracing causal theory, of the sort he attributes to the psychologists to whom the term is due. Nor do I take it to be inapplicable

to *action*, even where it does involve causation; cf. his "Emotions and the Category of Passivity," *op. cit.*, for the view of emotional behavior as something other than action, apparently because it results from a *wish*. Cf. ch. 3, n. 8.

⁷ An early version of this argument was given in my "Emotions, Reasons, and 'Self-Involvement'," *op. cit.*, pp. 165–167. Here, however, the "self-centered" judgment reflects my analysis of emotion into affective and evaluative components. On the present account the content of this judgment reinforces the evaluative content of emotion with awareness of intentionally connected affect.

⁸ This represents another application of my argument in "Conditional Oughts and Hypothetical Imperatives," *op. cit.*, pp. 272–273; cf. ch. 5, n. 1 for the restriction to optional ends. The challenge the argument poses to rational commitment to action on affectless desire may be thought of as allowing for a variety of weakness that reverses the standard picture of an agent overcome by *emotional* desire.

⁹ Note that the content of the self-centered judgment, which the argument does *prescribe* for the agent, might sometimes just be included in the evaluative component of a higher-order emotion—perhaps amounting to a "tamped-down" variant of fear of continuing discomfort. This would allow for a kind of reflex response, without time for reflection.

My reconstruction of the agent's reasoning as well as the argument drawn from it can be extended to evaluation short of belief as long as we recognize inferential relations among contents of emotions. In fact, this is presupposed by my treatment throughout this essay of action requirements as arising in context from the evaluative components of emotions not essentially involving desire, even in the absence of their corresponding beliefs, as in the fear of Fido case in Chapter 2.

¹⁰ Cf. "Behavior Control and Freedom of Action," *Philosophical Review*, 87 (April 1978), 225–240; cf. ch. 6, n. 15. I should note that "pressure" may be used as a noun form for *either* "to press" or "to pressure"—the latter more clearly connoting a kind of coercive force as opposed to simple temporal urgency. I take emotional pressure to involve both of these elements, the former built upon the latter, in a way indicated by my discussion of the "mounting" cost of postponing action under pressure.

¹¹ The objection from "expansive" action was raised, with a similar example, by Karen Hanson. I avoid Hanson's other example of marrying out of love, since I make out love as essentially involving a desire for closeness. Since the desire is analyzed as discomfort at a requirement of action to minimize distance, at least some of the motivational force of love may indeed be explained by reference to a need to escape discomfort, even supposing that the emotion is pleasurable on the whole.

In what follows, by contrast, joy itself is assumed to be "unalloyed," in the sense of not *essentially* involving a motivating desire, though I do allow that it gives rise in context to a particular desire for expression. The reader should bear in mind, though, that joy sometimes serves as a *goal* of action, rather than as a *goad* towards action, as I assume here.

¹² Comments from William Lyons on an early version of the present work led me to give special treatment to this example. It is commonly used as an example of a passive emotion—cf. ch. 3, n. 8—but Lyons directed my attention to the special problems it raises by seeming to be aimed *towards* discomfort. My discussion of it here, as a case of emotional "subjection," was prompted by Karen Hanson's further comments along the same lines. A later, expanded version of this discussion has been presented to a University of Michigan Philosophy Department Colloquium on "Emotions in Art and Life" in March, 1988.

¹³ I take it that this need not always amount (though it often does) to an expectation of lesser long-range discomfort. In general, the fact that there are other ends of action besides avoiding discomfort rules out any necessary conflict between the self-sustaining

aspect of uncomfortable emotions like sorrow and my conception of discomfort as a state that an agent would want to get out of; cf. ch. 2, n. 7. The need to *justify* putting up with discomfort, though, is what makes the case of grief different from joy and other positive emotions, whose objects might also be said to be incapable of improvement in some cases, though work may still be needed to sustain the emotions themselves.

[14] For other cases, this is what allows us to give concern for his own emotional discomfort as one of the agent's reasons for action, even though it might be ridiculous—as well as unseemly, as in the case of grief—for his attention to be focused on it while he acts. Cf. Shaffer, "An Assessment of Emotion," *op. cit.*, p. 205. Note, though, that unconscious emotions of the sort in question here will not involve "masked" *irrational* desires—as on an alternative explanation of grief behavior on which the agent is thought of as trying in vain to recover the love-object, or something similar. On the view of unconscious emotion defended in Chapter 2 we would need further behavioral evidence—of a frustrated attempt at recovery, say—for attributing this sort of irrational motivation to the agent.

Even if its self-interested aspect is made out as subliminal, let us also note, my proposed twofold explanation of grief behavior does involve emotional pressure just insofar as it turns on escape from discomfort. What its altruistic aspect supplies is not just the thought that one ought to express a sense of loss, but particularly that one ought to do so in a way that undercuts deliberative control. The result is a reason *for* emotion *as* a reason for action, and a kind of "double-action" account of grief motivation, with the emotion serving both as goal and as goad. To represent escape from discomfort as a "secondary mechanism" is thus not to minimize its importance. I owe thanks to Daniel Farrell, my commentator at the Michigan colloquium cited in ch. 6, n. 12, for forcing me to spell out this point more fully.

[15] See "Behavior Control and Freedom of Action," *op. cit.*, esp. pp. 230–233; cf. "Unfreedom and Responsibility," *op. cit.* My full view in the first piece extends unfreedom to other cases where action might be *unreasonable* to expect of an agent, even if not "too hard"; see my discussion of manipulation, esp. "Behavior Control and Freedom of Action," *op. cit.*, pp. 236–239, which might be applied to unconscious emotions. However, the version of the view given here is that relevant to compulsion, or the sort of unfreedom that involves a "push" towards action, as on my account of motivation in the present work.

[16] See Plato, *Republic*, in E. Hamilton and H. Cairns (eds.), *The Collected Dialogues of Plato*, pp. 576–844. (New York: Pantheon, 1963), esp. Book IV, pp. 682–683, 439e3–441c3. Cf. David Hume, *A Treatise of Human Nature*, *op. cit.*, p. 415.

INDEX